The New Silk Road

CHALLENGE AND RESPONSE

RICHARD T. GRIFFITHS

ISBN: 978-9-4924-3904-8 (sc)
ISBN: 978-9-4924-3905-5 (hc)
ISBN: 978-9-4924-3906-2 (e)

Library of Congress Control Number: 2019904542

HIPE Publications
PO Box 1005, 2302 BA, Leiden, The Netherlands

Lulu Publishing Services rev. date: 05/09/2019

Advance praise of the Book

'Despite the vast and ever growing literature related to China's Belt and Road Initiative, there has been a lack of hard facts and details around the many different rail, road and pipeline projects on the East-West axis between China and Western Europe, lumped together under the vast "Silk Roads umbrella". In his new book Professor Griffiths has filled a considerable part of this void, by systematically examining ongoing infrastructural improvement in 28 Eurasian countries. An important conclusion is that the BRI should not be seen solely as a Chinese policy initiative, since it comprises also a large number of projects that are implemented outside China's direct influence. This important book contributes to a more informed and better grounded distinction between what is "real" and what is "dream" in the Chinese BRI rhetoric, and provides us with an excellent platform to a deeper understanding of current and future Silk Road narratives.' *Claes G. Alvstam, Professor Emeritus Economic Geography, University of Gothenburg.*

'A valuable and distinctive contribution to the burgeoning 'Belt and Road' literature, this book shifts our perspective on the forces currently integrating the spaces of Eurasia. Offering fresh insights into the history and geography of these new interconnections, Griffiths persuasively argues that the new Silk Roads are not merely a Chinese initiative but the product of many actors collectively transforming Eurasia and the world.' *Charles Armstrong, Professor of History, Columbia University.*

'Professor Griffiths' timely and incisive study shifts the debate over BRI away from geopolitics and, by focusing on what is actually happening on the ground, it challenges the dominant Chinese and Western narratives. Through a detailed analysis of trade, infrastructure and overall connectivity, he reveals who is building and financing what, where and when. This reveals that BRI is a very much more inclusive and collaborative development than official Chinese or Western pronouncements would have us believe. A most welcome addition to the BRI literature.' *Chris Dixon, Professor of International Development, Director of the Global Policy Institute, London.*

'A book on China's Belt & Road beyond China's hyperbole and the West's angst! Griffiths strips China's bold initiative to its basics, and puts its implementation in the perspective of other infrastructure projects that sought and seek to unlock the Eurasian land mass. The book makes a compelling argument for Belt & Road's complementarity with other initiatives to enhance transport connectivity and facilitate trade.' *Pierre van der Eng, Associate Professor in International Business The Australian National University.*

'A must-read book with comparative insight, historical wisdom and intellectual sharpness!' *Baogang He, Alfred Deakin Professor and Chair in International Relations, Deakin University, Australia.*

'A highly recommendable read and excellent up-to-date reference source for students, scholars and practitioners alike.' *Michael Kaeding, University of Duisburg-Essen and Chairman of the Trans European Policy Studies Association (TEPSA), Brussels.*

'This really deep, engaging, critical and challenging book offers diverse examples of the flexibility of China's initiative of "Belt and Road" and demonstrates the interconnectedness of Chinese political culture, new economic challenges and geopolitical vision. Richard Griffiths, a brilliant and wide-ranging scholar, marches briskly through China, Central Asia to Europe and back. A glorious read.' *Alexey Maslov, Professor, Head of the School of Asian Studies, Russian National Research University "Higher School of Economics".*

'Amidst the proliferation of the academic studies on the current polarized debate on China's 'Belt and Road Initiative'(BRI), this volume provides novel and in-depth information on the complex network of the past and present Silk Road(s) connecting China to Western Europe. Richard T. Griffiths' accomplished vision and nuanced narrative unveil the broad spectrum of sometimes overlapping infrastructural investments, forgoing projects and aid programmes implemented by different countries and institutions a quarter-century earlier that so far have been largely ignored in most previous scholarship. An excellent collection of detailed maps, charts and other relevant data on transport connectivity and trade facilitation also makes this volume an essential resource for students, academics, business people and policy-makers globally.' *Isabel Morais, Professor Emerita, University of Saint Joseph, Macau Special Administrative Region of China.*

'A really stimulating book which offers new interesting analysis about the new Silk Road and main internal and international challenges and responses to this multidimensional policy instrument. Particularly innovative are the chapters which focus on two of the five main objectives identified by Xi Jinping, that is trade facilitation and the provision of transport infrastructure.' *Guido Samarani, Professor Ca'Foscari University Venice, Director Marco Polo Centre for Global Europe-Asia Connections.*

'The second book on Belt and Road Initiative by Professor Richard Griffiths is a great contribution to the studies of BRI. His analysis on roads, rail and pipelines especially provides a clearer view on the challenges and opportunities confronting China.' *Prof. dr. Xinning Song, Jean Monnet Chair ad personam, Renmin University of China.*

CONTENTS

Preface xi

Introduction...xvii

Chapter 1 The New Silk Road.. 1

China's Belt and Road Initiative.. 2

Western Reactions to the Belt and Road 4

The Ancient Silk Road.. 9

The Soviet Silk Road 12

Conclusions 16

Chapter 2 Challenge and Response 25

The Objectives of the BRI 26

The Countries of the New Silk Road 29

Trade Facilitation 32

Infrastructure.. 39

Conclusions 43

Chapter 3 Roads... 49

Versatile Roads... 50

Heading West from China... 52

Central Asia... 55

Caucasus...61

Heading East from Europe 64

The New EU Member States.. 64

Western Balkans.. 67

Ukraine, Belarus and Russia.. 68

Conclusions 71

Chapter 4 Rail... 81

Speedy Trains 81

Heading West from China... 86

Routes from China 87

Central Asia.. 91

Caucasus... 96

Russia, Belarus and Ukraine.. 98

Heading East from Europe 102

The New EU Member States.. 102

Western Balkans... 107

Conclusions 109

Chapter 5 Pipelines... 123

The Power of Pipelines.. 123

From Russia and Central Asia to Europe 126

Kazakh Oil... 127

Turkmen Oil and Gas... 129

Azerbaijan Oil and Gas 133

Russian Gas.. 134

From the West to China 138

Kazakh Oil... 138

Central Asian Gas 139

Russian Gas...141

Conclusions 144

Final Reflections 153

About the Author..157

PREFACE

There sometimes comes a moment, when working on a book, that you realise that you have been asking the wrong question. This happened to me when researching for my book *Revitalising the Silk Road* (Leiden, 2017). I was writing a book on China's 'Belt and Road Initiative' (BRI) that was intended to escape from the political science/security studies literature that viewed the BRI in terms of rising powers and challenges to the established international order. I wanted to discover what was actually happening – what were the belts and roads that China seemed so intent on building? It took some effort, but I located most of the road, rail, pipeline, port and power projects that were being developed at the time. However, whilst doing the research I kept stumbling across projects that were being developed by other countries and institutions – national governments, private financiers and international development banks. I included some of these in my book, which better reflected the reality but did not make the book any easier to read. Gradually, I realised two things. First, other people, besides the Chinese, were building the 'belt and road' but their efforts were not being included in China's narrative. Equally disconcerting was the fact that these countries (and the international institutions that they supported and financed) did not seem to have a narrative of their own. Worse still, China was appealing to other parties to join it in building the belt and road, while ignoring the fact that they were already doing so, and everyone seemed to buy into this version of events. China's belt and road was the only show in town. Second, I had broken the advice that I give my own students – do not focus on the policy, focus on the problem it is supposed to solve. How many times had I said words to the effect that the poor do not exist simply so that the rich can have a policy towards them?

Yet here was I falling into exactly the same trap. It was little consolation that almost everyone else seemed to have done so.

This book is the one I did not write before. It traces the infrastructural projects along a broad span of countries identified in China's BRI and the efforts to promote trade among them. It was too complex to cover all of the countries, so it focuses on twenty-eight of the sixty-four countries identified in China's original concept – twenty-eight countries lying on the East-West axis between China and the edge of Western Europe - countries overlapping, in part, the routes of the ancient Silk Road. The book introduces the rest of the world into China's narrative, but, in the process, it also helps de-demonise China's policy initiative. It shows that we have all been helping to revitalise the Silk Road, albeit focusing at different times on different areas and on different priorities. It suggests that all sides have lessons to learn from each other. There is still much more work to be done, especially in the countries of South- and South-East Asia that lie outside the scope of this volume. There is so much we can still do together.

There are many people to thank for helping to bring this book into existence. First I must thank the staff and fellows at the International Institute for Asian Studies at Leiden University for welcoming me into their midst and providing me encouragement to continue my research. I would like also to thank my friends and colleagues at Sichuan University and Shandong University for the conversations we have had and for lending me their students upon whom to practise my ideas. My thanks also go to David Kurtz of the Timetric Construction Intelligence Center for allowing me access to information in Timetric's valuable databases, to Nathaniel Young of the European Bank for Reconstruction and Development for giving me access to the databases that served as the basis for his own calculations of Eurasia's infrastructure investment needs, and to the staff at RailFreight.com for allowing me to attend their conferences where I learned answers to questions that I had not even formulated. I would also like to thank, in alphabetical order, Joyce Griffiths, Nynke van der Heide, Stian Krook, Clémence Overeem and Jake Potter for their contribution to the book and Luke Sky for the art-work on the cover. Finally, there is a little sports bar in Leiden which probably hosts the highest concentration of people who are familiar with China's Belt and Road initiative on the entire planet and who are responsible, when my head is in the clouds, for helping to keep my feet firmly on the ground. Thanks guys!

Leiden, 10 April 2019

Abbreviations

ADB Asian Development Bank
AIIB Asian Infrastructural Investment Bank
BCP Border Crossing Point
BOT Build-Operate-Transfer
BRI Belt and Road Initiative
BRICS Brazil, Russia, India, China and South Africa (country grouping)
CAREC Central Asia Regional Economic Cooperation Program
CEE Central and East European countries
CNPC China National Petroleum Corporation
COMECON Council for Mutual Economic Assistance
CPC Caspian Pipeline Consortium
CRBC China Road and Bridge Corporation
EBDR European Bank for Reconstruction and Development
EIB European Investment Bank
ERDF European Reconstruction and Development Fund
EU European Union
EU(15) The fifteen member states of the European Union between 1995
    and the enlargement of 2004
EXIM Bank Export-Import Bank
FDI Foreign direct investment
FEU Forty foot equivalent unit (container size)
GATT General Agreement on Tariffs and Trade
GDP Gross Domestic Product
HKTDC Hong-Kong Trade Development Council
HSR High-speed railway
ICT Information and Communications Technology
Inh/km^2 Inhabitants per square kilometre
IMF International Monetary Fund
JICA Japan International Cooperation Agency
kms Kilometres
km/h Kilometres per hour
LPI Logistics Performance Index
NTM Non-tariff Measures
OECD Organisation for Economic Cooperation and Development

ppp Purchasing power parity

SDR Special Drawing Rights

TEU Twenty foot equivalent unit (container size)

TEN-T Trans-European Network - Transport

TIR International Transport of Goods (international truck certification)

UN United Nations

UNESCAP United Nations Economic and Social Commission for Asia and the Pacific

USA United State of America

WE-WC Highway West Europe-West China Highway

WTO World Trade Organisation

All currency units are in current US dollars (unless otherwise stated)

INTRODUCTION

In September 2018, *China Daily* published an opinion-piece by Wolfgang Schüssel, the former Chancellor of Austria (2000-2007). The article was part of a celebration of President Xi Jinping's speech in Astana in September 2013 which launched what was later to become known as China's 'Belt and Road initiative'. In that speech President Xi summoned the spirit of the ancient Silk Road to present a vision of a blooming and prosperous Eurasian continent based on policy cooperation among nations, the promotion of trade, the provision of infrastructure and exchange of insights among different peoples. China would employ its own experience in economic development and its reserves of capital to help make the dream become reality. President Schüssel readily endorsed China's plans and argued that Europe should stop being so suspicious and start cooperating in 'making a two-way Silk Road'. He ended his piece with a call to action: 'Let's start it'![1] Inside my head I wanted to scream, not just at him but at all the countless other politicians, journalists and academics who have written on the Belt and Road initiative (BRI). I wanted to scream: 'What do you think we have been doing these last five years? Come to that, what do you think we've been doing these last twenty-five years? Who do you think has been building the new Silk Road?'

Let me explain the source of this frustration. I consider the evocation of the Silk Road a masterstroke of branding for the BRI. Ever since the term was first coined, over a century ago, the 'Silk Road' has embodied all the mystery and romance of long-distance travel. Where once the arrival of a new camel train heralded excitement in an ancient market, it was now the arrival of the first container train, sometimes bedecked with a red banner, that announced the opening of a new trade route. It is a heady mixture. This branding of Chinese infrastructural investments as the embodiment of the spirit of the Silk Road has been pursued with relentless efficiency, probably unmatched since the days of the Marshall Plan half a century earlier. Scarcely a speech by Chinese politicians and administrators passes without some reference to it and the Belt and Road has resurfaced, time and again, in newspaper reports, think-tank papers and academic articles. Not a stretch of road or railway, nor power plant nor port could be financed or built by China without it being part of the BRI. Gradually the initiative's scope expanded to incorporate the terrain previously occupied by foreign aid, foreign direct investment and mergers and acquisitions. Then it burst the bounds of Eurasia and began to cover everything from bridges in Latin America, railways in Africa and nuclear power stations in England.

In this way what began as a simple policy initiative assumed all-consuming dimensions. It epitomised the rise and rise of China. It accompanied the nation's forward march. It challenged the existing world order. It had to be met and responded to. In academic circles its analysis was increasingly prefixed by geo-, as in geo-economics or geo-politics. The initiative threatened countries' independence and pushed them into debt slavery. Every perceived set-back was gleefully reported as a pit-fall or a pot-hole on the Belt and Road. Political scientists and security analysts had a field day. Most frustrating of all, everyone began to talk as though there was nothing in the world before, and after, China's BRI.

China had successfully branded a policy, but what was it for? Most Western analysis, and certainly most American analysis, started to answer that question by looking for an explanation inside China. There are two versions in the most common analysis. In the first version, in order to save the Chinese economy/state industries/the party's authority over the country (delete where appropriate) the government starts creating demand abroad. This probably will not work (the jury is out on that one) but one bonus (or possibly even an intended consequence) is that it increases its influence over neighbouring countries. A second version portrays a more belligerent China using its rising economic power to create a quasi-imperialist relationship (akin to the former 'tribute system') with countries abroad by pandering to a network of corrupt client states or else by trapping them into unsustainable borrowing and creating a modern version of 'debt-bondage'. In both versions, the idea that the policy might actually be beneficial to the foreign economy scarcely gets a mention. Far less does anyone start from the premise that there might actually exist real problems in trade and infrastructure that require some solution.

This book starts from that premise. There is something seriously wrong with the functioning of the trade routes that lay along the path of the ancient Silk Road- something wrong with the new Silk Road. The development of international trade and the provision of necessary infrastructure in the Eurasian continent docs indeed pose challenges. The book concentrates on the countries lying along the direct overland trade route between China and Western Europe.[2] It contends that these challenges long predate the announcement of China's BRI in 2013. It starts its analysis some twenty years earlier, with the collapse of the Soviet Union and the trade bloc created among countries within its sphere of influence. New frontiers were erected, with new policies and new trade restrictions. The transport infrastructure that had served the previous trade network was ill-equipped for the new situation, dedicated as it was to sending goods that were no longer competitive to markets that no longer existed. Into this vortex stepped the European Union (EU). Its response took two forms. First the EU provided financial assistance and trade preferences to the neighbouring countries in the Baltic and in Central and Eastern Europe that eventually culminated in their EU membership and to the Balkan states preparing for eventual membership. Second, through bilateral aid programmes and contributions to Western aid agencies, it provided financial support for building roads and railways elsewhere along the new Silk Road. It is still doing both, but much still remains to be done. China's entry into this world means that it is committing its financial and political capital to the efforts to promote development in the counties involved. Moreover, it has helped raise the entire issue to a whole new level. Suddenly trade and infrastructure have become core concerns of policy and debate.

This book is not about *China's* Belt and Road initiative. However, it would not have been written without it, and it will certainly include it within its scope. By changing the perspective of analysis, by looking at the building of roads, railways and pipelines and by examining the initiatives to reduce barriers to international trade, this book will accomplish two things. First, it will give Europe a narrative. Since 1993 the EU has been building infrastructure in neighbouring states and removing barriers to their trade. Yet in its response to China's BRI, the EU has been cautious almost to the point of invisibility and hesitant to the point of weakness. By continuously stressing the needs for care and caution, of openness and transparency whilst offering, at some time in the future, 'cooperation' on a project or two, the EU has undersold its own achievements. It has completely integrated nine of the states included by China in its BRI into a single market, where all frontier barriers to trade have been eliminated. It has concluded free trade agreements with five of the others. Finally, in January 2019, it included a further six in its plans for an integrated European transport network. Europe's own 'belt and road' extends to the borders with Russia and to the shores of the Caspian Sea.

The book's second accomplishment is that this new perspective restores China's BRI to more 'normal' dimensions. It constructs a more inclusive narrative in which China plays an important, but not exclusive, role. China is also financing the development in neighbouring countries and is helping to move frontier barriers to trade and transit. In the process it hopes to gain sympathy for its culture and its policies. So do Western countries and the international institutions that they promote. It is the success of China's narrative, but also perhaps its greatest fault, that it has constructed a narrative that is so China-centric. It is very much China's Belt and Road – China's narrative tells only of projects financed by China, built by China or directly benefiting China. It is the fault of Western commentators to buy into this narrative so completely. Like children, they seem to relish the grisly fairy stories of witches and goblins that they are told at bedtime, embellishing the details further in their minds, and then they complain afterwards that they have nightmares.

Chapter One examines the emergence of China's BRI, starting in 2013 with the presentation of a sweeping vision of the benefits to be derived from mutual cooperation among the countries of the Eurasian land-mass. It was only in 2015, however, that the main contours of the initiative began to emerge. The debate had already begun. Chinese scholars tended to emphasise the altruistic features of the BRI whilst American observers remained more cautious on the motivations. The new Trump administration, however, soon became downright negative. The EU was also guarded in its response and slow to react. Eventually, in 2018, it presented its own strategic vision for Central Asia and, in a remarkably low-key event in

January 2019, it identified the priority projects required for integrating Belarus, Ukraine, Moldova and the countries of the Caucasus into its own transport network. The chapter ends by sketching earlier epochs during which the ancient Silk Road flourished before presenting its truncated 20th century counterpart in the form of the Soviet Union and the COMECON trading network it created. It was the collapse of this Soviet Silk Road, and the problems created in its aftermath, that revealed the challenges faced in rekindling its prospects for future prosperity.

Chapter Two deliberates on the challenges facing the new Silk Road, and the responses to them. It introduces the five components of the BRI, before concentrating on two of them: transport connectivity and trade facilitation. In particular it emphasises the role played by roads, railways and gas and oil pipelines, and their importance in promoting trade and transport. The area covered by the new Silk Road is immense, stretching from the East China Sea to the Mediterranean. The countries that lie in between are confronted by high 'trade costs'. These include the costs in time and money of international transit, crossing borders and domestic logistics. These are still high on the eve of BRI, but twenty years earlier they were higher still. In 1993 the EU opened the prospect of membership to the countries of Central and Eastern Europe and began the process of eliminating import duties. At the same time it advanced grants and loans worth billions of dollars for upgrading their administrations and infrastructure. Insufficient infrastructure remains a constraint on growth and development for the countries along the new Silk Road. The Asian Development Bank drew attention to this problem for all of Asia, suggesting that (excluding China) they would need between $9.4 trillion and $10.8 trillion over the period 2016 and 2030. Calculations by the European Bank for Reconstruction and Development, for a shorter period (2018-2022) suggest an 'infrastructure gap' of $1.6 trillion for the countries of the new Silk Road. The following three chapters consider how these challenges are being met.

Chapter Three examines the challenge posed by roads. These offer the most flexible medium for trade, but they often present a problem of finance. Roads that appear to be free of costs distort competition with other forms of transport and can impede government policies to reduce emissions by shifting goods to rail. Moreover, starting from the Xinjiang

Autonomous Region in China and continuing to the more urbanised areas of Western Russia, most of the region is sparsely populated. In recent years, many of the main highways in Central Asia have been improved, mostly with the assistance of Western development banks, which ploughed $10 billion into road improvement in Kazakhstan alone. However, problems still persist at border crossings and the chapter describes in some detail the problems at Khorgos, on the China-Kazakh border. These were eventually relieved by Chinese investment in the facilities. At the Western end of the new Silk Road, the EU has ploughed almost $100 billion in loans and grants for road improvements in the countries of Central and Eastern Europe and almost $12 billion in the Western Balkans. Recently, western development banks have invested over $2.5 billion in roads in Ukraine and over $1.2 billion in Belarus, where China, too, has also loaned $0.8 billion in road improvements. In January 2019, the EU anticipated a further investment of $8.5 billion in roads in these countries and the Caucasus between now and 2030.

Chapter Four concentrates on railways, which are potentially faster and capable of carrying greater loads than roads. For land-locked countries, especially, they are vital for economic development. However, trains do have their limitations and they require good logistical management to function effectively. Fast passage across borders, from one rail system to another is exceptionally important, as is demonstrated by the discussions on the improvements made by China in the management of freight trains, especially the express trains destined for Europe. The freight carried by these trains to Europe has increased exponentially, ironically causing problems for Malaszewicze in Poland, where most of those trains cross into the EU. Much of the building of the railway tracks along the new Silk Road has been executed with domestic funding, although Western and Chinese development banks' support has never been far away. In Central and Eastern Europe, between 1990 and 2014, the EU invested only $28 billion in the railways (less than one third the funding given to roads) and proportionately even less in the Western Balkans. Nevertheless, for most of the period, the priority of policy-makers has been with roads. This may be about to change. The EU is preparing to spend $33 billion on railways in these two regions by 2020. Russia has announced a $40 billion infrastructure scheme that would include vastly increasing the freight capacity of the Trans-Siberian railway, and talks are also progressing on starting the construction of the High Speed Railway (HSR) between Russia and Kazan, that could eventually form part of a high speed line stretching from Berlin to Beijing.

Chapter Five focuses on the development of the pipelines carrying oil and gas across the Eurasian continent. These are the hidden work-horses of modern economies, carrying tons of fuel that would otherwise overwhelm the transport network. They cover vast distances, often through challenging environments such as frozen tundra and deep sea-beds, and the expenditures involved dwarf those involved in railway improvement. Yet they remain unnoticed in much of the literature (unless China happens to be building them). However, they do not grant producers automatic rights of access, and disputes can prove costly.

The book finishes with some final reflections on the main thrust of its arguments. On this basis it then offers five pieces of advice to the policy-makers of the European Union, and one request (for clearer data) and one piece of advice for the Chinese authorities.

In March 2019, the *China Daily* published an opinion piece by the political scientist Sun Jisheng, vice-president of the China Foreign Affairs University (Beijing) under the headline, 'Belt and Road story has to be better told'. Having repeatedly stressed the need for a better BRI narrative to help dispel misconceptions over the initiative, she proclaims, 'Although it has been more than five years since the Belt and Road Initiative was launched, many people around the world still don't understand its real essence. Actually, the Belt and Road is a kind of public good that China is providing to the world.'[3] This book provides a new narrative, but not in the direction Sun Jisheng would wish.

The story told in this book starts with a shattered and fragmented Eurasian trading bloc. It shows how the international community, including China, has devoted finance and expertise to help resolve it. It demonstrates the role played by western aid agencies in Central Asia and the role played by the EU in the countries in its neighbourhood. All of these parties shared a belief that coordinating policies, facilitating trade, building infrastructure and promoting greater people-to-people exchange would boost peace and prosperity. All of them have helped build roads, railways and pipelines and they will all have experienced setbacks along the way.

The book also helps shift the perspective in other ways. It dispels the illusion that China is pouring tons of concrete and steel into roads and railways across the Eurasian land-mass. Indeed, outside its own frontier, China is noticeable for its absence for much of the story. It dispels the notion that 'Europe' or, more specifically the EU, has been tardy or lacking in its response to the challenges posed along its eastern borders. It demonstrates that improved logistics may be as important as improved infrastructure in expanding international trade. It also reminds us that in an era of increasing globalisation, and of literature on hyperglobalism, international borders still matter. It is my hope that it will also contribute to the development of a deeper international effort to resolve the manifold challenges that still remain before the new Silk Road recovers the glory of the old.

1   W. Schüssel, 'A Silk Road in both directions', *China Daily*, 21.9.2018. Available at: http://www.chinadaily.com.cn/a/201809/21/WS5ba44609a310c4cc775e773a. html.

2   This book covers 28 countries as opposed to the 64 included in China's Belt and Road initiative.

3   Sun Jisheng, 'Belt and Road story has to be better told', *China Daily*, 6.3.2019. Available at: http://www.chinadaily.com.cn/global/2019-03/06/content_37444439.htm.

CHAPTER ONE

THE NEW SILK ROAD

The Chapter will begin by describing the plans launched by China in 2013 for enhancing political and economic cooperation among the states of Asia and Europe, specifically by improving the transport infrastructure and facilitating trade. To this end, China pledged to provide substantial financial support and expertise to recreate the peace and prosperity that had characterised the ancient Silk Roads. The next section will look at the reactions in the USA and in Europe. Perhaps not surprisingly, the official claim of China's altruistic intentions in conceiving the scheme, and its mutually beneficial outcomes, has attracted criticism from Western observers and policy-makers. In the United States the reaction of the Trump Administration has reached almost visceral proportions. The reactions in Europe have been more muted, but fall far short of a full-hearted endorsement. Indeed the European Union (EU) has resorted to launching its own strategy for trade and connectivity in Central Asia, based on its own sets of principles, and concrete proposals for extending its integrated transport network beyond the borders of the EU and even beyond those of EU applicant countries. This effectively means that there are now two plans for enhancing trade and transport in Eurasia, both covering the territory occupied by the Silk Roads of old.

The third section describes the ebb and flow of trade and peoples along the old trade routes, highlighting the three periods of growth and prosperity that punctuated their centuries-long existence. The fourth section describes yet another, more modern period when trade flowed along the economies of Eurasia. That era covered the years between 1917 and

1992 when trade and investment was channelled through the Union of Soviet Socialist Republics (the USSR) and later through the Council for Mutual Economic Assistance (COMECON). It was the collapse of these arrangements, and the policies of the new states that were formed in the chaos and turmoil that ensued, that provided the challenges still faced by policy-makers today. The chapter concludes with some reflections on the nature and context of China's policy initiative.

China's Belt and Road Initiative

In September 2013, President Xi Jinping of China addressed the leaders of Central Asia at Nazarbayev University. The vision he outlined on that occasion, and the principles underlying it, have echoed through the articulation of China's foreign policy ever since.[1] In that speech he evoked the spirit of the ancient Silk Road to demonstrate 'that countries with differences in race, belief and cultural background can absolutely share peace and development as long as they persist in unity and mutual trust, equality and mutual benefit, mutual tolerance and learning from each other, as well as cooperation and mutually beneficial outcomes.'[2] Beijing would help revive the old trade routes between China and Europe. He suggested that China's deepening relations with Asian and European countries over the preceding twenty years had imparted a new vitality to the ancient Silk Road. He reminded his audience that China's foreign policy had always been based on respect of countries' chosen development paths and non-interference in their internal affairs. The new Silk Road Economic Belt would be a step-by-step operation. The main steps were:

- Improved communication of national policies
- Improved transport connectivity
- Improved trade facilitation
- Improved currency convertibility
- Improved people-to-people exchanges

He exhorted his audience, together, to 'turn the advantage of political relations, the geographical advantage, and the economic complementary advantage into advantages for practical cooperation and for sustainable growth, so as to build a community of interests. We should create new brilliance with a more open mind and a broader vision to expand regional cooperation'.[3]

This was the first of a series of speeches made by China's leaders on the theme of what was to become known as the 'Belt and Road Initiative' (BRI). However, for the next eighteen months little information was forthcoming over the exact scope and nature. Meanwhile in October 2013, at the Asia-Pacific Economic Cooperation Summit in Bali, China proposed the formation of an Asian Infrastructure Investment Bank (AIIB) with an initial capital of $100 billion and in the course of 2014 many Asian countries signed memoranda of understanding that they would join the new organisation.[4] Hard on the heels of the AIIB's creation, in July 2014 the so-called BRICS countries (Brazil, Russia, India, China and South Africa) had signed an agreement to create their own New Development Bank with an initial paid-up capital of $50 billion.[5] To cap a busy year, in November 2014 Beijing announced that it was contributing $40 billion to the creation of a Silk Road Fund.[6] All this while, there was still no solid information of what was envisaged by the BRI itself.

When it finally appeared, the 'Vision and Action Plan' described a series of development corridors, building largely on existing initiatives and regional grouping to which China adhered, as well as a maritime Silk Road, linking China's prospective commercial port developments together.[7] In April 2015, at the annual Bo'ao forum (Asia's equivalent of the annual Davos Forum in Europe), President Xi spelled out for the first time the geographical range of the BRI. There were to be 65 countries (including China) on three continents, with a combined population of 4.4 billion people. However, at the time, he failed to reveal which countries.[8] By June the background information had been expanded to reveal that the 64 countries accounted for 29 per cent of the World's GDP, but still without naming the countries involved.[9] Allowing for rounding errors, this led commentators to include any number of small African countries into the equation. It was only later that the Hong-Kong Trade Development Council's (HKTDC) on-line portal published a list based on 'information from government sources',[10] which was later confirmed by publications from the China's National Reform and Development Commission that had oversight over the Initiative.[11] This revealed that the BRI covered all the countries on the mainland Eurasian Continent, stretching from China in the East to the former Socialist states of Central and Eastern Europe, many of which had become member states of the EU. The latter owed their inclusion in the BRI to the so-called '16 Plus One' arrangements of annual meetings of national leaders of former socialist countries and China, established when Premier Wen Jiabao visited Poland in April 2012.[12]

The lack of detail that emerged during the first two years of the BRI's existence did not deflect professional academics and commentators from debating it. However, the absence of specific information helped shape the parameters of the discussion. Not surprisingly, most Chinese academics endorsed the official line, that the scheme was altruistic in its intent and neutral in its execution. China had pulled itself out of poverty, and was ready to lend its expertise and resources to helping others share its dream of national renewal. BRI was an example of enlightened self-interest, creating a win-win situation for all concerned. Only on the fringes of the debate was there any questioning of the scheme. These critics asked whether China had the resources to implement such a vision, and whether those resources might not be better employed eliminating residual poverty at home.[13] Now, it is possible that the official discourse accurately reflects the reality of poli-cy-makers in Beijing. Indeed, one academic has convincingly demonstrated a logic whereby the BRI forms a coherent and consistent response to the opportunities and constraints on China's policies.[14] However, policies do have consequences. It is one thing to deny that they were intended; quite another to deny that they exist altogether. Foreign aid does afford the lender leverage over local authorities. Large-scale projects do deliver pres-tige, both for the donor and for local politicians. First-mover advantage in infrastructure can help establish standards that facilitate subsequent commercial ventures. Domestic businesses and personnel can benefit from their employment in projects abroad. Finally, whether by bad management or ill-fortune, loans may not always be easy to repay.

Western Reactions to the Belt and Road

There is a trend in the debate among Western commentators to view the BRI in terms of national power, and to convert any consequences, intended or unintended, into deliberate motivations. This came about partly because much of the American international relations specialists tend to be 'realists', who view the world in terms of state power and who argue that states do what they need to do, thus obviating the need to seek a deeper layer of motivation.[15] The tendency was doubtless aided by the absence of any other concrete information that would have allowed the construction of an alternative motivation, and it was certainly reinforced by a tendency in the American Administration to bolster America's role in Asia. The USA's 'pivot to Asia' had started in 2011 and initially Hillary Clinton, then Secretary-of-State, had seen China as a potential partner. However, within two years, as the US backed its traditional allies in disputes over islands in the East China Sea, this open approach had hardened into a need to 'counter' China's increasing economic and military strength in the region. The US also stayed aloof from the AIIB, and tried to persuade its European allies not to join. By the start of 2018, the Trump Administration began the unilateral imposition of tariffs on Chinese imports in order to promote industrial production at home. It is no surprise that this hardened attitude also included the BRI. In October 2018 Vice-President Pence directly accused China of using 'debt diplomacy' to expand its influence, advancing 'hundreds of billions of dollars' in infrastructure loans 'on terms that are opaque at best, and the benefits invariably flow overwhelmingly to Beijing'.[16] One month later he was offering $30 billion extra in aid to Indo-Pacific countries. He went on to characterise Chinese infrastructure loans as follows, '… (The) projects they support are often unsustainable and of poor quality. And too often, they come with strings attached and lead to staggering debt. (Applause.)… We don't drown our partners in a sea of debt. We don't coerce or compromise your independence. The United States deals openly, fairly. We do not offer a constricting belt or a one-way road.'[17] Meanwhile a security report to the US Congress characterised the Initiative as 'being designed to finance and build infrastructure and connectivity around the world' with the strategic aim of exporting its model of authoritarian governance and encouraging and validating authoritarian actors abroad.[18]

The EU has been slow to adopt a position on the BRI. In one respect, this is curious since the EU has a connectivity plan of its own – the Trans European Transport Network, affectionately shortened to TEN-T. No famous names or legends have been attached to its conception. Outside the circles of the policy-makers involved, a handful of academics and representatives of commercial interests hoping to benefit, few people even know of its existence. Nonetheless in November 2014 the EU trumpeted a major investment push to help realise its creation.[19] The President of the European Commission, presenting the plan to the European Parliament exclaimed, 'Europe is back in business. This is not the moment to look back. Investment is about the future. We are offering hope to millions of Europeans disillusioned after years of stagnation. Yes, Europe can still become the epicentre of a major investment drive. Yes, Europe can grow again.'[20] Here, surely, was a scheme to match the scale and scope of the BRI. Separated on opposite sides of the Eurasian landmass, Beijing and Brussels seemed to share the same vision. However, on the occasion of the EU-China summit in July 2015, nothing was said. The only outcome was a decision to establish a Connectivity Platform to promote 'seamless traffic flows' and to explore the possibility of identifying joint projects.[21] Another opportunity was missed at the First Belt and Road forum, held in Beijing in May 2017 when a succession of world leaders walked onto the stage to announce their appreciation and support for the BRI. The EU had sent its Vice-President Jyrki Katainen whose speech focused on outlining all the principles that needed to be matched before the scheme could fulfil its promise.[22] A year later, in April 2018, 27 of the 28 EU ambassadors to China signed a report declaring that the BRI 'runs counter to the EU agenda for liberalising trade and pushes the balance of power in favour of subsidised Chinese companies.'[23]

Unlike in the USA, there has been little enthusiasm for casting the policy issue in terms of global shifts in political and economic power. Although the EU shares many of the USA's frustrations with China's trade and investment policies, its leadership is wary of the Trump Administration's turn towards protectionism and its cavalier attitude to international agreements. In many ways the EU shares the concerns voiced in China's rhetoric on the need to respect international trade rules and the importance in tackling climate change, but it is slow to ally itself with China's position. It interprets the BRI largely in terms of transport and connectivity, and more explicitly in the links between China and Europe (thereby excluding the implications for South and South-east Asia). On the other hand, whenever reacting to China, its statements tend to veer away from the issues immediately to hand and to include such topics as democracy, environmental standards, and human rights. This might all appeal to the European Parliament, which is important in shaping the EU's foreign policy, but it irritates Chinese officials.[24] One specific worry shared in European policy-making circles is China's engagement with the new member states of East-Central Europe through the '16+1' mechanism for regular high-level discourse. These meetings are often followed by announcements of new Chinse investments. These new bilateral ties are often show-boated by the nationalist leadership in some of these countries, and may also have influenced their voting on issues critical of China.[25]

In August 2018, the EU outlined its own strategy for infrastructure and connectivity in Asia. It starts by suggesting that 'for both Europe and Asia, growing global interdependence is an opportunity for increased cooperation, for peaceful political cooperation, fair and stronger economic relations, comprehensive societal dialogue and collaboration on international and regional security. Europe and Asia, together, can be the engines of a more cooperative approach to world politics, global stability and regional economic prosperity.'[26] If these conditions were met, the EU would cooperate with other countries in establishing priority corridors, in designing rules and standards and in helping to reduce the investment gap. It is interesting to note that the EU's plans for Eurasia are presented as unconnected with China's BRI. China is only mentioned four times in the entire text. The EU does, however, leave open the option that China and Europe 'should strengthen the existing cooperation on the respective infrastructure and development cooperation initiatives, promote the implementation of the principles of market access and a level playing field, as well as rely on international standards within initiatives on connectivity.'[27]

In April 2019 the leaders of China and the EU met in Brussels for the 21st summit. Expectations beforehand were not high and the EU had approached the meeting with a robust statement on the state of bilateral relations. It made clear that, whilst cooperation was welcome, in some policy areas China and Europe were competitors, or even rivals.[28] This more confident approach, coupled with mutual rejection of American protectionism, seems to have produced significant progress on many fronts - with clear objectives and fixed deadlines.[29] This new realism also penetrated the joint connectivity platform where the two sides reached an agreement to jointly fund a study of the possible railway-based transport corridors (including possible inter-modal transport hubs) between China and Europe. The aim was to determine the most sustainable corridors and to identify the related key projects. The study should be completed by the end of the year and the projects that were identified would be open to investors and contactors from all sides.[30] If the date and conditions are met, the agreement will mark a major shift in the implementation of China's BRI in this part of the Eurasian continent.

Meanwhile, the EU had been preparing for a significant extension of its engagement with its neighbours. The Eastern Partnership was a body formed in 2009 associating the EU with Belarus and Ukraine, Moldova and the three countries in the Caucasus. The aims were to promote trade and international cooperation, and to act as a framework for some (limited) financial support.[31] In 2017, a little noted passage in the minutes of a summit meeting underlined the importance attached to 'inter-modality and interoperability of transport links, to improved connections with the TEN-T network across all transport modes and... defining the indicative maps on the core networks.'[32] Then, almost unnoticed by the press, in January 2019, the EU published a document that effectively identified itself with an integrated international transport network extending from the Atlantic coast to the borders of Russia and to the western shores of the Caspian Sea. The new vision extended the EU's core network into the Eastern Partnership countries, all of which were targets of China's BRI and two of which (Belarus and Armenia) were members of the Russia-led Eurasian Economic Union. It also significantly increased the amount of financial support. It outlined 47 projects, costing $5.9 billion to be undertaken by 2020 and a further 41 projects, with a price-tag of $8.6 billion to be completed by 2030. Most of the expenditure would be supported by international development banks (73 per cent) and by public-private partnerships (23 per cent).[33]

The Ancient Silk Road

The plans of both China and the EU address issues of trade and connectivity across the land-mass separating the two regions. Both schemes stress their contribution to peace and prosperity. Both cover the same geographical space – the space occupied by the ancient Silk Road. The name 'Silk Road' was appended to the complex networks of trading routes spanning the distance between China and Western Europe in 1877 by the German geographer Baron Ferdinand von Richthofen. Despite the fact that it is only tangentially supported by the historical record, the name and the image has stuck in popular imagination. Silk was probably never the most important item in long-distance trade between East and West, either in volume or in value. Tea, salt, copper and iron each probably exceeded the volumes of silk traded. However, then, as now, high value, low bulk items predominated the long-distance, overland trade. Relatively few people or camels travelled the full distance from East to West. It was the goods that moved, from market to market, from trader to trader, gathering value along the way. More important than the goods that moved, was the transfer of knowledge – of foods and diets, of architecture and urban planning, of technologies and beliefs, of languages and literatures, and of laws and societal systems.[34] Possibly it is the memory of the great civilisations that rose and fell along the ancient 'Silk Roads', rather than the image of camel trains carrying their exotic loads along its routes, that have stamped themselves on the public's imagination. The Silk Road is a myth[35], but myths also have their uses if they function as a short-hand for a complex collection of hopes and ambitions.

An overland trade route connecting China with the West long predates its 'opening' under the aegis of the first Han emperor in the second century BCE. Ancient silk, probably from China, has been discovered on Egyptian mummies dating from 1000 BCE.[36] Certainly the silk for the purple-dyed robes in which Alexander the Great (356-323 BCE) liked to dress came from China, with the dye produced by the Phoenicians in Tyre.[37] An exhibition of ancient Egyptian funeral art held in Brooklyn in 2010 featured a jade carving less than seven centimetres high of a dwarf standing with each foot on the head of an alligator, and gripping a snake by the neck in each hand. He was supposed to protect the dead in the afterlife. Just like the silk, the jade probably came from China.[38] Trade, therefore, already existed before 138 BCE when Emperor Wu, the seventh emperor of the Han dynasty, who had first unified the territory that we know as modern China, sent his envoy Zhang Qian at the head of a large delegation to establish an alliance with the Yuezhi nation, in what is now modern Tajikistan. When, thirteen years later, the unfortunate diplomat returned[39] to the Imperial Court he was still without the desired alliance but full of stories of the existence of vast sophisticated trading economies to the west of the Chinese empire. The news he brought prompted the Emperor to start establishing commercial as well as military alliances with his neighbours, and to tie the Empire to the trading routes that stretched infinitely westward to lands and cultures then unknown.[40]

The opening of trading routes west to China coincided with the first recorded growth of trade with the West. At the same time as the Han dynasty succeeded in negotiating treaties with local tribes and rulers, the Roman Empire was extending its own reach into Asia Minor and to the edge of the Indian sub-continent. Silk, indeed, began to appear as an item of luxury apparel among the richer citizens of Rome.[41] Few people at that time travelled the vast distance to Europe. Nor was there much of a road. The camel trains followed rough tracks and paths that skirted deserts in the Winter and crossed mountain ranges in the Summer, and which became more comfortable as they approached small towns and large trading cities along the route. These settlements provided markets and lodgings, camels and provisions, rest and protection. At these points trade was regulated and taxes were levied, and with the revenues raised the local rulers built magnificent cities. When times were peaceful, trade prospered and art and culture flourished. This first golden period of the Silk Road finished in the years after 220 CE, which marked the collapse of the Han dynasty and the division of China into warring kingdoms.[42] Rome, too, was beginning to lose its powerful status and, after 376 CE, it was to become prey to vast marauding horse-borne armies from Asia.[43]

The second golden era of the Silk Road coincided with the rule of the Tang dynasty (619-907 CE) which is often seen by Chinese historians as a golden age of Chinese cosmopolitan culture.[44] It was also a period when the Empire had largely defeated the threat from outside. With the increasing population size and prosperity of the country, trade along the

Silk Roads once more revived. This time the Western pivot was the rich Persian Empire[45], and there was a brisk trade in silk, but this was pushed by unique supply conditions rather than by some insatiable demand. In those days bolts of silk had been used as a currency – the silk was produced in standard size and quality, and its value was more stable than bronze coin. It was used to pay the wages of the considerable troops stationed to guard the border, and employed in cross-border transactions for food and other provisions. However, what impressed the Chinese in those days was the quality of the horses ridden by the steppe peoples. For some reason the grasses in China did not make the horses strong enough to carry a person. The magnificent horses, reputed to sweat blood when ridden hard, were in high demand, and the currency used to buy them was silk. Not surprisingly, some of that silk began its journey overland westward, moving slowly in small steps from market to market.[46] Meanwhile, local uprisings were proving increasingly difficult and costly to suppress, and towards the end of the eighth century the capital of Chang'an was lain waste. When, in 907 CE the emperor himself was slain, the small market towns along the Silk Road also fell upon more frugal times.

In the last quarter of the twelfth century the horse-borne hordes of the Mongolian steppe gathered round a leader later known as Genghis Khan (1162-1227 CE), who led them in a series of military ventures that eventually brought the entire area from Northern China to the Caspian Sea under his control. His successors extended the area under Mongol control to cover as much of modern China and, in the West, the territories of Hungary and Poland.[47] Following their campaigns of unprecedented savagery,[48] the Mongol rulers settled down to establishing peace and stability, and a low cost trade regime, across their lands. In the West, the first to seize the new opportunities were the mercantile city states of Renaissance Italy, such as Venice and Genoa.[49] Trade across the Eurasian continent flourished until the late fifteenth century when the Mongol Empire began to fragment, and the intermittent conflict between the Ottoman and Persian Empires cut off the overland routes to the East. At the same time, European sailors established direct sea links to the Indian Ocean and later to South East Asia, China and Japan.[50] Gradually the volume and value of goods carried by sea eclipsed those carried by land and they have done until the present day. Other regional trading networks continued to rise and die along the ancient cities of the Silk Road, but the overland route between the extremities of China and Europe sank into the stuff of legend until the early twentieth century, when it remerged in a completely new guise.

The Soviet Silk Road

In 1917 the Soviet government seized power and, after a bloody civil war, imposed its authority over much of the constituent territory of the former Russian Empire, shorn of the territories (large parts of Poland, Finland and the Baltic states) it had lost through the peace treaty concluded with the Germans at Brest-Litovsk. Following a period of reconstruction in the 1920s, the Soviet authorities imposed a system of central planning on the economy and dictated a regime of forced industrialisation throughout Russia and the constituent republics.[51] The plans placed a priority on the development of heavy industry and the attainment of autarky, or independence from the rest of the world. Roads and railways spread over the region but all were directed towards facilitating the fulfilment of the central plans.

Figure 1.1: The Soviet Silk Road

Victory in the Second World War released the Soviet Union from its isolation. One effect was that Russia reabsorbed the territories that it had lost in 1917 into the Soviet Union. It also installed communist governments in the Central and Eastern European countries (Bulgaria, Czechoslovakia,

East Germany, Hungary, Poland, Romania) that had been reconquered by its troops and established central planning mechanisms in each to control their economies. In 1949 these countries created the Council for Mutual Economic Assistance (also known as COMECON) as a framework for conducting their mutual foreign trade.[52] Joseph Stalin and his successors had established hegemonic control over the old Silk Road that at the time spanned the distance from the coast of the Pacific Ocean to the borders of Western Europe. Within the COMECON system trade was bilaterally negotiated between partners with the aim of venting (planned) surpluses at agreed (artificially determined) prices and designed individually to balance (i.e. a surplus on trade with one partner could not be used to pay for a deficit with another). Exports outside the area would earn foreign currency but that usually flowed to the national bank, and not to the enterprise involved.[53] For the first decade after the Second World War the emphasis on heavy industry in Russia was also placed upon all members of the Soviet bloc. This helped skew their industrial structures in a similar direction and further reduced the scope for specialisation and trade. Gradually, however, conditions were relaxed and, especially in the 1970s and 80s, some of the Central and Eastern European countries succeeded in expanding their trade with the West.[54] This was as much a result of the slow-down in the Russian economy as of a need to earn convertible currency.

The effect of the socialist foreign trade regime was to create a region with high levels of intra-area trade (the proportion of imports and exports traded with other nations in the bloc) but low levels of foreign trade dependence (the share of imports and exports relative to GDP). The extent to which this was the result of the COMECON regime is difficult to determine. For a start, Soviet era statistics are a minefield. The system of national accounts differed from that of the West and prices bore little relation to economic conditions. Add to this the complication that the data appears often to be deliberately inflated and that each state maintained its own price level, and one can begin to appreciate the difficulties in reconstructing the situation.[55] The World Bank has attempted to answer the question of how far the distortion of trade patterns was a consequence of the planning system. The results for the mid-1980s suggest that the Central and Eastern European states were the closest to 'normal' (in so far as they approached the predicted results of 'gravity models of trade' based *inter alia* on economic size and distance from markets). Their best performance was a trade with China at 95 per cent of normal, but their trade with Western markets (OECD member states) was only 36 per cent of normal. By contrast, intra-trade was more than six times higher than predicted. Central Asia's trade with the West was only 20 per cent of the level expected, and that with China was a little better at 35 per cent, but intra-trade was almost nine times higher than 'normal'. Finally, to complete the picture, the Caucasus only traded with the West at nine per cent of the expected level and China at 25 per cent, but its trade within the group was almost eight times the 'normal level.[56]

Most observers at the time were agreed that the Soviet system was inefficient and that levels of productivity were surprisingly low, but few were prepared for what happened next. First the system strained, then it cracked and finally it imploded.[57] Within a year (1989) all the Central and Eastern European states had broken free from Russian influence and were engaged in transforming their political and economic systems. In June 1991 the COMECON states voted to disband the organisation and six months later the Soviet Union itself was dissolved.[58]

As the Soviet system collapsed, the countries along the Silk Road suffered several crises simultaneously. Within the former Soviet Union, the collapse of central planning cast state enterprises adrift from their supply chains and many collapsed before they could find new markets. In Russia and elsewhere there was an increase in trade with Western economies, but insufficient to compensate for the loss of domestic demand. Moreover, the search for new markets was disrupted by the simple fact that most countries were producing the goods for which there was little demand, in plants that had low productivity and at prices that were too high. On top of this many faced problems of international liquidity, trying to finance burgeoning balance-of-payments deficits whilst being unable to borrow at affordable rates. Russia itself experienced three banking collapses in the space of a decade, and the currency union that had bonded the former Republics was quickly dissolved.[59] Those Republics that had been dependent on trade with Russia found themselves dragged into the vortex of Russia's own deepening depression. The states of Central and Eastern Europe, which had had better commercial connections with Europe and which had higher levels of development found themselves trying to manage a transition to a market economy by privatising former state enterprises but without any experience with modern business methods. Their economies also started sliding into a recession.

The collapse of Soviet state power at home and its influence over its neighbouring states also contributed to a series of violent conflicts that tore across the region. From 1991 Yugoslavia, itself a union of separate republics which had been under increasing strain since the death of its leader Marshall Tito, suddenly convulsed along ethnic (Serb, Croat, Bosniak, Slovenian and Albanian) and religious (Orthodox, Catholic, Islamic) lines as the constituent republics declared their independence against the wishes of the dominant Republic of Serbia. A series of savage wars were only finally terminated in 1999, in two cases after the intervention of European and American forces.[60] Within the former Soviet Union the borders of the constituent republics had been drawn with scant attention to the ethnic composition of the territories involved and the situation had been aggravated by the large-scale migration of Russians into neighbouring countries. In 1991-1992 Georgia faced brief but inconclusive civil wars with Ossetian and Abkhazian separatists in the north-east and north-west of the country, which had left both regions with a large degree of de facto autonomy. When in 2008, Georgia launched a military operation to regain control of the regions, the Russian army intervened on the separatists side, bringing the war to a rapid close and occupying both regions. The border has been closed ever since.[61] In Azerbaijan the region of Nagorno-Karabakh began to agitate for its inclusion into Armenia. In 1992 ethnic unrest escalated into a full-scale war between the two countries and by the time a ceasefire was eventually agreed in 1994, Armenian troops occupied most of the disputed territory. Since then Armenia's borders with both Azerbaijan and Turkey have been closed.[62] The most recent manifestation of unrest came in 2013 when the Russian minority in the east of Ukraine reacted to the deposition of the pro-Russian leadership of the country by occupying local government buildings and claiming independence. With Russian military support, the insurgents started a civil war which still simmers to this day, but in March 2014, Russian troops intervened and annexed Crimea, and the naval base leased from Ukraine.[63] In retrospect it is something of a miracle that, in 1993, Czechoslovakia managed to arrange its own peaceful separation into two separate states, the Czech and Slovak Republics.[64]

In Central Asia, the Ferghana Valley is a fertile but ethnically mixed region whose territory is shared among three states- Tajikistan, Kyrgyzstan and Uzbekistan.[65] In 1992 a civil war broke out in Tajikistan, stirred by a mixture of ethnic, ideological and religious tensions. The war was aggravated and prolonged by the involvement of Islamic forces that had been radicalised by fighting alongside the Taliban in Afghanistan. By the time that a peace was brokered in 1999 tens of thousands had died and over a million people had been driven from their homes.[66] Towards the end of the 1990s, Islamic forces started organising in Uzbekistan, making incursions into both Tajikistan and Kyrgyzstan and, in 1999, were behind an attack on the capital in Uzbekistan. Meanwhile the pockets of Taliban control in several areas in the North bordering Turkmenistan, Uzbekistan and Tajikistan served to provide a continuous threat to stability in the region.

Conclusions

It is difficult to exaggerate the impact of China's BRI on the framework for policy formulation among the developing countries of the world, or the resonance of its message of mutually beneficial cooperation on their populations. To see it simply as a means for advancing an increasingly assertive Chinese foreign policy, as do most 'realist' commentators, ignores the very real dimension of needs to which the policy is addressed. Official US policy is now highly dismissive of China's BRI, and that is a mistake. The reactions in Europe are different, and operate at several levels. The representatives of the transport and logistics firms engaged in trade with China are generally welcoming of the opportunities that increased overland trade represents. The reaction of the EU is ambivalent. On the one hand it recognises the benefits of infrastructural investment and trade facilitation, which it has been promoting in its own neighbourhood for the previous twenty-five years. On the other hand it resents the exclusion of European firms from bidding for the construction contracts that accompany Chinese investments. Behind the caution of its official statements, however, the EU has staked out an ambitious geographical reach for the development of its own priority transport networks.

The view of the history of the ancient Silk Road serves to emphasise the need for peace (or, better put, the absence of war) in order for the full benefits of international communication to emerge. For this reason the book has included the Soviet Silk Road in the survey, where peace was imposed on the region by the never distant threat of Soviet intervention. It was a 'shadow' Silk Road characterised by the low volume of trade relative to the size and wealth of the countries involved, but also its intense concentration among the countries within the geographical limits of Soviet power. It may not have been much, but it was better than what followed in the immediate aftermath of its collapse.

The 'end of the Cold War' was portrayed at the time as some kind of moral victory the superiority of western values or the western economic system. It is generally remembered as being 'a good thing'. However, for the socialist countries involved, it was a deeply disruptive event, and for their populations it felt like anything but a victory. New nations established new frontiers. Economies collapsed, trade shrank, unemployment and poverty soared. In places long-simmering ethnic and religious divisions spilled over into open warfare. In 1990-92 the entire area covered by the Soviet Silk Road was in crying need of international help.

1   In December 2018 the Central Party Literature Press published a book contain-
     ing no less than 42 speeches and articles by President Xi himself on the issue
     of China's Belt and Road initiative, covering the period September 2013-July
     2018. See announcement at Xinhua.net 11.12.2018. Available at: http://www.
     xinhuanet.com/english/2018-12/11/c_137666561.htm.

2   J Xi, *Promote People-to-People Friendship and Create a Better Future*, speech at
     Nazarbayev University, Kazakhstan, 11.9.2013. Available at: https://www.fmprc.
     gov.cn/mfa_eng/wjdt_665385/zyjh_665391/t1078088.shtml.

3   *Ibidem.*

4   N. Lichtenstein, *A Comparative Guide to the Asian Infrastructure Investment Bank*,
     Oxford, 2018; M. Dian and S. Menegazzi, *New Regional Initiatives in China's
     Foreign Policy: The Incoming Pluralism of Global Governance*, London, 2018,
     47-66; M. Wan, *The Asian Infrastructure Investment Bank: The Construction of
     Power and the Struggle for the East Asian International Order*, Basingstoke, 2016.

5   *Agreement on the New Development Bank – Fortaleza, July 1*, 15.7.2014.
     Available at https://www.ndb.int/wp-content/themes/ndb/pdf/Agreement-
     on-the-New-Development-Bank.pdf; J. Gu, A. Shankland and A. Chenay
     (eds..) *The BRICS in International Development*, Basingstoke, 2016; A.N.
     Sakar, *BRICS New Development Bank: A Game-changer for the Emerging
     Economies*, Avon Publications, 2016. See also *The Economist*, 29.9.2018.
     Available at: https://www.economist.com/finance-and-economics/2018/09/29/
     the-beleaguered-brics-can-be-proud-of-their-bank.

6   *China Daily*, 9.11.2014. Available at: http://www.chinadaily.com.cn/
     china/2014-11/09/content_18888916.htm.

7   PRC, National Development and Reform Commission, *Vision and Actions
     on Jointly Building Silk Road Economic Belt and 21st-Century Maritime Silk
     Road*, 28.3.2015. Available at: http://en.ndrc.gov.cn/newsrelease/201503/
     t20150330_669367.html.

8   *South China Morning Post*, 2.4.2015. Available at: https://
     www.scmp.com/comment/insight-opinion/article/1753773/
     one-belt-one-road-initiative-will-define-chinas-role-world.

9   *Foreign Policy*, 23.6.2015. Available at: https://foreignpolicy.com/2015/06/23/
     south_china_sea_beijing_retreat_new_strategy/

10   http://china-trade-research.hktdc.com/business-news/article/The-Belt-and-
     Road-Initiative/The-Belt-and-Road-Initiative-Country-Profiles/obor/en/1/1X-
     000000/1X0A36I0.htm

11   PRC, National Development and Reform Commission, 一带一路 大数据报
     告, Beijing, 2016. (One Belt One Road. Big Data Report).

12   Huang Ping, Liu Zuokui (eds.) *How the 16+1 Cooperation promotes the Belt
     and Road Initiative*, Beijing, 2017. Available at: http://www.16plus1-thinktank.
     com/u/cms/cepen/201802/281459352q2e.pdf; M. Musabelliu, 'China's Belt and

Road Initiative Extension to Central and Eastern European Countries - Sixteen Nations, Five Summits, Many Challenges', *Croatian International Relations Review*, 23, 78, 2017, 57-76. Available: https://content.sciendo.com/view/journals/cirr/23/78/article-p57.xml; K. Brown, 'China's Geopolitical Aims: The Curious Case of the 16-Plus-1', *The Diplomat*, 3.5.2017. Available at https://thediplomat.com/2017/05/chinas-geopolitical-aims-the-curious-case-of-the-16-plus-1/; A. Bachulska, 'What's Next for China's 16+1 Platform in Central and Eastern Europe?', *The Diplomat*, 3.7.2018. Available at https://thediplomat.com/2018/07/whats-next-for-chinas-161-platform-in-central-and-eastern-europe/.

13   M.D. Swaine, 'Chinese Views and Commentary on the "One Belt, One Road" Initiative', *China Leadership Monitor*, 47, 2015. Available at: https://www.hoover.org/sites/default/files/research/docs/clm47ms.pdf; R.T. Griffiths, *Revitalising the Silk Road. China's Belt and Road Initiative*, Leiden, 2017, 36-38; J. Wuthnow, *Chinese Perspectives on the Belt and Road Initiative: Strategic Rationales, Risks, and Implications*, INSS China Strategic Perspectives, 12, 2017. Available at: https://inss.ndu.edu/Portals/68/Documents/stratperspective/china/ChinaPerspectives-12.pdf.

14   F.J. Leandro, *Steps of Greatness: The Geopolitics of OBOR*, Macao, 2018.

15   A. Chance and A. Mafinezam, *American Perspectives on the Belt and Road Initiative, Sources of Concern and Possibilities for Cooperation*, ICAS, November 2016. Available at https://chinaus-icas.org/wp-content/uploads/2017/02/American-Perspectives-on-the-Belt-and-Road-Initiative.pdf. T. Miller, *China's Asian Dream*, London, 2017; N. Rolland, *China's Eurasian Century. Political and Strategic Implications of the Belt and Road Initiative*, Washington, 2017. For a European example see B. Maçães, *Belt and Road. A Chinese World Order*, London, 2018.

16   *Remarks by Vice President Pence on the Administration's Policy Toward China, Hudson Institute*, Washington DC, 4.10.2018. Available at: https://www.whitehouse.gov/briefings-statements/remarks-vice-president-pence-administrations-policy-toward-china/. The following day the New York Times commented that the speech sounded as though the USA was declaring a new 'Cold War' on China. *New York Times*, 5.10.2018, Available at: https://www.nytimes.com/2018/10/05/world/asia/pence-china-speech-cold-war.html.

17   *Remarks by Vice President Pence at the 2018 APEC CEO Summit Port Moresby, Papua New Guinea*, 16.11.2018. Available at: https://www.whitehouse.gov/briefings-statements/remarks-vice-president-pence-2018-apec-ceo-summit-port-moresby-papua-new-guinea/.

18   *2018 Report to Congress of the U.S.-China Economic and Security Review Commission*, 2.11.2018. Available at: https://www.uscc.gov/Annual_Reports/2018-annual-report.

19 In fact the European Union has had a Trans-European Network for transport (TEN-T) since 1996. The originality in its reincarnation lies in its supposed 'European' character, rather than an accumulation of nationally negotiated and agreed projects.

20 *Investing in Europe: speech by President Juncker in the European Parliament plenary session on the €315 billion Investment Plan*, Strasbourg, 26.11.2014. Available at: http://europa.eu/rapid/press-release_SPEECH-14-2160_en.htm.

21 European Council, *EU-China Summit joint statement. The way forward after forty years of EU-China cooperation*, Brussels, 2015. Available at: https://www.consilium.europa.eu/media/23732/150629-eu-china-summit-joint-statement-final.pdf.

22 *Speech by Jyrki Katainen, Vice President of the European Commission at the Leaders' Roundtable of the Belt and Road Forum for International Cooperation*, Brussels, 15.5.2017. Available at: http://europa.eu/rapid/press-release_SPEECH-17-1332_en.htm. I was there. If there was ever a wrong speech before the wrong audience, this was it.

23 *Handelsblatt*, 17.4.2018 Available at: https://chinacircle.handelsblatt.com/eu-ambassadors-band-together-against-silk-road/.

24 A. Saarela, *A new era in EU-China relations: more wide ranging strategic cooperation?*, European Parliament, Directorate-General For External Policies, Policy Department, July 2018. Available at http://www.europarl.europa.eu/RegData/etudes/STUD/2018/570493/EXPO_STU(2018)570493_EN.pdf; A. García-Herrero, K.C. Kwok, Liu Xiangdong, T. Summers and Zhang Yansheng, *EU–China Economic Relations to 2025 Building a Common Future*, London, 2017. Available at: https://www.chathamhouse.org/sites/default/files/publications/research/2017-09-13-eu-china-economic-relations-2025-garcia-herrero-kwok-liu-summers-zhang-final.pdf.

25 A. Budeanu, *The "16+1" Platform China's Opportunities for Central and Eastern Europe*, IRIS, October 2018. Available at: https://china-cee.eu/wp-content/uploads/2018/11/161-cooperation.pdf; D. Pavlićević, '"China Threat" and "China Opportunity": Politics of Dreams and Fears in China-Central and Eastern European Relations', *Journal of Contemporary China*, 27,113, 2018, 688-702; F. Godement and A. Vasselier, *China at the Gates: A New Power Audit of EU-China Relations*, European Council on Foreign Relations, 1.12.2017. Available at https://www.ecfr.eu/page/-/China_Power_Audit.pdf.

26 European Commission, High Representative of the Union for Foreign Affairs and Security Policy, *Connecting Europe and Asia – Building blocks for an EU Strategy, Joint Communication to the European Parliament, the Council, the European Economic And Social Committee, the Committee of the Regions and the European Investment Bank*, Brussels 19.9.2018, JOIN(2018) 31 final. Available at: https://eeas.europa.eu/sites/eeas/files/

joint communication - connecting europe and asia - building blocks for_an_eu_strategy_2018-09-19.pdf.

27 *Ibidem*. It is worth noting that China's declared policy towards the EU, while loaded with 'red lines' on the recognition of Taiwan and Tibet, and interference in bilateral (maritime) disputes, also endorses the need for joint rules and principles. *China's Policy Paper on the European Union,* Full text, *China Daily*, 18.12.2018. Available at: http://www.xinhuanet.com/english/2018-12/18/c_137681829.htm.

28 *EU-China Strategic Outlook: Commission and HR/VP contribution to the European Council (21-22 March 2019)*. Available at: https://ec.europa.eu/commission/sites/beta-political/files/communication-eu-china-a-strategic-outlook.pdf.

29 *Joint statement of the 21ˢᵗ EU-China summit*, 9.4.2019. Available at: https://www.consilium.europa.eu/en/press/press-releases/2019/04/09/joint-statement-of-the-21ˢᵗ-eu-china-summit/. *Remarks of President Juncker at the joint press conference with Mr Li Keqiang, Premier of the State Council of the People's Republic of China, and Mr Donald Tusk, President of the European Council, following the EU-China Summit*, 9.4.2019. Available at: http://europa.eu/rapid/press-release_SPEECH-19-2078_en.htm.

30 *Meeting Minutes of the 4ᵗʰ Chairs' Meeting of the EU-China Connectivity Platform* (plus appendices), 4.9.2019. Available at: https://ec.europa.eu/transport/sites/transport/files/4th_chairs_meeting_minutes_en.pdf.

31 The Eastern Partnership has its own website; https://eeas.europa.eu/diplomatic-network/eastern-partnership_en.

32 Council of the European Union, *Joint Declaration of the Eastern Partnership Summit (Brussels, 24 November 2017)* 14821/17. Available at: https://www.consilium.europa.eu/media/31758/final-statement-st14821en17.pdf.

33 European Union Press Release 18.1.2019. Available at: https://eeas.europa.eu/headquarters/headquarters-homepage/56763/eastern-partnership-new-indicative-ten-t-investment-action-plan-stronger-connectivity_en. *Eastern Partnership, Indicative TEN-T Investment Action Plan*, 2018. Available at: https://ec.europa.eu/neighbourhood-enlargement/sites/near/files/ten-t_iap_web-dec13.pdf. The sums in euro are €5.2 billion and €7.6 billion respectively.

34 A.H. Dani, 'Significance of Silk Road to human civilization: Its cultural dimension', *Journal of Asian Civilizations*, 25, 1, 2002, 72-79.

35 T. Chin, 'The Invention of the Silk Road, 1877', *Critical Inquiry*, 40, 1, 2013, 194-219; L. Raw (ed.), *The Silk Road of Adaptation: Transformations across Disciplines and Cultures*, Cambridge, 2013.

36 G. Lubec, J. Holaubek, C. Feidl, B. Lubec and E. Strouhal, 'Use of silk in Ancient Egypt', *Nature*, 362/25, 1993, 25.

37 J. Yang, 'Alexander the Great and the Emergence of the Silk Road', *The Silk Road*, 6, 2, 2009, 15-22. Available at: http://www.silkroadfoundation.org/newsletter/vol6num2/srjournal_v6n2.pdf.

38 K. Johnson, 'Taking it with you in Ancient Egypt', *New York Times*, 11.3.2010. Available at: https://www.nytimes.com/2010/03/12/arts/design/12ancient.html.

39 Zhang Qian was captured by the Xiongnu, a people in the Northern steppes against whom the alliance was to be directed, and held in slavery for ten years. Eventually he was able to escape and find his way to the Yuezhi nation, only to discover its rulers were disinclined to disrupt their comfortable lives for military adventure. Zhang Qian spent the best part of a year with the Yuezhi people before setting off on his return journey, only to be recaptured by the Xiongnu. After a further two years in captivity he managed again to escape.

40 X. Lui, *The Silk Road in World History*, Oxford, 2010, 1–19.

41 B. Hildebrandt, *Silk: Trade and Exchange along the Silk Roads between Rome and China in Antiquity*, Oxford, 2016.

42 M. Pirazzoli-T'Serstevens, *The Han Dynasty*, Oxford, 1982; M.E. Lewis and T. Brook, *The Early Chinese Empires*, Cambridge Ma, 2009; J.E. Hill, *Through the Jade Gate to Rome: A Study of the Silk Routes during the Later Han Dynasty 1ˢᵗ to 2ⁿᵈ Centuries CE*, Lexington KY, 2009.

43 R. McLaughlin, *The Roman Empire and the Silk Routes: The Ancient World Economy and the Empires of Parthia, Central Asia and Han China*, Barnsley, 2016; B. Ward-Perkins, *The Fall of Rome: And the End of Civilization*, Oxford, 2006.

44 M.E. Lewis, *China's Cosmopolitan Empire: The Tang Dynasty*, Cambridge Ma, 2012; C.D. Benn, *China's Golden Age: Everyday Life in the Tang Dynasty*, Oxford, 2004.

45 S. Frederick Starr, *Lost Enlightenment: Central Asia's Golden Age from the Arab Conquest to Tamerlane*, Princeton, 2013.

46 T. Barfield, 'Steppe empires, China, and the Silk Route: Nomads as a force in international trade and politics' in A. M. Khazanov and A. Wink (eds.) *Nomads in the Sedentary World*, Richmond, 2001, 232-249; Tan Mei Ah, 'Exonerating the Horse Trade for the Shortage of Silk: Yuan Zhen's "Yin Mountain Route"', *Journal of Chinese Studies*, 57, 2013, 49-95.

47 P. Kalra, *The Silk Road and the Political Economy of the Mongol Empire*, Abingdon, 2018; B. Shagdar, 'The Mongol Empire in the Thirteenth and Fourteenth Centuries' in V. Elisseeff (ed.), *The Silk Roads*, New York NY, 2000, 127-144.

48 D. Croner, *Chingis Khan Rides West: The Mongol Invasion of Bukhara, Samarkand, and other Great Cities of the Silk Road, 1215-1221*, 2014.

49 J. Brotton, *The renaissance bazaar: From the Silk Road to Michelangelo*, Oxford, 2002.

50 S. Chaudhury and M, Morineau, *Merchants, companies and trade: Europe and Asia in the early modern era*, Cambridge, 2007.

51 Philip Boobbyer, *The Stalin Era*, London, 1970; A, Nove, *The Soviet Economic System*, London, 1977; F. Hirsch, *Empire of Nations: Ethnographic Knowledge and the Making of the Soviet Union*, Ithaca, London, 2005.

52 They were joined by Mongolia in 1962. Albania and Yugoslavia also established communist regimes but they remained largely outside Russia's influence and control.

53 M. Kaser, *Comecon : integration problems of the planned economies*, Oxford, 1967; F.D. Holzman, 'Comecon: A "Trade-Destroying" Customs Union?', *Journal of Comparative Economics*, 9, 1985, 410-423; W. Loth and N. Paun (eds.) *Disintegration and integration in East-Central Europe: 1919 - post-1989*, Baden-Baden, 2014.

54 M. Lavigne, 'The Soviet Union inside COMECON', *Soviet Studies*, 35, 2, 1983, 135-153.

55 M.V. Belkindas and O.V. Ivanova (eds..) *Foreign Trade Statistics in the USSR and Successor States*, Washington D.C., 1995. Available at: http://documents. worldbank.org/curated/en/172291468752103344/pdf/multi0page.pdf.

56 B. Kaminski, Z. Kun Wang and L.A. Winters, *Foreign Trade in Transition. The International Environment and Domestic Policy*, Washington DC, 1996, 10-14. Available at: http://documents.worldbank.org/curated/ en/848091468769322143/pdf/multi0page.pdf.

57 R. Strayer, *Why Did the Soviet Union Collapse?: Understanding Historical Change*, Abingdon, 1998; D.R. Marples, *The Collapse of the Soviet Union, 1985-1991*, Abingdon, 2004.

58 K. Lányi, 'The Collapse of the COMECON Market', *Russian & East European Finance and Trade*, 29, 1, 1993, 68-86; O. Havrylyshyn and R. Wissels, 'Reviving Trade Amongst the Newly Independent States', *Economic Policy*, 9, 19 (Supplement: Lessons for Reform) 1994, 171-190.

59 R.T. Griffiths and V. Sergeev, Экономическая реконструкция. Сравнение послевоенной Европы и постсоветской России, Moscow, 2003; T.P. Gerber and M. Hout, 'More shock than therapy: Market transition, employment, and income in Russia, 1991–1995', *American Journal of Sociology*, 1998; L. Klein and M. Pomer (eds.)*The New Russia : Transition Gone Awry,* Stanford, 2002.

60 L. Silber and A. Little, *Yugoslavia: Death of a Nation*, London, 1997; C. Baker, *The Yugoslav Wars of the 1990s*, New York, 2015; R. Craig Nation, *War in the Balkans, 1991-2002*, Washington DC, 2016.

61 B. George Hewitt, *Discordant Neighbours: A Reassessment of the Georgian-Abkhazian and Georgian-South Ossetian Conflicts*, Leiden, 2013; T. German, *Abkhazia and South Ossetia: Collision of Georgian and Russian Interests*, IFRI, Russie.Nei.Visions 11, 2006. Available at: https://www.ifri.org/sites/default/files/ atoms/files/germananglais.pdf; *Independent International Fact-Finding Mission on the Conflict in Georgia, Report*, 3 Volumes, Heidelberg, 2009. Available at: http://www.mpil.de/en/pub/publications/archive/independent_international_ fact.cfm.

62   M. Kambeck and S. Ghazaryan (eds..) *Europe's Next Avoidable War: Nagorno-Karabakh*, Houndmills, 2013; O. Geukjian, *Ethnicity, Nationalism and Conflict in the South Caucasus: Nagorno-Karabakh and the Legacy of Soviet Nationalities Policy*, Burlington, Vt, 2013; S, E. Cornell (1998) 'Turkey and the conflict in Nagorno Karabakh: a delicate balance', *Middle Eastern Studies*, 34, 1, 1998, 51-72; E. Melander, 'The Nagorno-Karabakh Conflict Revisited: Was the War Inevitable?', *Journal of Cold War Studies*, 3, 2, 2001, 48-75.

63   R. Menon and E. B. Rumer, *Conflict in Ukraine: The Unwinding of the Post–Cold War Order*, Boston Ma, 2015; T. Ash, J. Gunn, J. Lough, O. Lutsevych, J. Nixey, J. Sherr and K. Wolczuk, *The Struggle for Ukraine*, Chatham House Report, London, 2017. Available at: https://www.chathamhouse.org/sites/default/files/publications/research/2017-10-18-struggle-for-ukraine-ash-gunn-lough-lutsevych-nixey-sherr-wolczukV5.pdf.

64   M. Stolarik (ed.)*The Czech and Slovak Republics: Twenty Years of Independence, 1993–2013*, Budapest, 2016; M. Kraus and A. Stanger (eds..) *Irreconcilable Differences. Explaining Czechoslovakia's Dissolution*, Oxford, 2000.

65   A. Borthakur, 'An analysis of the conflict in the Ferghana valley', *Asian Affairs*, 48, 2, 2017, 334-350; R. Gabdulhakov, *Geographical Enclaves of the Fergana Valley: Do Good Fences Make Good Neighbors?*, Central Asia Security Policy Briefs, 14, 2015. Available at: http://osce-academy.net/upload/Policy_briefs/Policy_Brief_14.pdf.

66   T. Epkenhans, *The Origins of the Civil War in Tajikistan: Nationalism, Islamism, and Violent Conflict in Post-Soviet Space*, Lanham Ma, 2018; R. Kevlihan, 'Insurgency in Central Asia: A case study of Tajikistan', *Small Wars and Insurgencies*, 27, 3, 2016, 417-439.

CHAPTER TWO

CHALLENGE AND RESPONSE

This chapter views the revitalisation of the Silk Road, not in terms of some romanticised historical cultural artefact but as a direct response to the disruption and dislocation caused by the collapse of the Soviet-led trade bloc a quarter of a century ago. It begins by reviewing the five objectives identified in President Xi's initial conception of the 'Belt and Road initiative' (BRI). From these five, the chapter explains the reasons behind the decision to concentrate on two - trade facilitation and the provision of (transport) infrastructure. The remainder of this chapter will introduce the countries that lie along the new Silk Road with a look at some of the basic statistics for the situation as it existed in 2011, on the eve of the announcement of China's BRI. It will then examine two quantitative indicators that capture the extent of trade disruption that still persisted almost two decades after the collapse of the Soviet Silk Road. These impediments to international trade occur at one of three stages of a good's passage from supplier to consumer – the journey to the importing country, the costs involved in crossing the border and, finally, the cost and efficiency of the domestic distribution network. The final section of the Chapter will discuss estimates for the future needs for infrastructural investment by the countries along the new Silk Road. The conclusion will summarise the implications of the chapter's findings on trade and infrastructure.

The Objectives of the BRI

The BRI is a multidimensional and multifaceted policy instrument based on experience in domestic development and foreign institutions and which is still evolving in both its content and its global reach. It has five dimensions – policy coordination, transport connectivity, trade facilitation, currency convertibility and people-to-people exchanges. Of these five dimensions, this volume has chosen to concentrate on only two – transport connectivity and trade facilitation which are the most innovative features of the scheme. Even then, not all aspects lend themselves for analysis.

Let us start by looking at the three aspects of the BRI that this book has excluded. First, the element of improving policy communication, as a prelude to closer cooperation, is not in itself new. Despite China's chosen self-effacement in international affairs since 1990,[1] it had not remained isolated from world institutions. In 1971 the Peoples Republic of China took its place in the United Nations (UN) and in 1986 it was accepted as a member of the General Agreement on Tariffs and Trade (GATT), the predecessor of the World Trade Organisation (WTO). Of particular importance for the new Silk Road, China is a member of the UN Economic and Social Commission for Asia and the Pacific (UNESCAP) and of the Central Asia Regional Economic Cooperation (CAREC) programme, formed under the aegis of the Asian Development Bank (ADB) in 1997. Both of these bodies promote cooperation in infrastructural improvement and trade facilitation, and China is active in both. Indeed CAREC's research branch has recently moved to Urumqi in China's western province of Xinjiang. Similarly, China has a long experience in bilateral relations with other nations. Since the first 'strategic partnership' agreement negotiated with Brazil in 1993, it has established over sixty-seven others, including one with each of the five countries in Central Asia, as well as agreements with Russia, Belarus and Ukraine, with four countries in Central and Eastern Europe and with Serbia.[2] Policy communication is an obvious precondition for the success of the BRI, but it is not an innovative component.

The drive towards attaining convertibility and reserve status for China's Renminbi is a relatively new ambition, but it is unlikely that the BRI alone will be sufficient to turn the dream into a reality. To put it simply, to become an international currency there has to be a lot of it in circulation so that foreign banks and businesses can accumulate it and use it in their own international transactions, but not so much that countries lose confidence in its value. The best way is to run a balance-of-payments deficit (which undermines confidence) or to recycle a balance-of-payments surplus by lending and investing abroad. BRI investment may assist in the process, but a more forceful motor is China's overall foreign direct investment (FDI). Investment abroad by Chinese companies has been actively encouraged since the 'going out' policy initiated in 1999[3] and, by 2017, it had resulted in an accumulated stock of FDI of $1.4 trillion dollars.[4] The decision by the International Monetary Fund (IMF) in 2013 to include the Renminbi among the basket of currencies used to calculate the value of Special Drawing Rights (SDRs) was an important step forward. Many countries hold some of their reserves in Renminbi, and China has currency swap agreements with the Central Banks of over 30 countries. Even so, today only two per cent of global transactions are made in Yuan, as opposed to 63 per cent using the US dollar.[5] Without a major shift in the World economy, it is difficult to see the situation changing rapidly, or even sufficiently, to be measureable, let alone being able to assess the role of the BRI in bringing that change about.

The fifth objective, of improving people-to-people exchanges is a laudable one but it is difficult to operationalise. The Chinese government's own attempt to measure the success of its efforts in this direction uses data on city-twinning, international cultural exchanges, tourist numbers, the existence of Confucius Institutes and bilateral cooperation agreements.[6] Fudan University, in its efforts to quantify progress on this front, takes as its indicators scientific and development cooperation, the number of foreign students studying in China, the number of twin cities and the outcomes of polling data on attitudes to China.[7] While all of these indicators capture part of the phenomenon of mutual understanding and respect, even together they fall short of conveying the intent of the Initiative. Moreover, none of them is unique to the BRI, and most of them certainly predate it. Einstein reputedly once wrote, 'Not everything that counts can be counted and not everything that can be counted counts' and with that in mind, it was decided to leave this particular facet of the Belt and Road outside the remit of this book.

Transport infrastructure has been part of the BRI from the very start. Even here, there are aspects that are difficult to follow. For example, the Vision and Action Plan of March 2015 called specifically for the creation of an 'information Silk Road'.[8] Chinese companies, facing overcapacity at home, have been active in expanding abroad through providing ICT services for other infrastructural projects, offering fibre cable- and satellite-based network and employing the internet to offer goods and services.[9] However, at present, the literature on the topic is scarce and it is difficult to compare China's development in this sector with those of other countries. For this reason, we have omitted it from the discussion. Similarly, despite the fact that the expansion of China's airline routes and the construction of airports both in China itself and abroad has been impressive,[10] it has also been omitted from the discussion. This is partly a reflection of the fact that much of the funding for airport terminal enlargement and fleet expansion along the Silk Road is from domestic sources.[11] Had this book been written a year or two later, both of these sectors would undoubtedly have warranted a chapter each.

Xi Jinping's original speech in Kazakhstan in September 2013 referred specifically both to 'road connectivity' and to a 'transport network'.[12] This book therefore concentrates on roads, railways and oil and gas pipelines and devotes separate chapters to each. The book also considers trade facilitation. This is related to, but not synonymous with, the provision of transport infrastructure. Improving transport may help trade either by reducing the costs of transactions or by shortening the time taken between destinations. However any advantage brought about by improvements in transport infrastructure can easily be nullified by high administrative costs or time-wasting bureaucracy. The EU Court of European Auditors offers a telling example of how to save 25 minutes on a 100 kms journey. One option would be to build in Germany a (shorter) 90 km high-speed rail (HSR) line between Nuremberg and Ingolstadt at a cost of $3.1 billion.[13] The second option would be to persuade the Italian authorities at the border with Austria to stop duplicating the safety controls that had already been performed in Munich, 220 kms earlier.[14] Many of the improvements in transport along the new Silk Road have come from the reduction or elimination of frontier barriers to trade and to improvements in bureaucratic efficiency at the borders.

The Countries of the New Silk Road

The countries of the new Silk Road are shown in Figure 2.1, together with some of the basic data on the size of their populations,[15] their land-mass[16] and their economies. The countries have been grouped together for ease of comparison. For this comparison the year 2011 has been chosen, because it offers two estimates for the size of the economy – the size in current dollars and the size adjusted for structural differences in prices (known as purchasing power parity, shortened to 'ppp'). The first measure reflects the value of incomes if they are all spent in international markets; the second is an estimate of the value of incomes if they are all spent domestically.[17] The first we assume is reasonably accurate; the second carries large margins of error. These could be as large as 25 per cent for countries with significantly different economic structures or located in different regions of the world, and they could still be as large as 10 per cent even between countries within the same clusters. However, simply because statistics are not completely accurate, this does not mean that they are useless. It means that they must be viewed and handled with care. Moreover, these errors are likely only to increase over time, so it is best to stay close to the original estimates (2011) until a new set appears.[18]

China anchors the Eastern end of the new Silk Road. It is the World's most populous country and rules over its second largest land-mass. Its population density is the highest of any country on the new Silk Road until one reaches Germany and the other developed countries of Western Europe. However, almost 90 per cent of the population live in the eastern half of the country. If we were to take the autonomous region of Xinjiang (population 21.8 million, landmass 1,665,000 km^2) that borders on Central Asia, the population density would be only 13.1 inh/km^2. When measured in current dollars, China is already the second largest economy in the World, surpassed only by the United States. Its per capita would place it just over the (arbitrary) threshold of 'upper middle income countries' as defined by the World Bank.

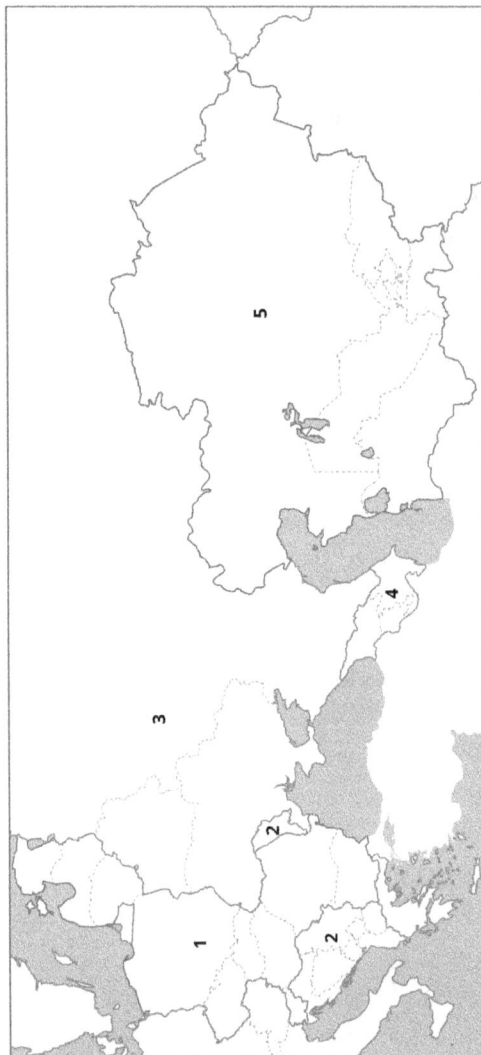

1 NEW EU
Bulgaria, Czech Republic, Estonia, Hungary, Latvia, Lithuania, Poland, Romania, Slovakia, Slovenia

2 WESTERN BALKANS & MOLDOVA
Albania, Bosnia, Croatia, Macedonia, Moldova, Montenegro, Serbia

3 RUSSIA, BELARUS, UKRAINE

4 CAUCASUS
Armenia, Azerbaijan, Georgia

5 CENTRAL ASIA
Kazakhstan, Kyrgyzstan, Tajikistan, Turkmenistan, Uzbekistan

Indicators (2011)	EU (15)	New EU	Western Balkans & Moldova	Caucasus	Russia, Belarus, Ukraine	Central Asia	China
Population (million)	398.3	99.9	24.4	15.9	198.1	64.4	1,344.1
Area (000km2)	3,127	1,078	288	186	17,909	4,003	9,597
Density (Inhr/K2)	127.4	92.7	84.5	85.6	11.1	16.0	140.0
GDP (Billion current $)	16,229.9	1,344.6	159.0	90.5	2,117.4	275.2	7321.9
Pc GDP (Current $)	40,748	13,460	6,527	5,966	10,686	4,273	5,456

Figure 2.1: The Countries of the New Silk Road (basic data, 2011)

As we move to Central Asia we cover another vast relatively under-populated land-mass with relatively average low incomes. Kazakhstan's high(er) income conceals far lower levels elsewhere. The Russian Federation forms the World's largest land-mass under the rule of a single country, but the area bordering Central Asia also consists of relatively underpopulated countryside. The average conceals the increase in population density after reaching the western end of the Russian Federation. Even so, both Belarus and Ukraine fail to match the figure reached in China. Turning south, and sandwiched between the Caspian Sea and the Black Sea lie the three countries known together as the Caucasus. The more mountainous countryside supports a higher population density, but the fact that per capita income levels approach those of China is largely attributable to the higher figures for Azerbaijan pulling up the rest. In the south of Europe lie a group of countries grouped together as 'Moldova and the Western Balkans'. With the exception of Albania and Moldova, all are successor states of former Yugoslavia. With the exception Croatia, their per capita incomes lie close to the average of that of China. China has included them in its BRI because it had penetrated their annual meetings, held together with countries of Central and Eastern Europe, to create the '16 Plus One' arrangements. By the time we reach the states of Central and Eastern Europe, which had all already become member states of the EU, the income levels are all significantly higher than those prevailing in China, even after taking account of large margins of error. Even these are dwarfed by those of the 'core' fifteen states of the EU which formed its membership before its enlargement. Although they had less than one third of the population of China, because of their prosperity, the overall size of their economy was more than twice as large.

In the previous chapter I suggested that there were two essential challenges; the breakdown in international trade and the deficiencies in infrastructural investment. The next section will examine the problems confronting their foreign trade.

Trade Facilitation

International trade is generally considered to be beneficial. This is easiest to appreciate when one considers its complete opposite – autarky, a situation in which each country strives for the greatest degree of self-sufficiency. As a result, there will be structural surpluses of some goods and shortages of many more. Some goods will be completely unattainable. Because of the lack of imports of raw materials and semi-manufactures many lines of production will become impossible. Attempts domestically to produce substitutes will drive up prices. Inability to buy or sell abroad will limit the scale of production for many items, forcing up costs and prices even further. With inflation rising, profits squeezed, employment falling and wages stagnant at best, the demand within the economy will fall. People will become poorer.

If we reverse the logic and make it more general, it is easy to see how international trade can boost overall output. However, this does not mean that countries will benefit equally. Some products command higher prices than others, and countries that specialise in those will benefit more from greater specialisation and trade. Industrial products generally fare better in this respect than agricultural items. Equally, control over resources and supply chains determine which businesses capture the gains from improved market access. The structural solution to these twin problems is to develop a more attractive range of goods that will command higher prices or profits and so to acquire market shares along the supply chain that will break oligopolistic positions. Basically that implies developing the higher value-added industries and becoming more efficient in the delivery of services. In the long-run both of these require capital investment and the provision of improved education. However, in the short-term many countries attempt to limit the effect of competition through policies of taxation, regulation and control.[19]

Over the years there has evolved a considerable literature on attempts to calculate the size of the extra costs involved in conducting foreign trade. One authoritative survey of the literature, based on information collected among (high-income) industrialised countries, suggested the cumulative cost of conducting international trade was equivalent to an import tariff of 170 per cent, a figure that included extra domestic distribution costs.

International transport costs raise the price of an imported item by 21 per cent. This figure comprises freight costs and an additional imputed 9 per cent cost for the interest on capital for the time lost in transport. Border costs would add 44 per cent to the initial price but the effect of import tariffs, which is the item most commonly in the news, only forms a small part of that. The remainder was accounted for by the costs of changing currency, the administrative costs and security checks which together added 55 per cent to the cost of imports. It is important to recognise that these estimates were made on the basis of a limited range of data and from a limited range of countries. Moreover, it is likely that the figure for poorer countries would be higher still, partly because they have higher frontier barriers to trade and partly because they enjoy lower levels of administrative and logistics efficiency.[20] These data were hard enough to obtain for rich countries with efficient administrations and it would be impossible to replicate the calculation for all the countries along the new Silk Road.

The World Bank has constructed its own estimates for trade costs using econometric models based on the substitutability between domestic production and foreign imports, and applying this to pairs of countries. The difference between predicted and observed results is converted into an imputed tariff equivalent. However, although this removes the need to measure separately many different variables, it does not allow a statement on which of the two countries is responsible for the difference, far less to quantify the source of the difference.[21]

The results for these trade cost calculations[22] for the year 2011 are shown in the top set of data in Figure 2.2. It shows the impact of trade costs on the bilateral trade of China, Russia and Germany (chosen as a proxy for the EU(15) since it was its largest single member state) with groups of countries along the new Silk Road. The results are expressed as tariff equivalents and, within each cluster, the country results have been weighted by the 2011 GDP data.[23]

If we travel westwards from China, on the eve of the BRI it is bilateral trade with China that incurs higher trade cost penalties than these countries face in their bilateral trade with either Germany or Russia. China's trade costs with the Caucasus and Moldova and the Western Balkan are eye-wateringly high. Russia enjoys the lowest trade cost penalties in its dealings with the countries of Central Asia, the Caucasus, Belarus and

Ukraine; all countries that had been part of the former Soviet Union. The footprint of history has proven surprisingly resilient in resisting the winds of time. Germany enjoys relatively low trade cost penalties with the new member states of the EU and with Moldova and the Western Balkans. It also trades more favourably with Russia than does China. It is interesting that the trade costs on the bilateral trade between China and Germany are relatively low, despite the huge distance separating the two countries. Indeed for China it is Germany that presents the lowest trade cost penalties of all the countries along the new Silk Road. This could be because the trade was largely ship-borne, where the penalties of distance were lower than over-land, and possibly because of lower penalties incurred in domestic distribution. One other point worth making is that, compared with a decade earlier, all trade-costs had fallen with the exception of Russia's bilateral trade with the Caucasus (where Russia has been involved in the ethnic conflict between Armenia and Azerbaijan, and in its own invasion of Georgia) and, interestingly, with the exception of both China and Germany.

Trade costs (2011, % tariff equivalent)	EU (15)	New EU	Western Balkans & Moldova	Caucasus	Russia, Belarus, Ukraine	Central Asia	China
With China	68.5	153.0	255.3	213.2	118.1	89.9	-
With Germany	-	51.3	100.3	152.8	89.7	128.1	68.5
With Russia	80.2	98.2	183.8	115.7	(50.1 Ukraine)	75.0	94.9

Logistics Performance (2010, score 1-5)	EU (15)	New EU	Western Balkans & Moldova	Caucasus	Russia, Belarus, Ukraine	Central Asia	China
Customs	3.75	2.88	2.37	2.19	2.15	2.27	3.16
Infrastructure	3.81	2.84	2.33	2.24	2.49	2.48	3.54
Logistics	3.92	3.29	2.76	2.78	2.73	2.93	3.56

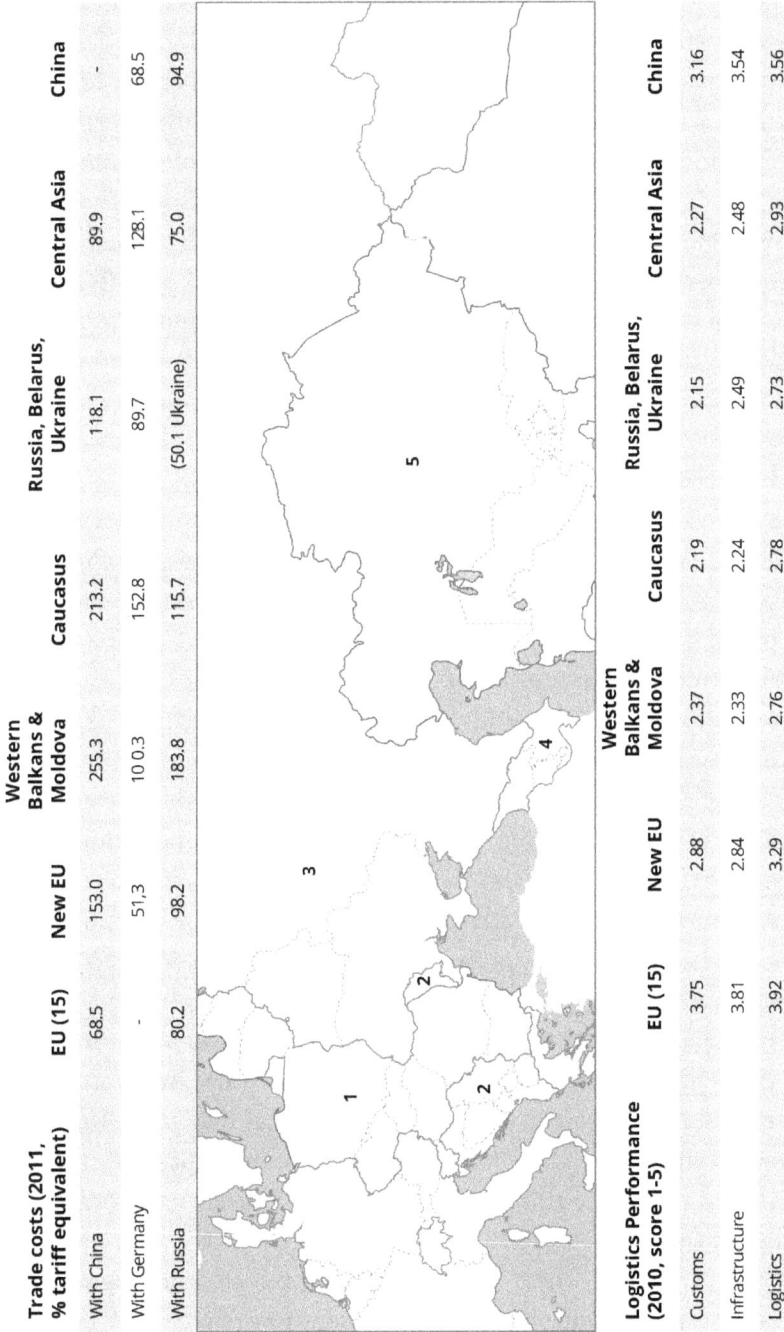

Figure 2.2: Trade Costs and Logistics Performance along the New Silk Road (2010 and 2011)

As explained earlier in this chapter, total trade costs comprise three elements – the costs of travel to the border of a partner country, the costs involved in crossing the border and the transport and distribution costs within the partner country. The World Bank has constructed a Logistics Performance Index (LPI), that allows for quantifying differences in the efficiency (and therefore, costs) of two of those components – namely the border crossing and the domestic infrastructure and logistics. The LPI is based on the opinions of logistics managers on the performance of the countries to which they export. The answers include assessments on the efficiency of customs and border clearance, on the trade and transport infrastructure and on different components of logistics and distribution (that I have averaged into a single number). The results for the clusters along the new Silk Road, in which the individual country results have been weighted according to their GDP size in 2011, are shown in the lower set of data in Figure 2.2.[24] The results are expressed as a score ranging from 5 (very good) to 1 (low).[25] For the countries along the Silk Road the margin of error in the overall score ranged from 4 per cent for the best performing countries to 25 per cent for the worst.

What even a cursory review of the data reveals is that China's performance on all aspects of the LPI is better than that of any cluster along the route until one reaches the EU. In fact China's performance is unmatched in any one of the three components by even a single one of the 28 countries. No margin of error 'correction' places this in any doubt. The performance of the new EU countries of East-Central Europe is out of reach of the rest, but still significantly below both that of China and of the EU countries to the West. The fact that every other country had a worse domestic distribution performance is important in explaining the relative disadvantage faced by imports once they are inside the domestic market. On the other hand the deficiencies in transport infrastructure are also important both for domestic distribution as well as for international trade since the same roads and railways are used for foreign consignments passing through the territory. Of course this also applies for the efficiency of border and customs procedures.

Borders are places where foreign goods and vehicles entering or transiting a country are controlled for health and safety dangers, for proof of ownership, for conformity with national regulations, for the imposition of any import taxes (commonly known as 'tariffs') and for the payment of the charges in the performance of these 'services'. All of this costs time and any corresponding delays (sometimes mounting to days rather than hours) depend on the organisation of the customs posts. The LPI data offers a clear picture of the relative efficiency of border operations with the EU(15) performing best, followed by the new EU member states and then by China. The rest have a fairly lamentable reputation and lie far behind. While this is important, it says nothing about other elements of border costs. For the year 2010, the LPI operation also collected information on border charges - the fees levied on a 20-foot container for the costs for documents, administrative fees for customs clearance and technical control, customs broker fees, terminal handling charges and transport to the road and rail network. The result for China was surprisingly exact - $299.80. This cost was also far and away the lowest. The result for the Central Asian cluster, GDP weighted, was a staggering $3,334, followed by the Caucuses with $2,660 and Russia, Belarus and Ukraine with $1,880. The average for the other three clusters lay between $1,218 and $1,027.[26] None of these charges includes import tariffs.

The suggestion in the literature is that the reduction of import tariffs after 1945 has diminished their importance for international trade and that other dimensions of 'trade costs' have become correspondingly more significant. Indeed, average tariffs appear low. Tariffs are measured by looking at the rates of duty actually applied on individual imported items and weighting them for the share of that item in total imports of the country concerned. If we do this, for 2011, for the countries of the new Silk Road, the highest results are for Russia (7.25 per cent) and China (5.99 per cent). The countries of the EU share a common tariff of 1.43 per cent for trade with non-member countries. The results for most of the other countries lay below 3.5 per cent.[27] Whilst this measure is better than an arithmetic average, the problem is that, if high tariffs reduce trade to almost nothing they will count for virtually nothing in the calculation. Behind these averages, therefore, lurk some highly restrictive tariffs. To take a couple of examples; six per cent of Russia's imports of agricultural products faced tariffs of more than 50 per cent, as did 4.7 per cent of those of the EU.[28]

Many countries also impose non-tariff measures (NTMs) at their borders in the form of regulatory restrictions or even outright prohibitions.

These include sanitary and phytosanitary measures, such as hygiene regulations and maximum pesticide residue limits. There are also technical barriers to trade such as requirements on labelling, product quality, packaging, and certifications. These are all designed to protect the consumer, but it is costly and time-consuming for firms to comply. This increases trade costs and potentially reduces trade. It also invites fraudulent customs declarations by falsely indicating product codes or places of origin.[29] Although the literature has suggested that these have become more restrictive than tariffs, the most recent research for the period 2012-2016 suggests that the richer countries have more recourse to NTMs, and have more complex regimes, than do the less developed countries. However, for most countries, the effect is that of a tariff equivalent of less than three per cent, although the data conceals peaks where the impact is nearly prohibitive. Moreover, although the average costs may be low, the impact is larger for small firms in poorer countries, where the time and labour costs of fulfilling the import requirements might be unduly heavy.[30]

Average tariffs may well be falling, but it would be better still to have no tariffs at all. With tariffs in existence, imports still need to be controlled, verified and subject to whatever (low) tariffs are still levied. Indeed, if the object were really to facilitate trade, it would be even better to have no borders at all - to have a single regulatory system covering all goods so that no controls are needed at national frontiers. This characterised the EU's response to the crumbling edges of the Soviet trading system. Already in 1990 former socialist East Germany had voted to unify with West Germany, thereby joining the EU. Despite the vast sums of aid pumped into the economy by West Germany, the output in the region sank and unemployment soared. This was a little surprising at the time since East Germany had been considered the most advanced of the socialist economies. Similar collapses were occurring throughout the economies of the former members of the Soviet trading system region. As a result, in 1993, the EU opened the prospect of membership to all European states that had made the transition to democracy, that were economically competitive and that were capable of implementing and enforcing the EU's rules and regulations. This had several implications. It opened the prospect of access to the more wealthy European markets on an equal basis and the EU offered administrative and financial help in meeting the criteria.

One of the first steps was to sign free trade agreements with potential member states which, from 1995, gave them immediate free access to sell their industrial goods in EU markets (with some exemptions[31]) and obliged them gradually to reciprocate over a ten year period. In addition, in the early years (1990-1997) the EU's pre-accession programmes provided $17.2 billion in foreign assistance to help prepare for market integration and European Investment banks and the individual member states, in the same period, provided a further $39.2 billion in bilateral aid.[32] As their economies began to recover, so European businesses started to invest in the region. By the end of 1997, they had invested $43 billion in various industries in these countries. This represented over 75 per cent of total foreign direct investment (FDI).[33] EU pre-accession funding continued even after the dates when the countries eventually joined the EU and became eligible for other European funding programmes. Full EU membership occurred in May 2004 for the Baltic states (Estonia, Latvia and Lithuania), the Czech Republic, Hungary, Poland, the Slovak Republic and Slovenia and in January 2007 for Bulgaria and Romania. In those ten years from 1997-2007, the EU had allocated $20.3 billion to its pre-accession programmes, with 80 per cent of it directed towards the ten new member states (Turkey and the former Yugoslav republics received much of the rest).[34] These sums were dwarfed, however, by the streams of FDI that flowed into the new member states, most of it coming from businesses in the existing fifteen EU member states. By 2012 the FDI holdings of the EU(15) in the new members totalled $361 billion compared with $30.7 billion from the USA, which was the next in terms of size.[35]

Infrastructure

To understand the potential of constructing transport infrastructure (roads, railways and pipelines) on economic development, it is necessary to distinguish between two so-called 'linkage effects'. A backward linkage effect deals with the benefits of an investment on the supplier – labour, raw materials, finance, research and development and so forth. The forward linkage deals with the benefits for the operator or the final consumer. The greater the backward and forward linkage effects, the greater is the potential of investment for stimulating economic growth.[36] The construction of real infrastructure are considered potentially powerful generators of growth. However the nature and distribution of the benefits depends on the relationship between client and contractor and between operator and customer.[37]

It does not necessarily require foreign funds, whether in the form of development assistance or private capital to pay for infrastructural maintenance and investment, but it helps. Nor do the funds necessarily need to be earmarked for that specific purpose. An injection of capital into the national income flow releases the equivalent amount to be spent in other directions. For example, if foreign aid is directed at providing a hospital, a government can employ the sums 'saved' on other projects. Moreover, once that initial injection of money begins to circulate in the economy (for example through wages, consumer purchases, shop-keeper income etc.) it raises the level of national income. If the authorities have an appropriate tax system in place, the government can harvest part of that income stream for other objectives.

Since the EU's assistance to the countries of Central and Eastern Europe has been described in the previous section, we can now focus on the international aid effort towards the countries of the Caucasus and Central Asia. Under the OECD's definition of 'official development assistance' the aid must be designed to promote welfare in the recipient country and include at least 25 per cent in the form of a non-repayable grant. The sums include all bilateral development programmes as well as aid channelled through international agencies.[38] About 75 per cent of the total of aid from the OECD member-states comes from European countries. In the twenty years before the launch of China's BRI, Western countries channelled $8,8 billion in development assistance to the Caucasus and $7.3 billion to Central Asia. Belarus and Ukraine were admitted to the scheme only in 2005, but in those eight years alone, they received $3.4 billion. Incidentally, over that same twenty years, China received $28.2 trillion in development assistance from Western donors.[39] Much of these funds went to projects other than transport infrastructure, but part of them did and their impact will be examined in the following chapters. Meanwhile it remains a fact that trade and transport in many regions along the new Silk Road are still handicapped by the lack of transport infrastructure.

The World's attention was drawn to the crying need for infrastructure in Asia by the Asian Development Bank (ADB) in 2009 and again in 2017. In its second approach to the question, the ADB suggested that over the period 2016-2030 the region would require $22.6 trillion ($1.5 trillion a year) to realise its growth trajectory; $26 trillion if measures were taken to reduce the impact on climate change. All the data was measured in 2015 dollars. Of this total only 60 per cent would be new investment; maintenance and rehabilitation would absorb the rest. The largest requirements was power generation, that accounted for 56 per cent of the investment; the remainder being made up of transport infrastructure (32 per cent), telecommunications (8.7 per cent) and water and sanitation (3.3 per cent).[40] However, all these figures also included China. If China were removed from the calculations, the two totals would have been $9.4 trillion and $10.8 trillion respectively over the fifteen year period. Of these totals, the combined needs of the five Central Asian countries along the new Silk Road were estimated at between $492 billion and $565 billion.[41]

Excluding China, which only needed a small percentage increase in investment levels to meet its requirements, the countries in the ADB analysis faced a problem. They were devoting 3.3 per cent of their GDP to infrastructural investment but would need to find 8.2 per cent to meet the challenges of population growth, economic development and climate change. The report suggested that, if they introduced fiscal reforms, national governments could cover 40 percent of the difference themselves. FDI was currently running at under 0.7 per cent of GDP so that figure would need to quadruple were international business to fund the rest of the gap. Otherwise the alternatives were borrowing from international development banks (hopefully at preferential rates), borrowing on the open-market or not investing sufficiently, with all the attendant costs to growth that this would entail. The two ADB reports had the effect of deflecting the world's attention away from a fixation with issues of good governance, complemented it with a gritty analysis that demonstrated that without the tools to do the job, no amount of good governance would suffice to drag economies along a path of sustainable development, or any development at all.

	New EU (excl. Czech Republic)	Western Balkans & Moldova (excl. Montenegro)	Caucasus	Russia, Belarus, Ukraine	Central Asia (excl. Uzbekistan)	Total
Total	340.7	79.4	55.4	842.1	273.8	1,591.4

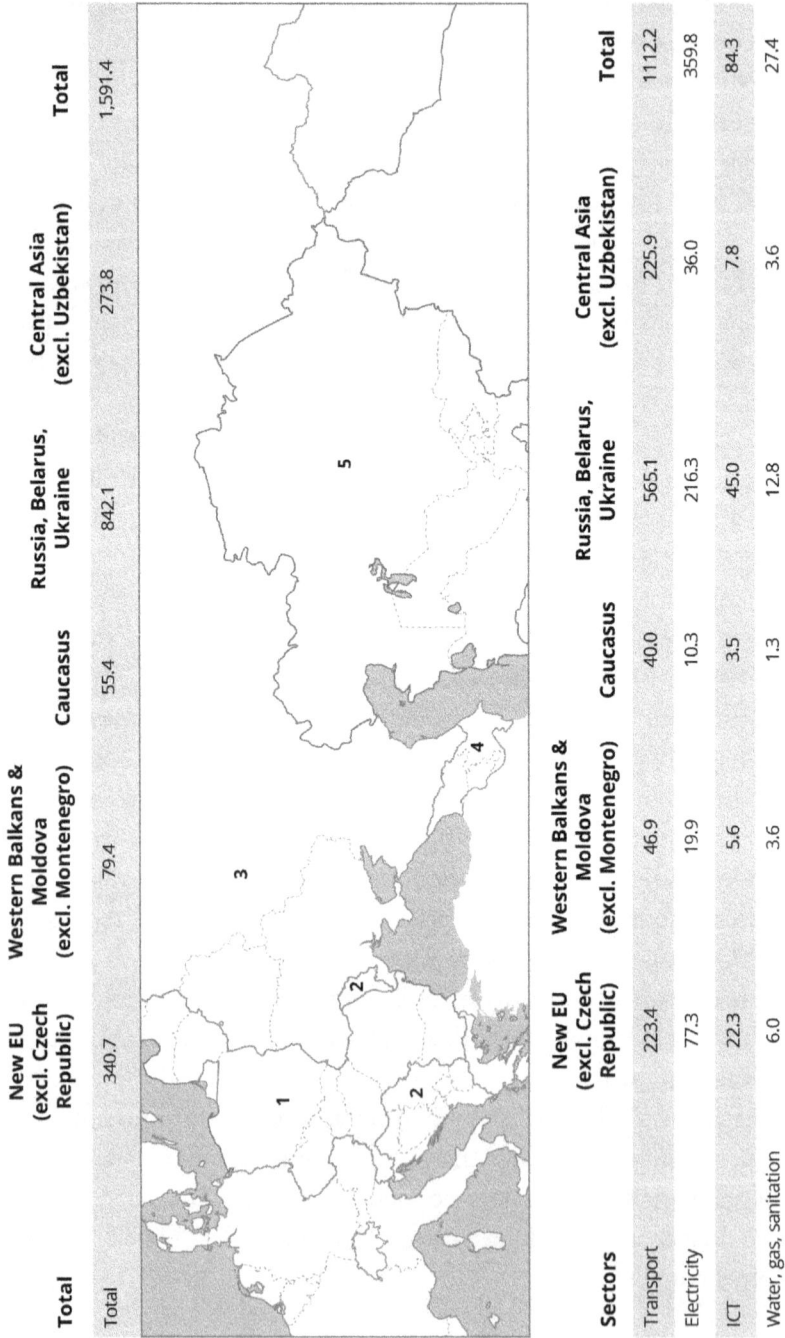

Sectors	New EU (excl. Czech Republic)	Western Balkans & Moldova (excl. Montenegro)	Caucasus	Russia, Belarus, Ukraine	Central Asia (excl. Uzbekistan)	Total
Transport	223.4	46.9	40.0	565.1	225.9	1112.2
Electricity	77.3	19.9	10.3	216.3	36.0	359.8
ICT	22.3	5.6	3.5	45.0	7.8	84.3
Water, gas, sanitation	6.0	3.6	1.3	12.8	3.6	27.4

Figure 2.3: The Countries of the new Silk Road. Infrastructure needs, 2018-2022 (millions 2015 dollars)

In May 2018 the European Bank for Reconstruction and Development (EBRD) made similar calculations for the five-year period, 2018-2022, for the countries under their remit, which coincidentally also includes almost all of the countries of the new Silk Road (minus Uzbekistan and Moldova, for which data was unavailable, and the Czech Republic). Measured in 2015 dollars the region would need to invest $1.6 trillion ($320 billion a year).[42] However, the distribution among sectors was strikingly different from that in Asia. Along the countries of the Silk Road, transport infrastructure accounted for 66 per cent of the total, and the provision of electricity absorbed a further 23 per cent. Telecommunications and water and sanitation absorbed the remainder. Also, compared with Asia, the share of maintenance in the total was slightly higher at 44 per cent, reflecting the higher levels of existing provisions in the more prosperous countries. Collectively, however, the countries shared Asia's problems in funding infrastructural investment. Their current investment levels in infrastructure are far below those required to sustain the necessary expansion.

Conclusions

This chapter focused on the barriers to trade and the inadequacies of the transport infrastructure among the countries that lie along the new Silk Road. In trying to quantify the impact of different impediments to trade it made use of the concept of 'trade costs'. Surveys based on real data suggested that the biggest disadvantage came in the distribution costs incurred once a product had already entered the country. Almost as large were the costs in time and money incurred in passing through the border itself, but the extra taxes levied on imports (tariffs) were not to be the largest factor. The costs of getting the goods to the border in the first place accounted for only 20 per cent of the extra costs. These insights were useful but the information is based on a limited number of richer countries and could not be reproduced for a larger group. Calculations on 'trade costs' made on the basis of econometric modelling revealed peaks of 'trade costs' in trade with China, Russia and (representing the EU) Germany that sometimes exceeded 200 per cent. Evidence on actual tariff rates and on the impact of non-tariff barriers suggested that they did not present any insurmountable problems, although in both cases the averages could conceal peaks that distort the results. By contrast, the costs in time and money in assembling the documentation needed to cross a border could be extremely high. It was here, on the impact of borders, that the EU started to ease the trade cost with its immediate neighbours, firstly by eliminating tariffs and later, through EU membership, by eliminating borders altogether. In addition it committed funds to the improvement of infrastructure.

The second part of the chapter looked at the infrastructure needs of the new Silk Road. It introduced the path-breaking studies by the ADB for Asia's needs, but these only covered the five Central Asian economies. They suggested that to keep pace with population growth and to develop their economies, they would need between $492 billion and $565 billion over fifteen years ($33 billion-$38 billion p.a.). The EBRD estimated that for five years they would need $274 billion ($54 billion p.a.); more if Uzbekistan were included. Altogether, all the countries along the new Silk Road would need $1.5 trillion ($300 billion p.a.) in infrastructural investment. Part of this they would raise themselves from taxation, but it is easy to see why China's emphasis on concessionary infrastructure loans is so appealing.

It is perhaps whimsical to reflect that the EU's experience in lowering/eliminating border costs and China's experience in its own domestic infrastructure boom could provide the perfect symbiosis for dealing with the needs of the new Silk Road. That instead on lecturing each other on how each is better than the other, they could benefit from learning from each other. Meanwhile, the development of the roads, railways and pipelines is moving apace, as we will see in the following three chapters.

1   Z. Chen, 'International responsibility and China's foreign policy' in M. Iida (ed.) *China's Shift: Global Strategy of the Rising Power*, Tokyo, 2009, 7-28. Since 1990 it had supposedly been following the prescription of Deng Xiaoping's '24 Character' foreign policy which urged the country to hold back from foreign engagement until it was ready to help promote and maintain harmonious world development.

2   G. Strüver, *International Alignment between Interests and Ideology: The Case of China's Partnership Diplomacy*, GIGA Working Paper, 283, March 2016. Available at: https://www.giga hamburg.de/en/system/files/publications/wp283 struever 0.pdf.

3   A.L Friedberg, *"Going Out": China's Pursuit of Natural Resources and Implications for the PRC's Grand Strategy*, National Bureau of Asian Research, 17/3, 2006; A. Yelery, *China's 'Going Out' Policy: Sub-National Economic Trajectories*, ICS Analysis 24, 201. Available at https://www.icsin.org/uploads/2015/04/12/e50f1e532774c4c354b24885fcb327c5.pdf; Y. Zhang, *China Goes Global*, London, 2005.

4   UNCTAD, Country Fact Sheet, China 2018. Available at: https://unctad.org/en/Pages/DIAE/World%20Investment%20Report/Country-Fact-Sheets.aspx.

5   J. Bateman, 'One Belt, One Road, One Currency', *Global Finance*, 1.6.2018. Available at: https://www.gfmag.com/magazine/june-2018/one-belt-one-road-one-currency. For expansion of the yuan's role in international transactions see Xinhua Economic News Service, 7.1.2019. Available at: http://en.silkroad.news.cn/2019/0107/126821.shtml and for a more sceptical note see D. Lubin, 'Waiting for the Global Renminbi', *Asia Sentinel*, 18.2.2019, Available at: https://www.asiasentinel.com/econ-business/waiting-global-renminbi/.

6   PRC, National Development and Reform Commission, 一带一路大数据报告, Beijing, 2016, 2017 (One Belt One Road. Big Data Report).

7   Fudan Institute of Belt and Road and Global Governance News Release, 25.12.2018. Available at: http://brgg.fudan.edu.cn/en/articleinfo 305.html.

8   PRC, National Development and Reform Commission, *Vision and Actions on Jointly Building Silk Road Economic Belt and 21st-Century Maritime Silk Road*, 28.3.2015. Available at: http://en.ndrc.gov.cn/newsrelease/201503/t20150330 669367.html.

9   Shen, H (2018) 'Building a Digital Silk Road? Situating the Internet in China's Belt and Road Initiative', *International Journal of Communication*, 12, 2683-2701. Available at: https://ijoc.org/index.php/ijoc/article/view/8405/2386; *China's Digital Silk Road*, Transcript of Presentation CSIS, Washington, 5.2.2019. Available at: https://csis-prod.s3.amazonaws.com/s3fs-public/publication/190211 Chinas Digital Silk Road.pdf.

10 Xinhua Silk Road Information Service, 29.1.2018 Available at: http://en.silkroad.news.cn/2018/0129/81482.shtml.

11 *Routes Online*, 13.9.2018. Available at https://www.routesonline.com/news/29/breaking-news/280353/aviations-role-in-boosting-silk-road-connectivity/.

12 J Xi, *Promote People-to-People Friendship and Create a Better Future*, speech at Nazarbayev University, Kazakhstan, 11.9.2013. Available at: https://www.fmprc.gov.cn/mfa_eng/wjdt_665385/zyjh_665391/t1078088.shtml.

13 The line does have nine tunnels with a total length of 27 kms. The original sum quoted was €2.3 billion.

14 European Court of Auditors, *Improving transport performance on trans-european rail axes: Have EU rail Infrastructure Investments been effective?* Special Report Nr 8, 2010, 41-42. Available at: https://www.eca.europa.eu/Lists/ECADocuments/SR10_08/SR10_08_EN.PDF. The controls also involved replacing the reflecting boards at the back of the train with electric tail lights.

15 World Bank Database https://data.worldbank.org/indicator/SP.POP.TOTL.

16 World Bank Database https://data.worldbank.org/indicator/AG.LND.TOTL.K2.

17 World Bank, *Purchasing Power Parities and the Real Size of World Economies. A Comprehensive Report of the 2011 International Comparison Program*, Washington DC, 2015, Tables 2 i-iv; 2.13 i-iv. Available at: http://siteresources.worldbank.org/ICPEXT/Resources/2011-ICP-Global-Report.pdf.

18 For an overview of attempts to calculate ppp GDP see R.T. Griffiths, *Configuring the World. A critical Political Economy approach*, Leiden, 2015, 90-98. For more detailed criticism of the latest data see A. Deaton and B. Aten, *Trying to Understand the PPPs in ICP2011: Why are the Results so Different?* National Bureau of Economic Research Working Paper, 20244, Cambridge Ma. 2014. Available at: https://www.nber.org/papers/w20244.pdf; R. Inklaar and D.S. Prasada Rao, *Cross-country income levels over time: did the developing world suddenly become much richer?* Groningen Growth and Development Centre Working Paper 151, 2014. Available at http://siteresources.worldbank.org/ICPEXT/Resources/Cross-Country-Income-Levels.pdf; M. Ravallion, *An Exploration Of The International Comparison Program's New Global Economic Landscape*, National Bureau of Economic Research Working Paper, 20338, Cambridge, Ma., 2014. Available at: https://blogs.commons.georgetown.edu/economicsofpoverty/files/2015/12/The-ICPs-new-global-economic-landscape.pdf.

19 For a useful introduction to international trade see R. Pomfret, *International Trade. Theory, Evidence and Policy*, World Scientific Publishing, New Jersey, 2016.

20 J. Anderson and E. Van Wincoop, 'Trade Costs', *Journal of Economic Literature*, 42, 3, 2004, 691-751. Available at: http://www.its.caltech.edu/~camerer/SS280/TradeCosts.pdf.

21 J-F. Arvis, Y. Duval, B. Shepherd, C. Utoktham, *Trade Costs in the Developing World 1995–2010*, World Bank Policy Research Working Paper 6309, 2013. Available at: http://documents.worldbank.org/curated/en/816351468338515230/pdf/wps6309.pdf.

22 World Bank Database, Available at: http://databank.worldbank.org/data/reports.aspx?source=escap-world-bank-international-trade-costs.

23 Because the data for one or both benchmark years was missing, Turkmenistan is omitted from the calculation for Central Asia, Bosnia, Montenegro and Serbia from the Western Balkans and Estonia, Hungary and Slovakia from the New EU states.

24 World Bank Database https://lpi.worldbank.org/.

25 World Bank, *Connecting to Compete, Trade Logistics in the Global Economy*, 2014, 51-54. Available at: https://openknowledge.worldbank.org/handle/10986/20399.

26 World Bank Database https://lpi.worldbank.org/domestic. The data was collected every two years. Turkmenistan is missing from the Central Asian cluster.

27 World Bank Database. https://datacatalog.worldbank.org/tariff-rate-applied-weighted-mean-all-products-2.

28 *World Tariff Profiles, 2012*, 76, 137.Available at: https://unctad.org/en/PublicationsLibrary/wto2012_en.pdf.

29 H.L. Kee and A. Nicita, *Trade Frauds, Trade Elasticities and Non-Tariff Measures*, mimeo, World Bank, June 2016. Available at: http://pubdocs.worldbank.org/en/315201480958601753/3-KEE-paper.pdf.

30 World Bank and UNCTAD, *The Unseen Impact of Non-Tariff Measures. Insights from a new database*, Geneva, 2018. Available at: https://unctad.org/en/PublicationsLibrary/ditctab2018d2_en.pdf.

31 Exemptions were in coal, steel and certain textiles.

32 Together this amounted to 75 per cent of the assistance they received in these years.

33 European Commission, *Towards greater economic integration. Central and Eastern Europe: trade, investment and assistance of the European Union*, Brussels, 1999, 4-5, 36-37, 43-63. Available at: http://aei.pitt.edu/43231/. Converted at the average of December exchange rates for 1990-1997, €16 billion converts to $17.2 billion, €37 billion to $39.2 billion and €40 billion to $43 billion. These sums would be 55 per cent higher if converted to current dollar prices.

34 Europa Database: http://ec.europa.eu/budget/library/biblio/documents/2015/internet-tables-2000-2015.xls. Converted at the average of December exchange rates for 1998-20077, €18 billion converts to $20.3 billion, or $24.8 billion if converted to current dollar prices.

35 Calculated from UNCTADSTAT database. http://unctad.org/en/Pages/DIAE/FDI%20Statistics/FDI-Statistics.aspx.

36 The concept was first developed by A.O. Hirschman, *The Strategy of Economic Development*, New Haven CT, 1958.

37 For a fuller exposition see R.T. Griffiths, *Revitalising the Silk Road. China's Belt and Road Initiative*, Leiden, 2017, 57-67.

38 OECD Glossary. Available at https://stats.oecd.org/glossary/detail.asp?ID=6043.

39 Asian Development Bank, *Infrastructure for a Seamless Asia*, Manilla: 2009. Available at: https://www.adb.org/sites/default/files/publication/159348/adbi-infrastructure-seamless-asia.pdf.

40 Asian Development Bank, *Meeting Asia's Infrastructure Needs.*, Manilla, 2017, 39-83. Available at: https://www.adb.org/sites/default/files/publication/227496/special-report-infrastructure.pdf.

41 OECD International Development Assistance Databases. Available at: http://www.oecd.org/dac/stats/idsonline.htm.

42 European Bank for Reconstruction and Development, *Transition Report 2017-2018, Sustaining Growth*, 53-55. Available at: https://www.ebrd.com/documents/oce/pdf-transition-report-201718-english.pdf. The author is grateful to the EBRD for providing a more detailed breakdown of the data. The original data has been increased by 10 per cent to match the ADB data which had been presented in 2015 dollar values.

CHAPTER THREE

ROADS

This chapter starts by exploring the versatility that roads offer in terms of locations reached, the times of access and the choice of vehicle. The chapter then divides into two main sections. The first section follows the progress of roads starting from China, travelling through Central Asia and ending in the Caucasus. Although the access to roads appears flexible, this changes dramatically when there is an international frontier in the way. The chapter explores the situation that developed in Khorgos, a crossing-point specifically developed by China for the promotion of trade. It then explores the new highways constructed in Central Asia and the sources of their funding. In the Caucasus it examines the role played by the closure of international borders, following the various conflicts in the region, on the pattern of highway construction. The second section of the chapter starts in East-Central Europe, passes through the Balkans before turning its attention to Ukraine, Belarus and Russia. It examines the timing of the European funding in neighbouring countries and the priority afforded to road construction. It also traces the gradual inclusion of neighbouring countries into the international corridors that reach through the European Union (EU) and the outreach of the initiative to the Caucasus. The concluding paragraphs will pull the evidence together and suggest that it is not the roads, themselves, that represent the problem, but the point at which they cross international borders.

Versatile Roads

Roads are as old as time. They come in a variety of forms ranging from primitive tracks worn into the ground by habitual use to fine, paved thoroughfares on the approaches to magnificent cities. They cross endless stretches of grassland, skirt vast deserts and climb towering mountain ranges. From time immemorial to the days when Baron von Richthofen made his own travels and coined the name 'Silk Roads', travellers had moved on foot, on horse or donkey, on camel or on cart. Until the invention of the internal combustion engine signalled the arrival of cars and trucks, things had remained largely unchanged for millennia. If the ancient Silk Road had taken the direct route from Xi'an, site of the original capital of China, in the east, to Antioch on the shores of the Eastern Mediterranean, the distance would be 6,461 kms. The shortest feasible overland route, however, was closer to 7,250 kms. Indeed, a recent geographical survey estimates that, when all the alternative roads and tracks and the various spurs were included, there were 75,000 kms of road in the corridors constituting the ancient Silk Roads.[1] Since 2003, the UN Economic and Social Commission for Asia and the Pacific (UNESCAP) has been running a project for the upgrading of a network of roads that would constitute an Asia Highway. In addition to China, the signatories include Russia, Mongolia and the countries of Central Asia and the Caucasus. Together these countries host 22,000 kms of international roads that form part of the Asia Highway (and a further 25,000 kms of roads of more regional importance), and there are still 2,000 kms to cover before reaching the shores of the Mediterranean.[2]

Roads are an exceptional form of transport infrastructure. They allow access to (almost) any wheeled vehicle along any arbitrary point in the network and, without any need to change the vehicle, to proceed to any destination that might be chosen. In addition, nowadays, most roads are free, in the sense that there is no direct charge for their use. By improving a road, the weight of the loads that can be carried and the speed of their delivery may substantially increase, and its use extended through the seasons. It is easy to see why road improvements should provide a stimulus to economic development, especially in areas where existing transport links are particularly primitive. The only problem, of course, is that roads are never truly free. Their construction always costs labour and materials. Even if the construction costs are covered from outside sources (central government grants or foreign development assistance) roads still need to be maintained. The question, therefore, is who should pay for them – the people where the roads are built (and should those closest to the road pay more, or those furthest away) or regional or central governments? Alternatively, the charge could be levied for the road's actual use (through tolls or taxes on fuel) or by a tax on those with the potential ability to benefit from their use (annual charges on cars or trucks) rather than on households and businesses along the route. Once the question of income is resolved, a further problem arises in the need to find a way to stop the authorities from using the income stream for other purposes. The result is often a road building cycle – build/neglect/decay/rebuild.

A second issue associated with the apparently 'free' access to roads is the impact that this has on other forms of transport which do levy a charge at the point of access. Since the cost of a vehicle (vehicle plus taxes) is fixed, the variable cost is time and fuel. Trains, by contrast, are also burdened by 'rail access' charges (a tariff for each kilometre travelled). This gives roads an artificial cost advantage which encourages their use. Unfortunately, in terms of passengers (passengers/kilometres) and freight (ton/kilometres) motor vehicles are heavier polluters than any other form of transport, whether by sea, land or air. Zero-charging for road access therefore undermines government efforts to reduce carbon emissions in order to improve health and to counter climate change.[3]

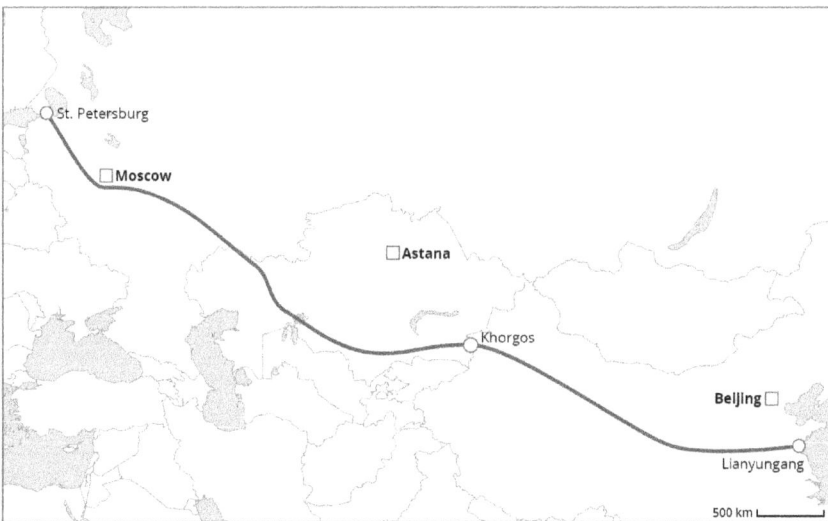

Figure 3.1 West Europe-West China Highway

In the October 2018 an article in the Times of London announced the completion of the West Europe – West China (WE-WC) Highway that stretches 8,445 kms from the port of Lianyungang in China all the way to the Baltic Sea at St. Petersburg, Russia. The article then continued by reminding its readers that the road represented part of China's $900 billion Belt and Road infrastructure investment scheme[4] despite the fact that, aside from the 4,243 kms Lianhuo Expressway inside China connecting Khorgos to Lianyungang, none of it was financed or built by China. Although most of the route will be used for short-haul traffic, in November 2018 the first trial TIR truck[5] made the journey along the road from Khorgos to the intersection to Poland and from there to Warsaw in thirteen days, which presaged a regular service to be launched in the new year. CEVA Logistics claimed that the service would be half the price of air freight, and 30-50 per cent faster than rail. Unfortunately, per ton/kilometre, it would be three times more damaging than rail traffic in the emission of green-house gases.[6] Sceptics also doubted whether an up-scaled service could regularly replicate the success of a single trial run. They suggested that breakdowns, customs delays and the sheer complication of arranging for shifts of drivers could not offer the reliability expected by customers.[7] In the next paragraph we will follow the building of the main highways from China to Europe.

Heading West from China

The Xinjiang Autonomous Region forms the Chinese territory bordering on the countries lying to the west. Situated in the north-west of the country it covers 1.6 million km² of territory. Much of it is desert, so it is not surprising that it only has a population of about 24 million people, most of whom are clustered in the west where the mountains provide a source of water. Beyond the capital of Urumqi, the region is flanked by the Alatau Mountains, with a natural crossing through the Alashankou Pass. This was one of the entry points for Silk Road travellers into ancient China, but it was not a favoured route. The sparse population and harsh climate made the journey perilous, and caravans were vulnerable to attack by bands of steppe nomads. Over 1,300 kms further south, the oasis town of Kashgar marked a more popular crossing point. This route led travellers into a more settled farming area, which was less dangerous and which offered better prospects for trade. Recently, a new town called Khorgos has risen from almost nothing and lies, literally, virtually in the middle of nowhere. The location is not far from the Eurasian pole of inaccessibility – the point on the Eurasian landmass that is furthest from the sea (46°17'N 86°40'E). Looking at this from another angle, one could say that it is at the centre of the Eurasian landmass. Supported by a $3.5 billion grant from the Chinese authorities, Khorgos has grown into a vibrant modern town of 85,000 inhabitants, with wide, tree-lined boulevards and, at the border, a huge free-trade shopping complex. On the other side of the border, in Kazakhstan, lies the Khorgos East Gate dry port, ready to act as the main hub for road and rail transport to the West.[8] It is also the point where the WE-WC Highway crosses from China to Kazakhstan.

Currently, 83 per cent of Xinjiang's total trade is focused on Central Asian states, and 80 per cent of China's total trade with Central Asia transits through the territory. In 2000 China inaugurated its 'Go West Strategy' to promote the economic development of its relatively less prosperous inland regions. After the riots in Urumqi in 2009,[9] the Xinjiang Autonomous Region was granted 'extraordinarily important strategic status' in the nation's development programme. A complex set of measures resulted in the establishment of the new Special Economic Zone in Kashgar and the creation of special trade zones at the land-ports of Alatau and Khorgos.[10] The five year plan for Xinjiang (2016-2020) envisages building 9,152 kms of roads to satisfy the infrastructural needs of the region, but not all of it to be completed within the five year period, involving an expenditure of $13 billion, more if extra funds were forthcoming from the Silk Road Fund or other sources.[11] The 4,243 kms road from the coast reached Khorgos in 2014.

The roads lying to the west pass through Central Asia, Russia and the Caucasus. The UNESCAP has identified 22,000 kms of major international transport corridors running through these countries. Much of the area is sparsely populated, traffic density is correspondingly light and this possibly explains why, in 2003 when the data was first collected, fully 86 per cent of international routes consisted of one lane in each direction. These roads were generally unlit and in poor condition. They were also highly dangerous either because they were narrow, twisting and unprotected mountain roads, or because they were endless, straight, flat and boring, with many drivers reliant on alcohol or drugs to help pass the time.[12] Ten years later, when China launched its BRI, road conditions had already improved. The proportion of two-lane roads had fallen to 80 per cent, and 42 per cent were described as being in good condition.[13] Speeds along most international routes averaged 35-40 km/h, depending on the season. However, put a border crossing point (BCP) in the way, and (measured on a standardised 500 km route) the averages plunged dramatically to 13-20 km/h, with trucks taking on average between 9 and 16 hours to pass through all the border procedures. The single longest delays were incurred in simply trying to enter the border facilities. Back-ups could occur because the arrival of a truck coincided with a build-up of traffic, or because of inadequate facilities or because of the inefficiency of operations once inside the facility. Here further delays accumulated. Customs clearance often requires a full physical examination, necessitating the unloading and reloading of the cargo. This often had to be done manually, because forklifts and pallet jacks were mostly absent. The paper-work all needed to be checked – passport, driving licence, vehicle ownership, vehicle inspection, insurance, cargo documentation and cargo delivery documents, all with the correct forms and with the necessary translations. Having passed through these stages, the truck would need to join a separate queue in a new location for phytosanitary and veterinary controls. Many of these procedures would then need to be repeated on entering the country on the other side of the border.[14] Such was the lot of the ordinary truck driver travelling along the modern Silk Road.

There was a way to fast-track these border procedures – bribes. In order to obtain a favour in expediting border security 67 per cent of drivers made an unofficial payment; 56 per cent slipped some money to help speed up customs clearance and 55 per cent thought it worth paying a little extra for help in obtaining phytosanitary clearance. The largesse did not stop at the border. Delays could also occur during the journey itself. There were spot checks along the route to control axle-weights and vehicle conditions, and 80 per cent of drivers thought it worth paying a little extra to encourage a flexible attitude. However, by far the most common illicit payment of all was to pass quickly through the police checkpoints stationed at regular intervals along many routes for vehicle or identity inspection, or possibly for the simple purpose of supplementing police pay.[15]

Central Asia

China's main access to Asian and European markets lies through Kazakhstan. For road traffic the major border crossing point (BCP) is at Khorgos. In 2009, approximately 200 trucks a day passed through the facilities, most of these carrying Chinese goods to the former capital of Almaty, a city with a population of 1.5 million lying 300 kms to the south-west. As traffic increased, however, the facilities strained to cope. The problem was that few Chinese trucks were allowed to enter Kazakhstan because the two countries had different truck specifications and the Kazakh authorities were reluctant to grant vehicle licenses for Chinese trucks. This meant that Chinese drivers were forced to unload their cargo into a bonded warehouse where it would be collected by a Kazakh driver. In his turn, the Kazakh driver would first have to pass (empty) through Khorgas (the name of the village on the Kazakh side) and into Khorgos (on the Chinese side). To complete all the formalities would take four hours or so. He would then have to queue to get to the warehouse, load the goods and pass through customs and health and quarantine checks. There then followed another queue to enter the holding area, still on the Chinese side of the border, and to re-enter the Khorgas facilities. Unfortunately the parking space on that side is limited and so another long wait would ensue. Once onto Kazakh soil, there would be yet another queue before starting and completing the customs clearance procedures.

It is not difficult to imaging small increases in traffic upsetting the routine. In 2009 activities such as customs clearance, queuing and loading/unloading each took between one and two hours. By 2012 the time to clear the facilities in Khorgos had risen to 65 hours, with some drivers reporting 120 hours to complete all procedures. Part of the reason was that the new Eurasian Customs Union was being implemented with new procedures and a new tariff schedule. This coincided with an increased severity exercised by the Kazakh authorities in granting Chinese vehicles recognition. Finally, the situation was complicated by a temporary move of the location of customs facilities on the Chinese side.[16] The move of the administrative

offices was part of a development that was destined to completely trans-
form an isolated border crossing into a site that would be described as a
'new Dubai'.[17] Under a bilateral agreement for an 'International Centre for
Border Cooperation', new facilities like warehouses, wholesale outlets, and
separate vehicle inspection zones were being built. The Almaty-Khorgos
highway was also nearing completion, including an enlarged and modernised entry into the border facilities.[18] The good news was that by 2016
the time taken for a Kazakh driver to complete all the operations involved
in his round-trip through the Khorgos/ Khorgas procedures had fallen to
ten hours; still high by international standards.[19]

Let's us turn our attention to the roads themselves. The main highway
improvements for Kazakhstan, Uzbekistan and Turkmenistan are shown
in Figure 3.2. As we saw, Khorgos was the start of the Kazakh section on
the WE-WC Highway. The 380 kms four-lane highway from Almaty to
Khorgos (Figure 3.2, route 1) was also intended as a section of the road.
The new highway cost $1,25 billion to complete and construction was fin-
ished by 2016, with a World Bank loan covering 85 per cent of the cost.[20]
From there, a modern four-lane express-way would be built covering the
remainder of the 2,787 kms distance to the city of Aktobe in the north
(Figure 3.2, route 2). The estimated cost of the project was $7.5 billion. The
World Bank provided $2.125 billion for the 1,322 kms for which it was
responsible.[21] The $4.4 billion for the development of the rest was funded
by a consortium of banks led by the Asian Development Bank (ADB)
and by the Kazakh authorities.[22] The $181 million needed for the last 102
kms section from Aktobe to the border (Figure 3,2, route 3) was funded
by the European Bank for Reconstruction and Development (EBRD).[23]
The road then crossed the border into Russia and continues its journey
towards Moscow.

Figure 3.2: Routes of Main Highway Improvements
in Kazakhstan, Uzbekistan and Turkmenistan

The World Bank had been planning to construct a brand new 1,014 kms highway south-west from Astana to Shalkar, at the cost of $1.1 billion, but in November 2016 Kazakhstan authorities cancelled the project. Given the hysteria which usually greets news of cancellations of Chinese infrastructural investments, it is perhaps worth pausing to see what happened. Basically, Kazakh government revenues had been hard hit by the fall in energy prices since 2014 and the government was becoming concerned that debt service was consuming too much of the budget. Rather than take on new commitments, it was determined to use its funds to complete the projects already underway.[24]

At the northern end of the WE-WC Highway, roads are being improved to link it to the Caspian Sea port of Aktau (Figure 3.2, route 4), with an annual handling capacity of 19.5 million tonnes. The port's main traffic is to Iran, from which goods can be transported to the port of Banda Abbas and onwards to Africa and the Indian Ocean. More interesting, recently, has been the development of trade to Baku, in Azerbaijan. Ferries can cover the distance to Baku in about 22 hours. However, room for expansion is limited and its location leaves the port exposed to high winds and ferries prone to delays.[25] In December 2016 a new port was opened in Kuryk, in a more sheltered location 50 kms to the south. Costing $101 million to build, the new port has an annual capacity of 5.1 million tonnes. By 2018 it was already handling 1.6 million tonnes of cargo, mainly grain, oil products, fertilisers and chemicals.[26] In 2010 the ADB agreed a loan of $800 million of the $1.2 billion required to upgrade the 790 kms of roads leading from Aktobe to the ports. It later advanced a further $317 million to improve connectivity in the area.[27] Meanwhile Uzbekistan's major road project involves improving 760 kms of the main highway from the South of the country to link up with the border town of Beyneu (Figure 3.2, route 5) and the renewed highway network in Kazakhstan. Once again the lead has been taken by the ADB with has advanced $955 million of the $1.1 billion funds reserved for the project, with the Uzbek government contributing $257 million from its own resources.[28]

Turkmenistan has long been the most isolated of all the Central Asian Republics, but it too has come, albeit belatedly, to realise the importance of securing a share in the burgeoning transit trade in the region. In May 2018 the Turkmen government opened a new passenger and cargo port in Turkmenbashi on the Caspian Sea with an annual handling capacity of 75,000 trailer trucks and 400,000 TEU (twenty-foot equivalent) containers. The contractor Turkish Gap Inşaat had started work on the project five years earlier and it had been completed at an estimated cost in excess of $1.5 billion.[29] In 2017 work started to link the port to the capital Ashgabat by a four-lane toll motorway (Figure 3.2, route 6a) built on a BOT (build-operate-transfer) contract by the Turkish company Polimeks Insaat Taahhut ve Sanayi Ticaret AS.[30] However, within months it had suspended work on the project because it had run into financial difficulties due to non-payment for government work done on previous contracts. The company's executives have left the country, but not after encountering a few local difficulties.[31] Seemingly undeterred by this setback, in January 2019 the government inaugurated the start of construction on a new 600 kms eight-lane highway stretching from Ashgabat to Turkmenabat near the border with Uzbekistan and then south to the rail hub of Tedjen near the border with Afghanistan (Figure 3.2, route 6b). The $2.3 billion required by the project is being advanced by the National Bank and the work is to be undertaken by a little known domestic company named Turkmen Awtoban.[32] The exorbitant cost of the project and the previously unknown contractor has led some commentators to wonder how the money will be spent and who will profit.[33] The answer to that question should not be long in coming.

If we travel southwards along the Chinese border we come to the mountainous country of Kyrgyzstan with which China shares an 858 kms border. There are two border crossings that connect the roads between the two countries, one in Torugart and the other at Erkeshtam, 165 kms further south. The road from Torugart cuts through the north of Kyrgyzstan to Bishkek and onwards to Tashkent. The approaches to the border were supposed to have been improved with the help of a $20 million grant from the ADB. However, because of a dispute between different government agencies over the exact location of the new facilities the improvements were never made.[34] As a result, by 2012 it was taking an average of 18 hours for a truck to complete all the customs procedures. The following year, however, Kyrgyzstan introduced new simplified customs procedures, whereby imports were assessed by weight rather than by declared values. Hereafter, the passage of a truck in either direction took a matter of a couple of hours, at most.[35] The second route through Kyrgyzstan passes through the Irkeshtam Pass. This used to be the main southern thoroughfare on the ancient Silk Road, leading to Kashgar. The border crossing at Irkeshtam was officially opened in 1998, but because of the difficult nature of the narrow, winding road, it is the lesser used of the crossings. The road itself is in good condition, having been resurfaced in 2013 at the cost of $600 million. The highway is intended to be part of an upgraded road reaching down into Pakistan.[36] The crossing is open for six hours on weekdays and is closed at weekends and, as a result, the waits are horrendous. In the late Summer of 2012, a truck passing from China spent an average of 51.5 hours crossing the border. By 2016, however, the time had fallen to 22 hours. If a Chinese truck wished to continue its journey beyond Kyrgyzstan, for example to Duschanbe, it would then be forced to drive five days on a circuitous 1469 kms route (via Batken) because the Kyrgyz government does not allow the shorter route (995 kms via Karamyk) to be used for transit purposes by Chinese registered trucks.[37]

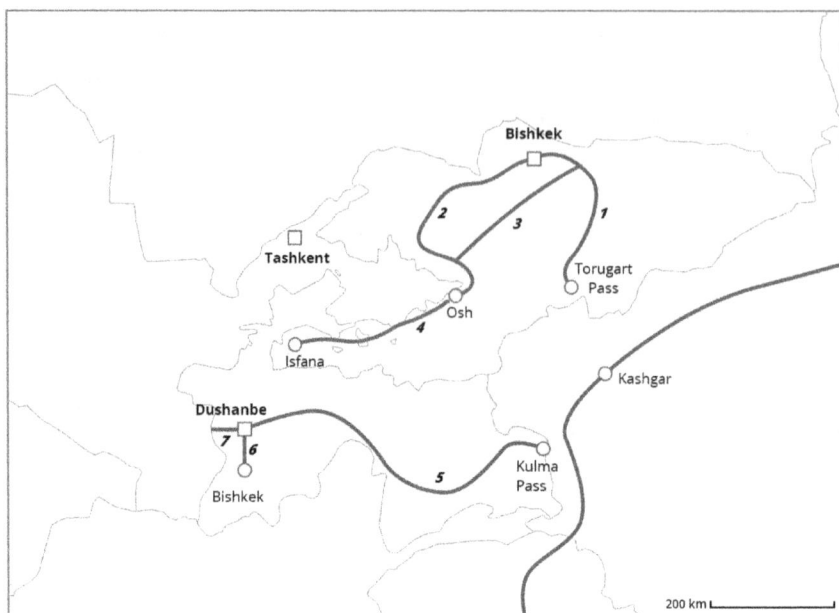

Figure 3.3 Main Road Improvements in Kyrgyzstan and Tajikistan

The main internationally financed road projects in Kyrgyzstan and Tajikistan are shown in Figure 3.3. There are four major road improvement schemes underway in Kyrgyzstan.[38] The first is from the Torugart crossing to the capital, Bishkek (Figure 3.3, route 1). The reconstruction of the 665 kms road was financed by loans from the EXIM bank of China ($200 million), the ADB ($150 million) and the Arab Coordinating Group ($75 million).[39] Work had started in 2010 and some 67 per cent had been completed by May 2017.[40] The second project involved improving the road linking Bishkek to the country's second largest city, Osh (Figure 3.3, route 2). The ADB acted as the main financier of the project with a loan of $140 million.[41] The old Bishtek-Osh road will always remain a long and winding highway, but a far more ambitious 'alternative route' is also envisaged, backed by a $850 million loan from the EXIM Bank of China. The plan calls for a route cut through the mountains that would slice 220 kms from the length of the current route (Figure 3.3, route 3). The China Road and Bridge Corporation (CRBC) started work on the new 154 kms road (including a 3.3 kms tunnel) in 2014.[42] The final project involved improving half of the 385 kms road connecting Osh to the Isfana (Figure 3.3, route 4) at the border with Uzbekistan. The $175 million in costs were shared by the ERBD and the World Bank.[43]

There is only one crossing point on the 414 kms border that Tajikistan shares with China and that is at the top of the Kulma Pass. Curiously, the Chinese control point is situated 14 kms away, next to the Karakorum Highway which links China to Pakistan. It is open from 11.00 to 17.00, with an hour's break for lunch, and it is closed at weekends. When the weather is bad it is closed altogether. This is an improvement on the previous situation, when it was open for only fifteen days a month. When it is open, the crossing takes about five hours.[44]

Tajikistan has three main projects. The first involves improving the road between the Kulma Pass and Dushanbe (Figure 3.3, route 5) which is funded by loans totaling $254 million from the EXIM Bank of China with the work undertaken by the CRBC.[45] A second project involves the reconstruction of a 90 kms four-lane highway between Dushanbe and the Kurgonteppa, to the south (Figure 3.3, route 6). The ADB is the main funder of the project, having invested close to $225.2 million.[46] The final project involves upgrading the road from Dushanbe to the Uzbek border (Figure 3.3, route 7) which had involved loans worth $220 million from the ADB.[47] What is interesting is that just outside Dushanbe a major multi-level road intersection is being built as part of the project with support of a $62.5 loan from the EBRD and a loan of $25.7 million from the Asian Infrastructural Investment Bank (AIIB). This was the AIIB's first ever development loan.[48]

Caucasus

Difficult though it may be to believe, the Caucasus were once considered the cross-roads of Eurasia. Until recently there were still policy maps portraying a potential North-South corridor linking the Baltic Sea with the Indian Ocean that cut right through its territory, but that is no longer a realistic option. There are no open border crossings at all between Armenia and Azerbaijan (or between Armenia and Turkey). In addition, with the exception of one crossing at the top of a mountain road, Russia is completely cut off from routes South through the Caucasus.

This is because no trucks are allowed through the secessionist regions of Abkhazia and South Ossetia. Nevertheless, the Upper Lars crossing is the main route for Armenian exports to Russia. The road conditions on both sides of the border are prone to landslides and the capacity of the border post is limited to about 80 trucks and 200 cars a day. The problem for freight is aggravated by the fact that priority is given to passenger vehicles. Any slight build-up in traffic and the effects could be dramatic. As recently as July 2018, as many as one thousand trucks were stretched along the road waiting to cross the border, with reserves of petrol to fuel refrigeration units running low.[49]

Since the option of a route to Western markets through Russia was not really feasible, Azerbaijan has become increasingly reliant on the sea route from Aktau to Baku. The port used to be located close to the city but since this restricted the room available for expansion, the government, in 2007, took the decision to completely demolish it and start afresh in Alyat, 70 kms to the south. Work on the new facilities began in 2010 and was completed in 2017 at the cost of $715 million. This would allow the port to handle 10 million tons of cargo and 50,000 TEU containers a year. Further expansion of the port was left dependent on the growth of traffic, but if all three phases were to be completed, the port could boast a capacity of 25 million tons and one million TEU containers.[50] In 2016 the volume of traffic only reached 3.1 million tonnes but it had grown to 4.4 million tons the following year, 86 per cent of it being transit traffic. The volumes were expected to rise further with the completion of a free trade zone inside the port that would simplify and speed-up logistics.[51]

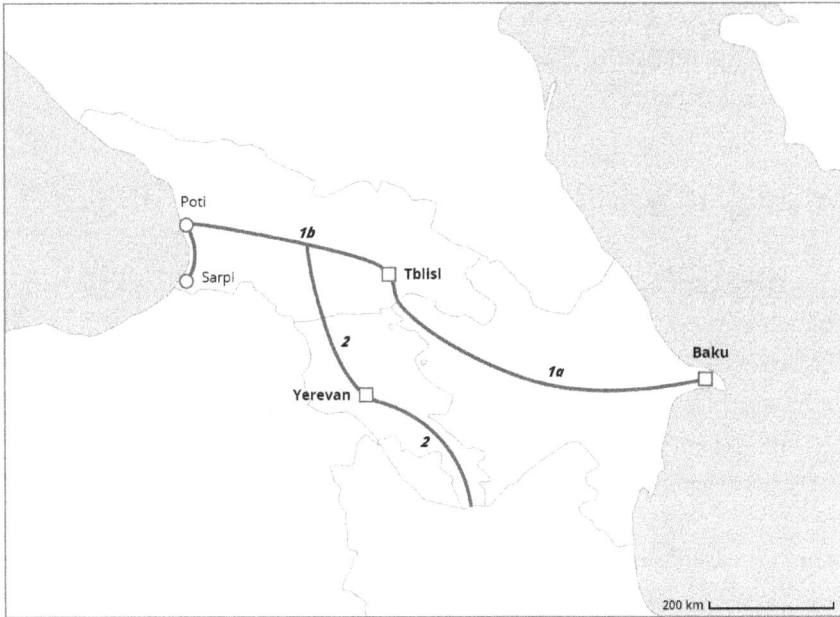

Figure 3.4: Main Road Improvements in the Caucasus

Figure 3.4 shows the main internationally funded road improvements in the Caucasus. Azerbaijan's main focus has been to improve the transit corridors either to the Georgian ports on the Black Sea or through Georgia and onwards to Turkey (obviously avoiding Armenia). Since 2007, the country has been upgrading the 321 kms road from Baku to the Georgian border (Figure 3.4, route 1a) from a two-lane to a four-lane highway, with the support of loans from the ADB ($945 million) and the World Bank ($382 million) and $386 million from its own coffers.[52] In its turn, Georgia concentrated on improving the 410 kms East-West road that stretched from the border with Azerbaijan, passed through the capital Tblisi and continued to Sarpi, on the Turkish border (Figure 3.4, route 1b). The project was supported by an ADB loan ($528 million) and by $183.2 million from the government.[53] Armenia's main concern was to improve the 500 kms North-South road, and more especially northwards to Georgia (Figure 3.4, route 2) and the port of Poti on the Black Sea. Once again the ADB ($680 million) was the main financier, together with the European Investment Bank (EIB) ($79.2 million) with a contribution of $103 million from national coffers.[54] This route is also a priority project in the Eastern

Partnership agreement, announced in January 2019 which anticipates a further expenditure of $2.25 billion to complete the southern stretch to the Iranian border.[55]

Heading East from Europe

As we turn our attention to Europe, or rather to the fifteen countries that comprised the EU at the time of the collapse of the Soviet Union, we have to shift both our spatial and our temporal orientation. The EU started building the new Silk Road earlier and in a different sequence – first trade facilitation, and then infrastructure. It also concentrated on the immediate neighbouring countries.

The New EU Member States

After the collapse of the Soviet Union and the emergence of Central and Eastern European (CEE) countries from the constraints of the Soviet trading system, the countries of Western Europe found themselves looking at their neighbours over militarised frontiers that no longer had any relevance. Borders had been to restrict access of their populations to the West, and unauthorised crossing could result in a jail sentence or even death. With an inward looking trade regime, the Eastern bloc did not have much need for many open freight corridors to the West. Quickly, the EU granted most of these countries limited, non-reciprocal free trade agreements that served to reduce some of the frontier barriers to trade. However, imports still had to be controlled for fraudulent declaration and for contraband. New border regimes were required, and more physical border posts.

Just as was the case in Central Asia, these efforts were not always crowned with success. In the years to 1998 the EU had sunk almost $1 billion into enhancing cross border connectivity. One of the largest projects was the construction of new border facilities on the Polish-German border near Frankfurt/Oder. The number of trucks crossing the border had trebled and waiting times had climbed to 30 hours. However, despite the expense of constructing a whole new freight terminal, the authorities initially only reduced the waiting time to ten hours (instead of the 30 minutes originally envisaged). The reason was that the Polish authorities failed to improve the access roads and the Polish side of the border post was understaffed.[56] The EU also tried to improve cross-border cooperation along the new borders separating the CEE countries (that were candidates for EU membership) from their former trading partners on the other side of the border. Unfortunately the sums (total 1996-2000 €132.5 million) were too small to support more than one or two large projects and there were interminable delays because local customs authorities were not equipped to handle the technical nature of many of the requirements. Matters were further complicated by the fact that the funding schedules for the CEE candidate countries were not synchronised with those for the new (external) trade partners. Despite the fact that the EU had already prioritised the major Hungary/Ukraine and Poland/Belarus border crossing points, where delays averaged 24 hours or more (rising occasionally to five days on the Polish/Belarus border), neither Ukraine or Belarus received any EU funding.[57]

Under the Soviet system, the authorities had tended to rely on rail for the transport of freight.[58] Car ownership was low and there was a heavy reliance on public transport. As a result, the CEE generally had a low density road network and the roads themselves were of poor quality. Initially, therefore, road improvement was the first priority. The political climate behind the EU funding these improvements was enhanced by the EU integrating transport into its 'single market' programme and the development of its own plans for an integrated international transport network.[59] However, when the official maps of the integrated road network appeared[60] although they included the CEE, the accompanying analysis and the recommendations were solidly focused on the existing member states.[61] The scheme included 75,541 kms of roads, that should reach motorway or expressway standards, of which 17,870 kms (23.6 per cent) were located in the CEE countries.[62]

From 1990-2007 the main source of funds was the EIB, which advanced loans worth $32.5 billion for the construction and rehabilitation of roads in CEE (representing 75 per cent of the total for the whole sector).[63] The EBRD and the World Bank together added close to another $1 billion to the total.[64] In 2004 eight of the ten CEE countries became members, and membership for the other two was imminent. As a result they all became eligible for funding from the EU budget, much in the form of non-repayable grants rather than loans. Between 2007 and 2014, the EU's European Reconstruction and Development Fund (ERDF) and Cohesion Funds had invested $43.3 billion in improving the roads in CEE.[65] This had resulted in the building of 3,452 kms of new roads and the upgrading of a further 18,640 kms. However, it is interesting that only half of the new roads were on routes identified by the EU's own international transport network programme (TEN-T).[66]

The discrepancy between the EU's own plans and the actual outcome requires a little explanation. There are three things to bear in mind. First, the EU is not as powerful as it may appear. It is individual governments that have the right to submit proposals for obtaining EU funding and they decide their own priorities. Second, governments never get funding for a whole project; a country always has to fund a percentage of the costs from its own budget. Finally, different funds have different rules, especially when it comes to the requirements for the percentages of 'matching' national contributions. Cohesion funds, aimed at regional development, generally cover 80 per cent of a project's costs, whereas the ERDF, which prioritises larger national and international projects, provides at the most 20-30 per cent. It is easy to see a government, with limited financial resources, opting to build local/regional roads since it will get more road for each unit of expenditure, especially since they will have a lower standard than major highways and, therefore, are cheaper for each unit of distance. Moreover, these roads will probably serve more (happy) constituencies and generate more votes for local government parties. They would then put the cash for major road projects into improving connections between larger cities, with perhaps the odd by-pass added to relieve congestion, again reaping the gratitude of the local citizenry. It becomes easy to see why routes dedicated mainly to international transit traffic would be neglected, especially if the borders were in rural areas.

For the period 2014-2020, the EU, through its European Structural Investment Fund envisages spending $36 billion on roads in CEE countries, with $22 billion specifically targeting TEN-T roads and motorways.[67] In addition, the 'Connecting Europe Facility' (a separate fund for European infrastructural investment in transport, energy and digital projects) would devote an additional $1.25 billion to be spent on road improvements. At the time of writing most of the spending still has to take place, so it will be interesting to see how much will actually be realised.[68]

Western Balkans

The western Balkans still pose a far more considerable challenge to the EU than had the CEE states. At some time or another, from 1991 to 1999, almost all the former territories that had comprised the state of Yugoslavia had been at war, mostly centred on secession from Yugoslavia or, more accurately, from the successor state of Serbia. After hostilities had ended, the state of war was replaced not so much by peace as much as by a hostile, resentful quiet. Where once there had been a single country there were now six separate states (not all universally recognised), six separate customs regimes and tariff schedules, 36 new border crossing points at the newly created frontiers, with each other, as well as 14 'external' border crossings with the EU member states. Given the tensions that were still smouldering, the waiting times at borders were surprisingly low. On the internal borders 47 per cent of crossings took less than thirty minutes, although 13 per cent took over an hour. At the 14 border crossings with the EU, the procedures seemed less onerous; at only two (on the Albania-Greece border) of them did delays average over an hour.[69]

Damage to roads incurred during the war was quickly repaired. Of the 6,520 kms network in the region only 15 per cent was considered to be in poor or very poor condition in 2006, and this figure had fallen to 7 per cent by 2011.[70] Between 2004 and 2012, EU and national and international partners had already invested $7.5 billion in improving the region's roads and they had committed a further $4.3 billion to ongoing and planned projects.[71] Since then, a further $6.5 billion has been ploughed into road improvements.[72]

It is perhaps worth looking at Montenegro in a little more detail – a small mountainous country with a population of 622,000 and the project that Reuters reporters have dubbed 'a highway to nowhere'. As far back as 2005, the government was considering a modern expressway connecting its port of Bar with its own impoverished northern regions and through to Serbia. Two independent studies had shown that, because of the low volume of traffic, the project was economically unviable and two efforts to attract foreign investors had failed. Notwithstanding these setbacks, in July 2013 the ministry of transport accepted a $935 million loan to cover 85 per cent of the cost from the EXIM Bank of China to construct the first (and most difficult) 41 kms section of the 165 kms road. It awarded the contract jointly to the China Communications Construction Company and the CRBC. The project should be completed by the middle of 2020. The question is, what then? Despite the favourable loan terms (an interest rate of 2 per cent and, after a 6-year period of grace, a repayments period of twenty years) the country lacks the estimated $1.2 billion required to finish the project, and without the rest of expressway, it can never get the traffic needed to generate the income to pay off the original loans.[73]

Ukraine, Belarus and Russia

To the east of the enlarged EU lie Ukraine, Belarus and Russia. Ukraine and Belarus both form part of the EU's 'neighbourhood policy' which offers them trade concessions and a measure of policy cooperation, but excludes them from EU membership. They also form part of Russia's 'near abroad' – the former Soviet states over which it expects to have primary responsibility. Indeed, in the case of Belarus, it is already part of the Eurasia Economic Union. These states, then, have the ability to play the two sides against each other, but the balance is a delicate one. When, in 2013, Ukraine adopted a more pro-European stance, it quickly found itself embroiled in a civil war that resulted in the loss of control over part of its country and the annexation, by Russia, of the Crimea. Although Ukraine has a 1,974 kms land border with Russia, because of the separatists in the Donetsk and Luhansk regions, the central government only effectively controls 1,565 kms of its length.

Figure 3.5 Main Road Improvements in Ukraine and Belarus

The main road projects in Ukraine and Belarus are shown in Figure 3.5. Since 2000, the EBRD and the EIB have lent $575 million to Ukraine for the upgrade from two- to four-lanes of 814 kms main highway between the capital, Kiev and Chop, on the border with Slovakia (Figure 3.5, route 1).[74] The work is still on-going. It is interesting, in this context, that in 2017, despite the finance originating from EU sources the Chinese firm Sinohydro won a $50 million contract to upgrade a 22 kms stretch of the highway.[75] In 2011 the EBRD and the EIB jointly funded a $1.15 billion loan for the upgrade of all the international road approaches to Kiev.[76] While the EU focused on road developments in the west of Ukraine, the World Bank concentrated on upgrading the roads to the east (Figure 3.5, route 2). In total, since 2009 it has loaned over $1.4 billion to upgrade the highway linking the industrial towns in Eastern Ukraine with Kiev and the main highways to Europe.[77] China was responsible for funding and repairing a section of the road along this route and building a new bridge over the Dnieper river, at an estimated costs of $340 million.[78] In 2019, the government anticipated upgrading an 80 kms section of the road from Kiev to Odessa (Figure 3.5, route 3), with loans of $240 million from the EIB.[79]

In Belarus, in November 2016 work finished on the widening from two to four lanes of two sections of the highway between Minsk and Bobruysk (Figure 3.5, route 4) which had been financed by a World Bank loan of $140 million.[80] In 2014 it approved a further loan of $250 towards the $450 million costs of improving the highway between Minsk and Grodno, and then to the Polish border (Figure 3.5, route 5). The project also envisaged doubling the capacity of the border facilities at Bruzgi.[81] The EXIM Bank of China, meanwhile, in 2011 advanced two loans worth $790 million to improve the highway between Minsk and Gomel, with the CRBC as the main contractor.[82] Finally, in December 2017 the EIB approved a loan of €110 million to upgrade the road from Minsk to Kamenny Log (Figure 3.5, route 6) on the Belarussian side to the border with Lithuania, and to finance the trebling of the capacity of the border facilities.[83] An interesting case of private financing of road improvements is offered by the section of road from Minsk to Smolensk which, despite being the most direct route to Moscow was, until 2016, little more than a 'gravel track', according to the Moscow Times. However, the road had been widened and raised, provided with more turning points and reinforced to carry heavier vehicles – all the work done by gangs of smugglers looking to avoid regular control points.[84]

From Ukraine and Belarus, the road to Central Asia lies through the territory of the Russian Federation. From Ukraine, the main road is a two-lane highway that travels 400 kms before reaching Volgograd, where it connects with the rest of the Russian network. The road was last upgraded over a decade ago and slightly over 20 per cent is classified by the Russian authorities as being in a bad condition. The main highway from Belarus passes through Smolensk before continuing to Moscow. This 450 kms stretch is a four lane-highway, described as being in good condition for its entire length which is not surprising since it was upgraded in 2014. From Moscow vehicles still have 2,300 kms to travel before reaching the border with Kazakhstan. Having been upgraded in 2009-10 for most of its length the road is described as being in good or fair condition. The last 450 kms, however, does not boast a single filling station.[85] The good news is that when, in August 2018, President Putin announced a major infrastructural investment programme worth $40 billion, spread over the coming six-year term of his presidency, the work included the reconstruction of the motorway from Moscow to Chelyabinsk (without mentioning that last 450 kms) and the motorways in the Volga region.[86]

Conclusions

Roads are mostly used for freight for domestic deliveries and for short-haul international freight movements. It is important to bear that in mind when faced with international road maps delineating single highways cutting their swathe through countries and continents. Such roads are expensive to build. The ADB suggested that in Asia four-lane highway cost on average $700,000 per kilometre, and a multi-lane expressway costing ten times that figure (measured in 2010 prices). Understandably, not many expressways were built.[87] Despite the high costs, roads across the Eurasian landmass were widened and upgraded, often with the support of foreign development loans. In Xinjiang, the Chinese government was planning to spend $13 billion in the five years between 2016-2020. The costs of the road improvements identified in the three largest Central Asian countries (Kazakhstan, Uzbekistan and Turkmenistan) totalled more than $14 billion, all of it provided by non-Chinese development banks. In Kyrgyzstan and Tajikistan, by contrast, China provided over half of the $2.4 billion in international funding to support road building. In the Caucasus, western development banks supplied $2.6 billion to support major road improvement schemes in the region. Over $3.4 billion has been provided to Ukraine for road development, with $340 million coming from China. In Belarus the positions were reversed, with China supplying over 60 per cent of the $1.3 billion advanced in support of road-building projects. Between 2007-2014 the EU invested $43.3 billion in road improvements in the new member states, mostly in the form of grants rather than loans, and it envisages spending a further $22 billion by the end of 2020. In the Western Balkans some $10.8 billion has been spent since 2012. These are considerable sums but whether measured in cash or in distance, the development of the 'road' section of China's 'belt and road' has been a very international undertaking. China's contribution was concentrated on neighbouring Kyrgyzstan and Tajikistan and on Belarus.

Much of this road-building effort, of course, also satisfied drivers of private cars, but the rationale of the funding bodies was driven by the needs of freight transport. The new roads could satisfy both needs. However, when they come into competition, it can derail even the best designed plans. The failure of the EU to establish a preference for its own international priority routes was testimony to the perverse effects of its own (unsynchronised) incentive schemes as a reflection of the political economy of keeping potential voters happy. The results so far would suggest the necessity for a recalibration of the funding rules, if the required backing of the member-states could be secured.

What else emerges from this chapter is the importance of borders. For people with a 'globalist' mind-set borders rarely intrude on their consciousness. Yet, regardless of the condition of a major highway, the crossing of an international border often results in lengthy and unpredictable delays as the vehicle and its contents are subjected to controls, often accompanied by widespread petty corruption by the officials involved. Slight increases in traffic, or small changes in the implementation of procedures, can lead to delays measured in days rather than hours. For short hauls, this can negate all the supposed advantages of better roads.

1 T. Williams, *The Silk Roads. An ICOMOS Thematic Study*, Charenton-le-Pont, 2014, 12–14, 31. Available at: https://www.icomos.org/images/mediatheque/ICOMOS_WHThematicStudy_SilkRoads_final_lv_201406.pdf.

2 Asian Highway Database 2003. Available at: https://www.unescap.org/our-work/transport/asian-highway/database.

3 Intergovernmental Panel on Climate Change, *Climate Change 2014: Synthesis Report. Contribution of Working Groups I, II and III to the Fifth Assessment Report of the Intergovernmental Panel on Climate Change* IPCC, Geneva, Switzerland. Available at: https://ar5-syr.ipcc.ch/ipcc/ipcc/resources/pdf/IPCC_SynthesisReport.pdf; Chapman, L. 'Transport and climate change: a review', *Journal of Transport Policy*, 15, 5, 2007, 354-367.

4 *The Times*, 9.10.2018. Available at: https://www.thetimes.co.uk/article/china-completes-new-silk-road-to-europe-highway-is-part-of-belt-and-road-initiative-n89q0ll3f.

5 TIR stand for Transports Internationaux Routiers. This is an international convention that allows trucks to move goods in sealed containers from a customs post at point of departure to another at point of arrival, without any intermediate border checks while, at the same time, guaranteeing the authorities the security of both the goods and the vehicle.

6 *The Load Star*, 28.11.2018. Available at: https://theloadstar.co.uk/china-europe-truck-service-gears-january-launch-successful-pilot/. In February 2019 the first TIR truck made a commercial run from Germany to Khorgos in twelve days, carrying a cargo of 12 tons of motor lubricants. *The Load Star*, 27.2.2019. Available at: https://theloadstar.com/first-tir-transport-from-europe-to-china-arrives-in-only-12-days/. In April 2019 it boasted covering the 13,600 kms from China to Spain in 16 days with a cargo of seven tons of clothing. *The Load Star*, 3.4.2019. Available at: https://theloadstar.com/milestone-for-one-belt-one-road-with-success-of-china-europe-overland-service/.

7 JOC.com, 30.11.2018. Available at: https://www.joc.com/trucking-logistics/new-china-europe-road-service-meets-forwarder-skepticism_20181130.html-0.

8 W. Shepard, 'Khorgos: Where East meets West', *The Diplomat*, 1.4.2016. Available at: https://thediplomat.com/2016/04/khorgos-where-east-meets-west/; B. Maçães, 'New Western Frontier, Conquered by China', *Politico*, 20.6.2016. Available at: https://www.politico.eu/article/khorgas-china-kazakhstan-new-silk-road-trade/; W. Shepherd, 'Horgos: The First New City Of The New Silk Road Emerges As A Robot Manufacturing Hub', *Forbes Magazine,* 7.1.2017. Available at: https://www.Forbes Magazine.com/sites/wadeshepard/2017/01/09/horgos-the-first-new-city-of-the-new-silk-road-becomes-a-hub-for-robots/.

9 The ethnic violence left 197 people dead and nearly 2,000 injured. The government responded by flooding the city with security forces and rounding up

Uyghur militants, but it also stepped up its infrastructural investment in the city itself.

10   A. Colarizi, 'China and Kyrgyzstan: So Near, Yet So Far', *The Diplomat*, 11.8.2015. Available at: https://thediplomat.com/2015/08/china-and-kyrgyzstan-so-near-yet-so-far/.

11   丝绸之路经济区核心区交通枢纽中心建设规划 (2016-2030), 2017, 45-47. Silk Road Economic Zone. core area transportation hub centre construction plan (2016-2030). Available at: https://www.yidaiyilu.gov.cn/wcm.files/upload/CMSydylgw/201708/201708250626019.pdf.

12   UNESCAP Asia Highway Database, 2003 (supplied to the author). 2003 was the first year for which comprehensive data was collected. Over 60 per cent of the roads of four lanes or higher were in the western areas of Russia.

13   UNESCAP Asia Highway Database 2013 (supplied to the author). Only 17 per cent of roads were described as being in poor condition, almost all concentrated in Russia and Mongolia.

14   CAREC, *CAREC Corridors Performance Measurement and Monitoring: Annual Report (April 2009 to March 2010)*, 12-16. (henceforth CPMM), Available at: https://www.carecprogram.org/uploads/CPMM-Annual-Report-2Q2009-1Q2010.pdf.

15   *Ibid.*, 19-20.

16   CAREC, CPMM, 2009, 35; 2010, 22-25 Available at: https://www.carecprogram.org/uploads/CPMM-Annual-Report-2010-Jan-Dec.pdf ; 2011, 13; 2012, 7, 17; 2013, 7,9, 16. Available at: https://www.carecprogram.org/uploads/2013-CAREC-CPMM-Annual-Report.pdf.

17   W. Shepard, 'Khorgos: Why Kazakhstan Is Building A "New Dubai" On The Chinese Border', *Forbes Magazine*, 28.2.2016. Available at: https://www.Forbes Magazine.com/sites/wadeshepard/2016/02/28/will-a-place-called-khorgos-become-the-next-dubai/.

18   W. Shepard, 'An Inside Look At China And Kazakhstan's 'Absurd' Cross-Border Free Trade Zone' *Forbes Magazine*, 26.7.2016. Available at: https://www.Forbes Magazine.com/sites/wadeshepard/2016/07/26/an-inside-look-at-icbc-khorgos-china-and-kazakhstans-cross-border-free-trade-zone/#3c2802145c8f.

19   CAREC, CPMM, 2016, 20. Available at: https://www.carecprogram.org/uploads/2016-CAREC-CPMM-Annual-Report.pdf.

20   World Bank Project Database, P128050. Available at: http://projects.worldbank.org/. Enter the project number to have access to all the relevant documentation.

21   World Bank Project Database, P099270. The total cost was estimated at $2.5 billion. At the time of writing, 1,110 kms have already been completed. See note 20.

22   ADB Project Database, 41121-013, 41121-023, 41121-043, 41121-053,, 43439-033,, 45150-001, 46145-001, 48424-002. Available at: https://www.adb.org/

projects. Enter the project number to have access to all the relevant documentation. The contributions were divided between the ADB ($3.1 billion), Islamic Development Bank ($443 million), the European Bank for Reconstruction and Development (EBRD)($196.5 million) Japanese development banks ($136 million) and a counterpart contribution from the Kazakh authorities ($500 million). At the time of writing only 87 kms of the work had been completed.

23   EBRD Project Database, 39258. Available at: https://www.ebrd.com/work-with-us/project-finance/project-summary-documents.html. Enter project number to have access to all relevant documentation. The total cost was $207 million cost. That section of the road was completed in September 2013.

24   World Bank Project Database P153497; *Note on Cancelled Operation Report (Ibrd-86190) on a loan in the amount of US$ 977.86 Million to the Republic of Kazakhstan for a Center West Regional Development Corridor Project May 11, 2017 Report No: Nco00004218.* See note 20.

25   *Project Cargo Weekly*, 17.8.2017. Available at http://www.projectcargo-weekly.com/2017/08/17/dp-world-port-aktau-kazakhstan-caspian-sea/ ; *PortNews.ru*, 3.10.2017. Available at: http://en.portnews.ru/news/246639/.

26   *Maritime Herald*, 29.3.2017. Available at: http://www.maritimeherald.com/2017/kazakhstan-started-new-ferry-line-with-azerbaijan-from-the-port-of-kuryk/; *Astana Times*, 6.2.2019. Available at: https://astanatimes.com/2019/02/kuryk-seaport-to-boost-shipment-capacity/.

27   ADB Project Database 43439-013, 43439-023, 43439-033. See note 22. At the time of writing 200 kms had been completed and work on a further 170 kms was still underway.

28   ADB Project Database, 42107-003, 42107-023, 42107-033, 42107-043, 44483-023, 44483-024, 44483-026, 444823-027. See note 22.

29   *Trend News Agency*, 2.5.2018. Available at: https://en.trend.az/casia/turkmenistan/2896894.html; J.C.K Daly, 'Turkmenistan's New Turkmenbashi International Seaport-Another Link in Expanding Eurasian Trade', *Eurasian Daily Monitor*, 15, 71, 9.5.2018. Available at: https://jamestown.org/program/turkmenistans-new-turkmenbashi-international-seaport-another-link-in-expanding-eurasian-trade/.

30   Хроника Туркменистана, 2.10.2017. Available at: https://www.hronikatm.com/2017/10/v-turkmenistane-nachali-stroitelstvo-platnogo-avtobana-ashhabad-turkmenbashi/.

31   Хроника Туркменистана, 27.2.2018. Available at: http://www.news-asia.ru/plugins/news/view/category/avto/id/11109.

32   *Business Recorder*, 26.1.2019. Available at https://www.brecorder.com/2019/01/26/469051/turkmenistan-launches-2-3bn-highway-in-bid-for-asia-europe-transit/. At the opening ceremony, President Berdimuhamedow's son deliberately included Uzbekistan as a potential beneficiary of the new highway.

State News Agency of Turkmenistan, 24.2.2019. Available at: http://tdh.gov.tm/news/en/articles.aspx&article16410&cat29.

33 *Eurasianet.* 25.1.2019. Available at: https://eurasianet.org/turkmenistans-latest-megaproject-a-road-to-the-future-or-white-elephant-grift.

34 ADB, *Kyrgyz Republic: CAREC Transport Corridor 1 (Bishkek–Torugart Road) Project, Evaluation Report*, PVR 351, 2014. See note 22.

35 CAREC, CPMM, 2011, 14; 2012, 19; 2013, 24.

36 M. Alymbekov, 'Kyrgyzstan and the Great Silk Road: Compatibility of Concepts', *Kabar*, 6.10.2013. Available at: http://old.kabar.kg/eng/analytics/full/11093

37 CAREC, CPMM, 2012, 33; 2014, 33. Available at: https://www.carecprogram.org/uploads/2014-CAREC-CPMM-Annual-Report.pdf; 2015, 35-36. https://www.carecprogram.org/uploads/2015-CAREC-CPMM-Annual-Report.pdf; 2016, 31(see note 19).

38 Kyrgyz Ministry of Transport and Communications. Investment Projects Implementation Groups, Database. Available at: http://piumotc.kg/en/news/.

39 ADB Project Database, 39674-012, 39672-022, 42399-013, 42399-023, 42399-024, 45169-001, 48401-007 and 48401-006. See note 22.

40 *AKIPress*, 4.5.2017. Available at: https://akipress.com/news:592106. At time of writing they were still working on the project.

41 ADB Project Database, 45169-001, 45169-002. See note 22. There were smaller contributions from the Japan International Cooperation Agency and Islamic Development Bank. Work on the 60 kms from Bishkek to Kara Balta, funded by the ADB only started in 2017 and completion was scheduled by 2021. Work on the 70 kms section from Madaniyak to Jalalabad still needed to begin.

42 *24.kg,*19.5.2017. Available at: https://24.kg/english/52135_Alternative_road_North_South_in_Kyrgyzstan_built_on_new_technology/. The project has subsequently become embroiled in a bribery scandal involving accusations of massive overpricing for cement and office space. *Open Democracy Russia*, 9.8.2018. Available at: https://www.opendemocracy.net/od-russia/satina-aidar/kyrgyzstans-north-south-road-to-corruption.

43 EBRD Project Database, 45508. Available at: https://www.ebrd.com/work-with-us/project-finance/project-summary-documents.html. Enter project number to find documentation. World Bank Project Database P107608. See note 20.

44 CAREC, CPMM, 2013, 34-35, 2014, 25-26 (see note 37).

45 ADB Project Database, 49042-005-dc.pdf (development coordination). See note 22.

46 ADB Project Database, 49042-004, 49042-005. See note 22. The other donors being the OPEC Fund for Development ($12 million) and the Tajik government ($17.5 million).

47   ADB Project Database, 49042-005-dc.pdf (development coordination); 42052-022. See note 22. In addition the OPEC Fund for Development funds $13 million.

48   AIIB Project Database. Available at: https://www.aiib.org/en/projects/approved/index.html. Document PD0002-TJK.

49   *JAM.news*, 6.7.2018. Available at: https://jam-news.net/thousands-of-armenian-trucks-on-georgia-russia-border/.

50   '21ˢᵗ Century Silk Road', *Visions of Azerbaijan*, Jan/Feb 2015. Available at: http://www.visions.az/business,613/; *AzerNews*, 21.1.2016. Available at: https://www.azernews.az/analysis/91916.html. See also W. Shepard, 'An Inside Look At The New Crossroads Of Eurasia: Azerbaijan's New Port Of Baku', *Forbes Magazine*, 3.11.2016. Available at: https://www.Forbes Magazine.com/sites/wadeshepard/2016/11/03/an-inside-look-at-the-new-crossroads-of-eurasia-azerbaijans-new-port-of-baku/.

51   *Trend News Agency*, 16.3.3018. Available at: https://en.trend.az/business/economy/2874076.html.

52   CAREC Project List. Azerbaijan. Available https://www.carecprogram.org/?page_id=4. World Bank Project Database P118023, P156377 See note 20.; ADB Project Database 39176-013, 39176-023, 39176-033, 39176-043, 39176-044, 45389-001, 45389-002, 45389-003, 54389-004. See note 22.

53   ADB Project Database, 41122-013, 41122-023, 41122-033, 41122-043, 50064-001. See note 22. The road was responsible for carrying 60 per cent of Georgia's international trade.

54   ADB Project Database, 42145-013, 42145-023, 42145-003, 42145-043, 49244-002. See note 22.

55   European Union Press Release 18.1.2019. Available at: https://eeas.europa.eu/headquarters/headquarters-homepage/56763/eastern-partnership-new-indicative-ten-t-investment-action-plan-stronger-connectivity_en. Eastern Partnership, *Indicative TEN-T Investment Action Plan*, 2018. Available at: https://ec.europa.eu/neighbourhood-enlargement/sites/near/files/ten-t_iap_web-dec13.pdf. The sum mentioned in the text is €2.1 billion of which the EU has earmarked €450 million from its own funding.

56   European Court of Auditors, *Special Report concerning cross-border cooperation (1994-1998) accompanied by the replies of the Commission*. Special Report 5/1999. Available at: https://eur-lex.europa.eu/legal-content/EN/TXT/PDF/?uri=CELEX:32000Y0221(01)&from=EN. The sum was €820 which has been converted to dollars at the average 1994-98 exchange rates.

57   European Court of Auditors, *Special Report concerning Phare investment projects in Bulgaria and Romania, together with the replies of the Commission*. Special Report 54/2006. Available at: https://publications.europa.eu/en/publication-detail/-/publication/89d8ff89-0a6d-45d2-8f92-759ffded12b9/language-en.

58 This was logical given the structure of domestic and international freight movements, with the concentration on raw materials and heavy industry products.

59 European Commission, *Growth, competitiveness, and employment. The challenges and ways forward into the 21st century,* COM (93) 700 final. Brussels: 05.12.1993.Available at: https://publications.europa.eu/en/publication-detail/-/publication/0d563bc1-f17e-48ab-bb2a-9dd9a31d5004.

60 European Parliament and European Council, *Community guidelines for the development of the trans-European transport network,* Decision No 1692/96/Ec, 23.7.1996. Available at: https://ec.europa.eu/transport/sites/transport/files/wcm/infrastructure/grants/2008_06_20/2007_tent_t_guidlines_en.pdf.

61 European Commission, *European transport policy for 2010: time to decide,* 2001. Available at: https://ec.europa.eu/transport/themes/strategies/2001_white_paper_en. To be fair, there was some acknowledgement of the need to look beyond the existing EU borders.

62 CEDR, *Future European Road Network,* 2009, 29. Available at: http://www.cedr.eu/download/Publications/2009/e_Future_road_networks_FERN.pdf

63 EIB, Project Database. Available at: http://www.eib.org/en/projects/index.htm. The €29.1 billion was converted on the basis of the average 1990-2007 exchange rate.

64 The EBRD advanced $504 million over the same period, all of it to projects in Hungary and Romania (EBRD, Project Database 2877, 24998, 33391, 35047). See note 23. The reported sum of €450 million was converted on the basis of the average 1990-2007 exchange rate. The World Bank advanced loans worth $476.7 million, most of it after 2000 and all of it concentrated on Poland and Romania (World Bank Project Database, P057960, P078170, P088824, P093812). See note 20

65 European Commission, *Transport, Final report. WORK PACKAGE 5 Ex post evaluation of Cohesion Policy programmes 2007-2013, focusing on the European Regional Development Fund (ERDF) and the Cohesion Fund (CF),* Brussels, 2016, 28. Available at: https://ec.europa.eu/regional_policy/de/information/publications/evaluations/2016/transport-final-report-work-package-5-ex-post-evaluation-of-cohesion-policy-programmes-2007-2013-focusing-on-the-european-regional-development-fund-erdf-and-the-cohesion-fund-cf. €31 billion was converted on the basis of the average 2007-2014 exchange rate.

66 European Commission, *Ex post evaluation of the ERDF and Cohesion Fund 2007-13,* SWD(2016) 318 final, Brussels, 28. Available at: https://ec.europa.eu/regional_policy/en/policy/evaluations/ec/2007-2013/.

67 ESIF Smart Specialisation Platform, Categories 028-034. Available at: http://s3platform.jrc.ec.europa.eu/. The ESIF combines five existing EU funding mechanisms. The ERDF and Cohesion Funds. This represented 92.5 per cent

of its total EU spending in the sector. €27.6 billion and €16.9 billion were converted on the basis of the average 2014 exchange rate.

68 EU, CEF, Project database. https://ec.europa.eu/inea/connecting-europe-facility/cef-transport/projects-by-country.Poland (€533.9 million) Hungary (€132 million) and Slovakia (€122.5 million) would be the main beneficiaries. The €960 million was converted on the basis of the average 2014 exchange rate.

69 South East Europe Transport Observatory (SEETO) *Report on Border Crossing Facilitation*, 2012, 13-14. Available at: http://www.seetoint.org/wp-content/uploads/2012/10/bc-facilitation-report-final.pdf.

70 SEETO, *Comprehensive Network Development Plan*, 2013, 11-12. Available at: http://www.seetoint.org/wp-content/uploads/2012/10/bc-facilitation-report-final.pdf.

71 SEETO, *Comprehensive Network Development Plan*, 2013, 19-20. €5.5 billion and €3.2billion was converted on the basis of the average 2004-2012 exchange rate.

72 SEETO, *Multi -Annual Plan 2018. Common problems- Shared solutions*, 2018, 31-33. Available at: https://www.seetoint.org/seetodocuments/1636 €5.4 billion has been converted on the basis of the 2010-2017 exchange rate.

73 N. Barkin and A. Vasovic, 'Chinese 'highway to nowhere' haunts Montenegro', Reuters, 16.7.2018. Available at https://www.reuters.com/article/us-china-silkroad-europe-montenegro-insi-idUSKBN1K60QX ; M. Grgic, 'Chinese infrastructural investments in the Balkans: political implications of the highway project in Montenegro' *Territory, Politics, Governance*, 2017, xx-xx

74 EBRD Database 2213, 31928, 36547. See note 23.

75 *China Daily*, 29.11.2017. It involved a section of the road near the city of Zhytomyr.

76 European Commission Press Release 17.5.2011, EBRD Database 40185. See note 23.

77 In 2009 it approved a $400 million loan to upgrade from 2- to 4-lanes 120 kms of the M03 between Boryspil and Lubny. The work on that section was completed in 2014 (World Bank Database, P100580). Meanwhile, in 2012, it approved a loan of a further $450 to expand the capacity of the 84 kms highway between Lubny and Poltava, and to build 22 kms of bypass along the route. Because of problems in land acquisition the project has fallen behind schedule and completion is now envisaged in 2020 (World Bank Database, P127156). Finally, in November 2015, it approved a loan of $560 million to upgrade 100 kms of the 146 kms highway between Poltava and Kharkiv. (Word Bank Press release, 3.11.2015). See note 20.

78 *UKRopNews*, 24, 21.3.2017. Available at: https://ukropnews24.com/ukravtodor-with-the-chinese-state-owned-company-will-build-a-road-detour-kremenchug-

bridge-across-the-dnieper/. See also Eastern Partnership, *Indicative TEN-T Investment Action Plan* (note 55).

79 *UNIAN News*, 10.1.2019. Available at: https://economics.unian.info/10403853-road-repairs-boom-2018-and-u-s-locomotives-for-ukrzaliznytsia.html. See also Eastern Partnership, *Indicative TEN-T Investment Action Plan* (note 55).

80 World Bank Database, P118375. See note 20.

81 World Bank Database, P149697.See note 20. Completion is envisaged in 2020.

82 China.AidData.org 42336,46413. The project was completed in 2016.

83 EIB Projects Database, Projects to be financed Belarus. Available at: http://www.eib.org/en/projects/pipelines/index.htm; Belarus News, 12.7.2018. Available at: https://eng.belta.by/society/view/reconstruction-of-belarusian-lithuanian-border-checkpoint-kamenny-log-to-begin-in-2019-113296-2018/. The main purpose of the border post reconstruction, which was set to start in 2019, is to triple the throughput capacity up to 6,000 vehicles daily. The border checkpoint would have a total of 32 vehicle clearance channels – 16 outgoing channels and 16 incoming ones, adjustable to match the traffic.

84 *Moscow Times*, 22.8.2016. Available at: https://themoscowtimes.com/news/traffickers-repair-russian-road-used-for-smuggling-55065.

85 UNESCAP, Asian Highway Database, Russia 2017. Information supplied to the author.

86 *RTNews*, 23.8.2018. Available at: https://www.rt.com/business/436633-russia-infrastructure-spending-economy/.

87 Asian Development Bank, *Meeting Asia's Infrastructure Needs.*, Manila, 2018, 99. Available at: https://www.adb.org/sites/default/files/publication/227496/special-report-infrastructure.pdf.

CHAPTER FOUR

RAIL

This chapter focuses on the railways that dominate long-distance overland freight transport. It starts by examining the advantages and disadvantages of railways compared with roads and the extra complications involved in crossing borders. It then examines the long-distance 'block trains' that carry freight from a hub in China to one in Europe, without discharging cargo elsewhere en route. Like the previous chapter, this chapter is also divided into two sections but the delineation is slightly different. The first section starts with examining the various crossings at different points along China's vast borders before turning to explore the construction and modernisation of railways in Central Asia and the Caucasus. This section, however, continues with a consideration of the railway plans for Russia, Ukraine and Belarus. The second section of the chapter starts with the new EU member states of Central and Eastern Europe, pausing to coincide the difficulties at Malaszwicze, which is the major crossing point for the China-Europe 'block trains', before moving to examine developments in the West Balkans. It ends by looking at problems facing the Chinese funded project for a Belgrade-Budapest High Speed railway (HSR). A final sectionsummarises the results and highlights the remaining issues.

Speedy Trains

Railways have many advantages over roads when it comes to the transportation of goods. They are potentially faster than moving heavily loaded trucks along busy highways, but whether that happens depends on the length of any delays. They can certainly carry more goods than a single truck-load, sometimes up to one hundred times more, and these scale economies make the unit cost of transport cheaper over longer distances. They are also considered to be less polluting than road transport, although much of the supposed benefits are lost if the loads have to be pulled by two heavy diesel locomotives rather than electric ones. They are also far safer. This is even more the case if we envisage a scenario where all the traffic moved by rail were to be transferred to roads, with all the contingent side-effects in terms of traffic jams and congestion.

Despite all these advantages, governments are finding it intractably difficult to shift traffic from road to rail. Unlike roads, railways rarely offer a seamless transport solution for traffic from the point of origin to the final destination. Of course there are exceptions, such as deliveries of coal directly to power stations or of ores and metals to smelting ovens, but for the most part all journeys begin and end on roads. The transition from road to rail is often not an easy one. Let us take the case of a single container. A truck will take the container to a depot from where it is conveyed to a flat wagon and coupled to a train. All of these functions take time and they carry a cost. They also have to be managed, and managed efficiently. The train itself cannot just enter a main railway line. The management must book a slot in the rail schedule for a journey to the end destination; preferably a regular series of slots to fit the rest of the timetable. More often than not, the train finishes at another depot, where the whole process of transferring the load to trucks is repeated in reverse. The efficiency of the logistical services determines the entire success of the operation – one where goods arrive undamaged, within a reasonable time-span and without delays. The entire operation is certainly more complex and time consuming, and possibly also more costly, than loading a container on the back of a truck and driving from A to B, especially if there is no charge for using the road. For short distances, therefore, roads remain the most feasible form of freight distribution. A good example of the effect of these considerations is afforded by data on distribution of total freight traffic (domestic and international) from Kazakhstan. In 2012, measured in ton/kms, rail was responsible for 49 per cent of the traffic compared with roads that carried 28 per cent and pipelines 22 per cent. However, when looking at the total tonnage carried, a quite different picture emerges. No less than 84 per cent of the total freight that moved around the country did so using roads, compared with 9 per cent travelling by rail and 7 per cent through pipelines. The reason for the discrepancy, of course, is that the average distance of a journey by road was far, far less than that made by rail and pipeline.[1]

Place an international frontier in the way, and the magnitude of the logistics problem for rail transport increases exponentially. Unless there is an international agreement to the contrary, crossing a border can mean changing drivers and trains. This may arise from differences in languages, rail management systems or safety regulations. If there is a change in the gauge of the track, or a difference in the maximum permitted length of train, crossing a border may also entail shifting the containers from one flat wagon to another. It also requires arranging a timetable slot in the rail schedule of the neighbouring country. At this point in the argument, it is worth reflecting on the fact that there are only a maximum number of trains that can run safely on a track within a specific time-frame. Most managers of rail systems will favour passenger traffic (including the return of empty passenger trains) over freight, which is often shunted to the night-time. With freight trains, they will often favour domestic customers over international customers. Domestic customers will represent a more regular business and, as larger customers, they will often also have the ear of the government to which they owe their licences.

In 2006 the US Chamber of Commerce surveyed the costs and time for transporting a forty foot (FEU) container from China to Europe by various means of transport. In all cases the destination was no more than 100 kms from the depot or port.[2] The data is shown in Figure 4.1. At the extremes, the results were not unexpected - air transport was fast but expensive while shipping was cheap but time-consuming. Trucks were more expensive than rail but the journey took longer by rail, even longer than time taken by ships to cover a much longer distance. Not only that, but rail journey times showed wide fluctuations, which made planning difficult at the final point of destination.

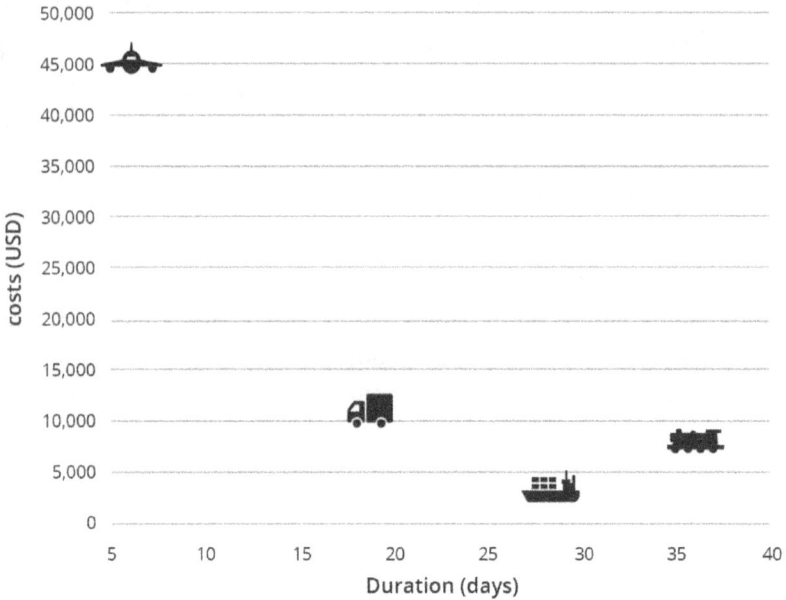

Figure 4.1 Typical price and time for transporting a FEU container from China to Western Europe by different means of transport (2006)

Despite all these difficulties, long-distance international rail container traffic has been increasing exponentially, albeit from a low base. The Yuxinou (渝 新 欧) railway lends its name from the Chinese acronym for Chongqing-China-Europe. In March 2011 it became the first regular commercial rail service between China and Europe, operated as a joint venture between Germany's national rail company Deutsche Bahn and the Russian Railways. That first train took 25 days to make the 11,179 kms journey Chongqing in China to Duisburg, in Germany. The time is now down to about a fortnight. At the end of August 2018 the 10,000th train to make the rail freight journey on the China-Europe route arrived in Wuhan from Hamburg. At the last count (March 2019) freight services connected 59 Chinese cities with 49 cities in 15 European countries.[3]

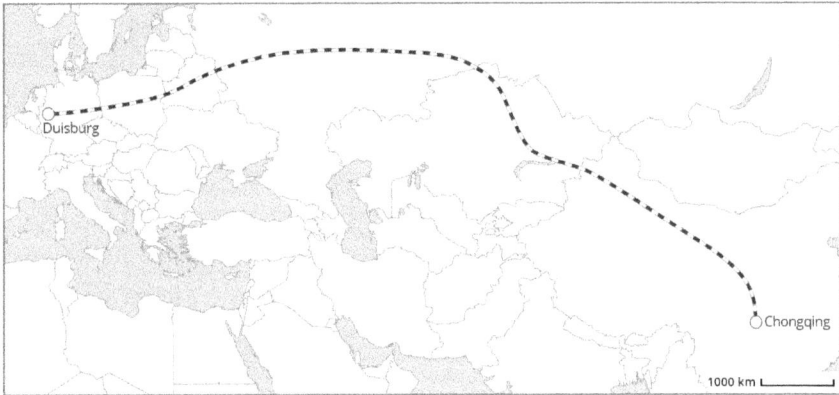

Figure 4.2 Route of the First Yuxinou Railway

The trains on the route were what is known as 'block trains', trains that travelled intact between two destinations and whose cargo was covered by a single customs declaration. This removes the need for any stops for decoupling and recoupling of wagons, and it also makes possible a single set of customs documents for the whole journey. These trains also received preferential treatment at customs facilities and enjoyed a guaranteed slot for the whole journey. These concessions not only reduced the time taken to cover the route, but they also made the journey more predictable and reliable.

If block-trains had made rail freight faster than container transport by sea, they still remained more expensive. Nevertheless, measured from Central China, the price of transporting a FEU container to Western Europe has fallen to about $5,500. However, this is only partly as a result of improved efficiency. Ever since the services began Chinese cities have been subsidising the costs of transport as they compete with each other for trade. Until recently no one knew how much this subsidy was worth. Some fragmented information from 2015 suggested that subsidies offered by Chinese cities averaged $3,500 for each FEU container (and $3,500-$4,000 for trains on the Chongqing-Duisburg route) which covered more than half the cost of the journey.[4] A more recent figure suggested that the level for a (smaller) TEU container was $2,000-2,500.[5] A source from the Russian railways suggested that twice as much would be needed if the Trans-Siberian railway were to run at a level where it could fund necessary improvements and make a profit.[6] One does wonder what would happen if China decided to reduce the level of its subsidies or even eliminate them altogether. In such circumstances rail might still offer advantages for high value goods by allowing firms to hold smaller inventories, but it would be uncompetitive for low value bulk traffic for which there is no premium for faster delivery.[7] What is happening, however, is that the Chinese authorities are restricting the subsidies to fully laden trains, which will mean either longer (and unpredictable) intervals between departures or fewer scheduled services, with longer dwell times at the depots.[8]

Heading West from China

The Yuxinou Express travels through Central Asia because it forms part of the government's strategy for moving the industrial balance of the economy away from the coast and towards the cities in Western China. Chongqing was the first city to launch a regular container service. Chengdu, 400 kms to the north-west, has recently become China's busiest rail container transport hub. One reason why the new rail routes have become important for the development of these two cities is that they lie far from the nearest sea-port in Shanghai, 1,700 and 2,000 kms respectively from the port. At $0.60 per km, the train journey to the coast for a FEU container would cost $1,000-$1,200 and take several days. Add the depot costs and delays at the port and the alternative of transport by sea becomes less compelling. Gradually, however, other industrial centres are awakening to the potential that the new routes can offer. This was foreseen in the plan drafted by the National Development and Reform Commission supervising the development of the BRI. It envisaged that cities in the far north of the country would try to access the Trans-Siberian railway as early as possible, while cities further south would transit first through Mongolia before joining it further to the west.[9] These options are shown in Figure 4.3

Figure 4.3 Exit points from China for Container Trains to Europe

Routes from China

Since 1916 the Trans-Siberian Railway has provided a direct rail line from the Pacific to the Baltic. The 10,555 kms Trans-Siberian Railway requires no changes in railway gauge on its route, nor any stops for customs duties and other border formalities. The passenger train runs on alternate days and it takes seven days to reach its destination. The freight train takes much longer. [10]

Figure 4.4 Rail Routes from Northern China

Direct access for Chinese freight trains to the start of the Trans-Siberian railway only began in 2016, when new trans-loading facilities required for switching gauge from the 1,435 mm standard gauge employed in China to the 1,520 mm gauge common in the former Soviet Union were opened in Suifenhe, on the Russian border (Figure 4.4 Route 1).[11] Since then, from an admittedly very low base, the volumes of traffic have increased substantially[12] prompting speculation over the construction of a 380 kms HSR line from Mudanjiang, in China's Heilongjiang Province, to Vladivostok at a cost of $12 billion.[13] The traffic is likely to increase further in the near future when the bridge over the Amur River, near the town of Heihe is completed(Figure 4.4 Route 1a). Negotiations for the bridge had started 28 years ago, but in March 2019 the two sections of the 2,200 kms bridge were finally linked and work has started on laying the railway track and building customs facilities. Since the bridge cuts 3,500 kms from the journey between the neighbouring town on either side of the river, Russian business is expecting to conduct a lively trade in iron ore, coal, fertilisers and timber through the new route.[14] Meanwhile, in the absence to the new connection, the growth in traffic over the Suifenhe crossing has been helped by an increase in the speed of the trains travelling on the Vladivistok/Moscow route has increased by 37 per cent to 490 kms/day. The main sticking point is the price that Russia charges for using the railway.[15] The $0.66-0.72 per km charged in Russia for an FEU container is higher than the $0.60 quoted in China, but far higher than the $0.23-0.32 for trains travelling through Kazakhstan.[16] To date, requests from the Chinese authorities to reduce it, in return for an increase in traffic have been rebuffed. For the time being, the more favoured route is to travel westward to the border crossing at Manzhouli, in the Inner Mongolia Autonomous Region (Figure 4.4, Route 2) and from there to connect with the Trans-Siberian railway at Chita. In 2018 a total of 2,853 China-Europe freight trains passed through this route, carrying 193,000 standard TEU containers. These figures were about 30 per cent higher than in 2017.[17]

For trains travelling from further south and trying to connect with the Trans-Siberian Railway, there is a route through Mongolia crossing the border at Erenhot/Zamyn Uud (Figure 4.4, Route 3). Because of the need to change railway gauge, the faulty equipment and the shortage of wagons, waiting times for trains could be measured in days, rather than in hours.[18] In October 2017 China started work on an economic zone covering nine square kilometres on each side of the border.[19] Upgrading the facilities on both sides of the border, increasing the supply of rolling stock and stream-lining the logistics all contributed to reducing the times involved at border crossings. As a result, the number of China-Europe Express trains using the route has climbed from 76 in 2015 to 161 in 2016 and 570 in 2017.[20] There was also a similar growth of traffic for minerals and other raw materials shipped from Mongolia to China, due in part to the speed in handling border traffic. A simplification in customs documentation and less diverse cargo carried on each train helped to increase the capacity of the station daily from six to ten such trains.[21] The main remaining bottleneck for the route through Mongolia is that the line is still single-track and has not been electrified. In June 2016, the leaders of China, Russia and Mongolia agreed a thirty-two project package for a China-Mongolia-Russia economic corridor. This also included plans for making the line double-track over its entire length and allowing for its electrification.[22] However the financial framework for the project has yet to be agreed. Another problem with the line is that the track cuts right through the centre of the capital city of Ulaanbaatar, reducing the speed of the trains and clogging up the city's traffic. The Asian Development Bank (ADB) is funding a technical assessment into the possibility of constructing a dedicated freight line to by-pass the city altogether, but the results are not expected until 2019.[23]

Despite the increased use of the northern routes, almost 70 per cent of the China-Europe trains still pass through the border crossing at Alashankou, in the autonomous region of Xinjiang. The journey times on the route within China have been reduced by the opening in December 2014 of the 1,766 kms HSR passenger line from Lanzhou to Urumqi, the capital of Xinjiang province. The 403 kms extension from Lanzhou eastward to Baoij became operational in July 2017, completing the link to the rest of China's HSR network (Figure 4.4, Route 4).[24] The five year plan for Xinjiang envisages the building of 5,017 kms of railways, not all of it to be undertaken within the five year period. Between 2016 and 2020, the local government foresees an expenditure of $5 billion on railways; more if extra funds were to be forthcoming from the Silk Road fund or other sources.[25]

The advantage of the HSR line is that it clears the conventional line for freight traffic – at least that is the rationale. In 2017 1,755 trains, carrying 895,000 tons of goods, passed through that route, representing an increase of 75 per cent on the previous year. Nowadays the block trains take 15 hours to pass through the customs facilities; down from nearly 24 hours when operations began, back in 2011.[26] From the China border town of Alashankou, the train travels through the long narrow pass in the Dzungaria/Ala-Tau mountain range, to the small town of Dostyk. Whilst delays in Alashankou have fallen, hardly any time-saving has taken place at Dostyk, where the average delay remains above forty hours.[27] The change in railway gauge requires that the containers have to be transferred onto the appropriate rolling stock. This operation is always performed at the incoming border crossing point (BCP), and the capacity at Dostyk in Kazakhstan is cramped (and its location unsuitable for enlargement).[28]

The Aleshenkou/Dostyk BCP had always threatened to become a bottleneck. As a result, the authorities had long planned a new BCP opposite the Kazakh village of Khorgas and a new route to Western Europe (Figure 4.4, Route 5). Initially it seemed that the new facilities simply duplicated the problems of the old. Passenger trains started arriving from China in September 2011 and the freight crossing became operational several months later. From the start the passage of rail freight through the BCP was held up by inadequate reloading facilities (note that gauge changes occur at the importing side!), compounded by a lack of space in the marshalling yards. Delays here could mount to close on fifty hours.[29] Central to the entire operation was the construction of a dry-port called Khorgos East Gate with four parallel railway tracks all equipped with gantries for transferring containers on through-trains. Trials were finally started in May 2015, and when fully operational the port will have a capacity of 540,000 TEU a year. The new gantries can make the gauge change in less than an hour. At present, however, most of the trains that pass through Khorgos stay in Central Asia, moving on by train and truck to markets in Uzbekistan and nearby countries like Iran.[30] The dwell-time at Altynkol station is now slightly under four hours, including ninety minutes for processing customs declarations and reloading cargoes.[31] Nonetheless, probably because of the contracts already in place with the Russian authorities, Aleshenkou carries most of the rail freight destined for Europe.

Central Asia

For the land-locked countries of Central Asia, railways are vital for their prosperity. Long before the BRI had even been conceived, 85 per cent of the volume of overland traffic crossing international borders had been carried by rail, compared with 15 per cent by road.[32] For much of the period after the collapse of the Soviet Union, officials from the Central Asian transport ministries, meeting under the umbrella of CAREC (Central Asia Regional Economic Cooperation) had focused their attention on road improvements. However, in October 2013 CAREC endorsed a new priority of shifting traffic from road to rail in an effort to improve regional competitiveness.[33] Three years later the transport ministers, meeting in Islamabad, endorsed a medium-term strategy document.[34] It isolated four 'designated railway corridors' for the southern route through Central Asia, all (theoretically) starting in China and three of them ending at ports on the Caspian Sea. The one exception was a planned route through Afghanistan and ending in Iran, but the current security situation has pushed its implementation into the future, and it will not be examined further in this chapter.

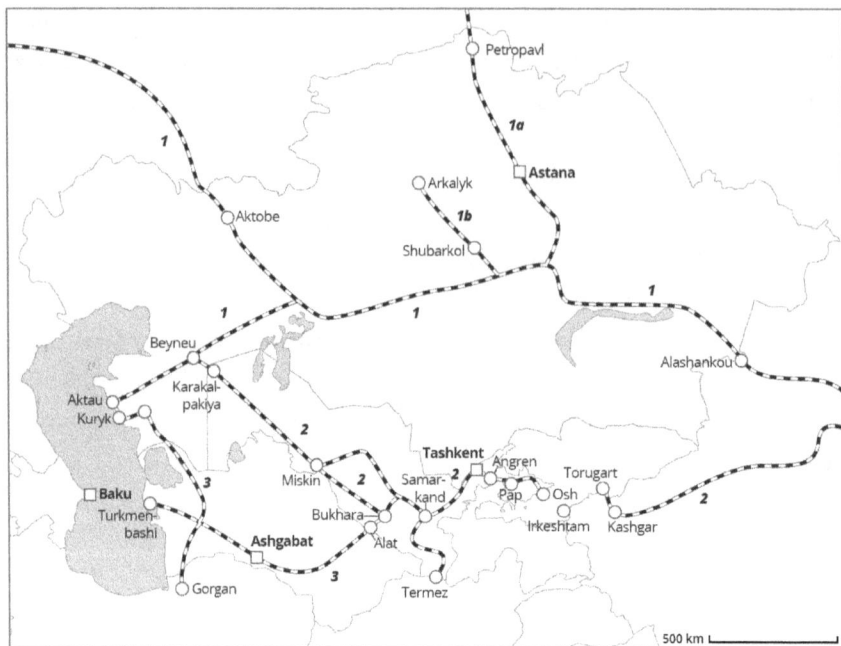

Figure 4.5: Main Railway Corridors in Central Asia

The first corridor crosses the frontier with China at Alashankou and for some of the route it follows the as the original Chongqing-Duisburg container route entering Russia near the border town of Petropavl (Figure 4.5, Route 1a). Much of the traffic, however, turns west at Astana and travels on a new east-west line from to Beyneu, across vast distances of steppe desert, sand and salt marshes (Figure 4.5, Route 1). Work on the line had started in June 2012 and it was finally opened for traffic in August 2014. In total it has shaved 1,000 kms (and one to three days) off the journey from China to the Caspian Sea. The main destination of this corridor, however, is the port of Aktau, Kazakhstan's key port on the Caspian Sea. By avoiding Russian territory altogether, the new route would allow Europe to ship foodstuffs to China that, at the moment are caught up in Russian counter-sanctions following the Ukraine crisis. At the same time a new 214 kms north-south route was opened between Arkalyk and Shubarkol which potentially allowed the building of a second branch into Russia and onwards to Europe (Figure 4.5, Route 1b).[35]

Aktau was essentially a 'tramp port' trading mainly in oil and dry cargo. Its equipment was outdated and it was already pushing its capacity limits. In 2012 it still had no ro-ro (roll on/roll off) facilities and no specific container handling berths. The only regular services was a rail ferry to Baku with a capacity for 28 or 52 wagons, but the service was so primitive that the rail cars had to be uncoupled from the train and loaded individually onto the ferry, and reassembled at the other end. With bad (winter) weather delays could amount to several days. The port has since been modernised and expanded. However, in 2016 construction began on a new ferry port at Kuryk, 70 kms to the south, at the cost of $104 million. At the same time, $30.3 million was spent building a 14 kms railway link to connect the port to existing rail network.[36] The new port, with an initial handling capacity of 4 million tonnes of freight, had the advantage over Aktau of not freezing in the winter, and of being less vulnerable to high winds. It also had room for further expansion. It started operation in March 2017[37] but in 2018 the volume of traffic was still only 1.6 million tonnes.[38]

The second rail corridor (Figure 4.5, Route 2) was intended to start from Kashgar and cross into Kyrgyzstan at Torugart before continuing by rail to Osh. It then passed through Uzbekistan, turned northwards, through Kazakhstan, and connected with the east-west line running to Aktau. The problem is that there is no railway between Torugart and Osh. In fact there is no direct rail crossing between China and Kyrgyzstan at all. This was not for want of trying. As long ago as 1996, the idea was first mooted for a rail line connecting the two countries, and extending from there to the rest of Central Asia. Technically there were two possible routes, both routes originating from Kashgar, with one travelling through the pass in Torugart and the other across the Irkeshtam Pass. Everybody wanted a piece of the action – the Russians, the Americans, the European Union (EU), different national rail consortia and, of course, China. This interest was a reflection of developments in the region in the aftermath of the Cold War and the on-going war in Afghanistan. After innumerable studies, the general consensus was that the route through Torugart would be easier and cheaper to realise. As the gigantic price-tag began to become clearer, and as the struggle for influence in the region ebbed, all the competitors disappeared from the scene until only China was left.[39] All this time various Kyrgyz governments had been blowing hot and cold on the entire project but, if anything, they began to favour the more expensive and more difficult route over the Irkeshtam Pass. This would dovetail better into the existing rail network and would connect to the improved domestic North-South rail link. The route through Torugart would be admirable for transit trade (and the revenues that would be collected) but for little else. However, with no other interested parties on the scene, negotiations began on the financial terms.[40] At various moments during the subsequent discussions on finances China offered a straight loan, a barter deal for funding in exchange for future deliveries of aluminium and iron, part-funding for a joint venture in which the Kyrgyz government would hold a 51 per cent stake or complete funding on a BOT basis.[41] In March 2019 Russia entered the equation. Kyrgyzstan is a member of the Russian-led Eurasian Economic Union. A state visit by President Putin brought promises of investments in the country worth $6 billion, as well as an undertaking to explore the joint development of Kyrgyz railways. The agreement specifically mentioned including a line running from China to Uzbekistan. At the time of writing there was no sign of how China would react.[42]

The second rail corridor, therefore, effectively starts at Osh before crossing into Uzbekistan some 28 kms further down the line. It then continues through Uzbekistan until it crosses into Kazakhstan. This, in itself, is no small achievement since the shorter route would have been to use the existing line that cut through Tajikistan. However a simmering dispute over water rights has long soured bilateral relations and, as a result, with the exception of oil and petroleum products, there has been no rail traffic between the two countries. In 2013, therefore, the Uzbek authorities started feasibility studies for a route to Tashkent and the Ferghana Valley that avoided passing through Tajik territory.[43] This would involve building a new 123 kms line between Angren and Pap. Most of the $1.5 billion cost was paid by the Uzbek authorities. The EXIM Bank of China contributed $350 million for the most difficult section (including a 19.2 kms tunnel, the longest in Asia) and the World Bank advanced $195 million for the line's electrification. Construction started in 2013 and the line was opened in June 2016. It carries eight freight trains a day and has succeeded in halving the cost of transporting bulk products as oil and fertilisers.[44]

Meanwhile in 2015 the Uzbek government had completed the electrification of the line from the border with Kazakhstan to Samarkand, but the trajectory southwards still operated with less powerful diesel locomotives, which placed restrictions on both speed and the lengths of trains. In 2018 the Japan International Cooperation Agency (JICA) and the ADB loaned $317 million to help cover the $500 million cost of electrifying the line between Samarkand and Termez, on the border with Afghanistan.[45]

At Bukhara, the line turns north, along a new stretch of line built to Miskin, near the border with Turkmenistan which was opened at the end of 2017. The single 355 kms single-track line cost $250 million to complete and is originally reserved exclusively for freight. It slices 75 kms off the existing, highly circuitous route and cuts the time between the two towns from three hours to one. There are plans for its electrification.[46] The line continues to Karakalpakia, where it crosses into Kazakhstan. It then travels a further 407 kms before meeting the first rail corridor at Beyneu and continuing to Aktau.

The third designated corridor (Figure 4.5, Route 3) follows the same route as the second until Bukhara where it turns south to cross the border into Turkmenistan at Farap/Alat. The train continues via Asghabat before turning north towards the Caspian port of Turkmenbashi. In 2013 the Turkmen government announced its intention to replace the outdated existing port. It was becoming badly silted, which restricted the size of vessels able to enter. The construction work had been undertaken by the Turkish company Gap Insaat.[47] In May 2018 the new port opened. It cost $1.5 billion to build and has a handling capacity of 17-18 million tons, including 400,000 TEU containers. Further expansion would raise the capacity to 28 million tons.[48] Some commentators saw the port as a left-over from commitments made when energy prices were high, and were sceptical about the port's (and the country's) self-proclaimed role at the 'heart' of the Silk Road, given that other routes were already well-established and that Turkmenistan lacked experience in handling large volumes of foreign trade.[49]

Access to Turkmenbashi was facilitated by the improvement in the North-South line between Kazakhstan (Uzan) and Iran (Gorgan). The track itself had been completed in 2011, with assistance from the Islamic Development Bank and the government of Belarus. In 2011 the ADB agreed to provide $125 million of the estimated $167 million for the electrification and signalling for 288 kms of the northern part of the line. The project was eventually completed, four years behind schedule, but below budget, in July 2016.[50]

Caucasus

The ships and ferries that depart from Aktau/Kuryk (Kazakhstan) and Turkembashi (Turkmenistan) used to have Baku (Azerbaijan) as their main destination but, because there was little room for expansion near the capital, the port has now relocated to Alyat, 70 kms to the south. It connected to the mainline the existing rail links running north, but which are seriously in need of modernisation. The real problem, however, lay in the rail link to the west. This had traditionally run through neighbouring Armenia, but since the end of the Nagorno-Karabakh war in 1994, Armenia's borders with Azerbaijan and Turkey had remained closed. In 2005, Azerbaijan, Georgia and Turkey together agreed on building a new railway (the Baku–Tbilisi–Kars Railway) by-passing Armenia (See Figure 4.6, Route 1). Both the EU and the USA had refused to help for the obvious reason that its effect would be to further isolate Armenia. The 838 kms rail line, involved the building or rehabilitation of 185 kms of track.[51] Most of the funding was covered by the three countries from their own resources, with Azerbaijan financing much of the work in Georgia, to the tune of $775 million. The European Bank for Reconstruction and Development (EBRD) also advanced $135.5 million to Georgia for the construction of a 10 kms dual-track bypass around the capital Tbilisi.[52] The entire work was originally scheduled to be finished by 2010. But it was not until January 2015 that the first test trains could run on the upgraded 721 kms section from Baku to Akhalkalaki. However, the trains could move no further because, although the groundwork had been completed on the Turkish side, no start had been made in laying the tracks, and the $400 million budget was virtually exhausted. A further $250 million was required to complete the project. The cause of both the cost overrun and the delay had been unexpected difficulties in tunnel construction owing to the harder rock encountered and the cessation of work while the contractor waited for payment. At the last minute the opening was further delayed when a landslide in Georgia destroyed part of the newly completed line.[53] Finally, in October 2017, the line was officially opened, with the expectation that it would transport five million tons of cargo annually, rising eventually to 17 million tons.[54] To prepare for the increased traffic between the Baku and Kars, Azerbaijan and Turkey agreed in July 2017 to construct a new a $26 million logistics centre in Kars region. Turkey expects 412,000 tons of cargo to move through the facility each year.[55] From Kars, the rail traffic could eventually travel along the Turkish railway system to Europe. In fact, in December 2018 the Turkish authorities initiated a scheme to connect Kars by rail to the West coast Mediterranean port of Izmir.[56]

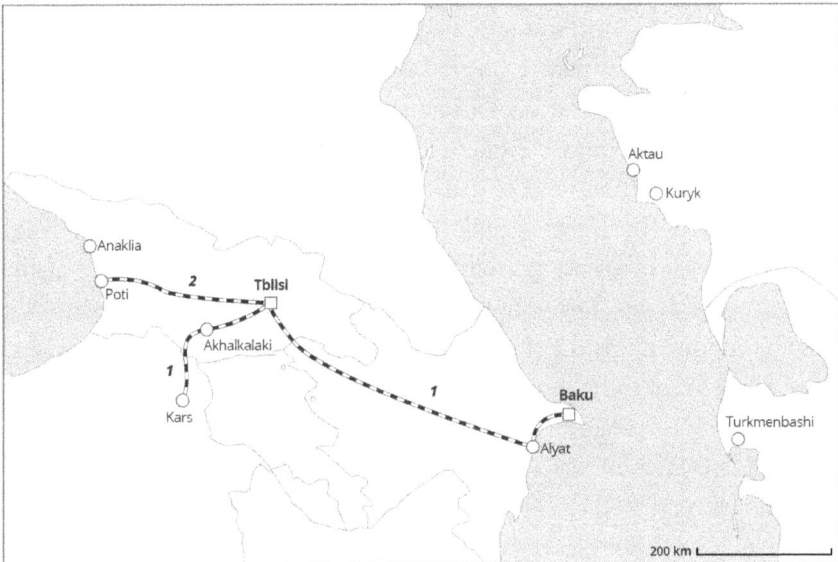

Figure 4.6 Railways and Ports of the Caucuses

The other alternative would be to head for Georgia's Black Sea ports of Poti (Figure 4.6, Route 2), which is run by APM Terminals (a subsidiary of Maersk). In 2014 the port authorities started a $100 million expansion to raise its capacity from 600,000 TUEs (which it considered being reached by 2017) to 1,000,000, and to make it capable of accommodating larger vessels of 10,000 containers.[57] Eighteen months later, it committed $250 million to improving the logistics chain in the harbour in order to remain competitive.[58] In September 2016, Georgia and Ukraine signed for direct international railroad services through the two countries' seaports and then on to China, aiming to cut the time for containers to travel from China to Ukraine's western border to 9-10 days.[59] It was a significant agreement.

Georgia had lost its direct rail link through Russia to Europe (after the breakaway of South Ossetia and Abkhazia in the 2008 civil war) and to Ukraine (after the annexation of the Crimea and the breakaway of Donetsk in 2014).

Another development which started in 2016 is the construction of a deep-sea port at Anaklia, in Georgia, at an estimated cost of $2.5 billion. The work is being undertaken by a consortium including the local firm TBC Holding and the US concern Conti International, which also holds the right to manage the port for 49 years. By 2019 the port should be capable of handling 7 million tons a year and accepting vessels with 10,000 container capacity. When completed it should be capable of handling 100 million tons annually and it will be the only Black Sea port capable of accepting post-Panamax container ships.[60] The work was delayed by the necessity to obtain an environmental impact report and only started in January 2018. There was speculation about accepting investment from China Railway International Group.[61] In March 2019, the future of the project was thrown into doubt when the government announced that it was considering returning the project to state control. The ostensible reason given was a list of eight 'new' demands by international development banks and the 'lack of progress' on the first phase of the port's construction.[62] However speculation was rife on darker forces at work. These included a vendetta being waged by the government against the owner of TBC Bank, agitation from other Georgian sea-ports and from Russia (and its port of Novorossiysk) that wanted the project killed for fear of the competition the new deep-sea port would offer, and pressure from China, anxious to preserve its chances of securing rail and road contracts against the possibility that international investors would insist on open competitive tenders. It is also suggested that by retaking control of the project would allow the government to farm it out anew, but this time to Chinese backers.[63] At the time of writing the outcome of the controversy was still uncertain.

Russia, Belarus and Ukraine

For Kazakhstan, the rail traffic runs through Russia until it reaches the borders of Belarus and Ukraine. Even before the unrest in Ukraine, most China-Europe trains passed through Belarus to reach Europe (Figure

4.7 Route 1). Since the collapse of the Soviet Union, Russia's railways had increased their share of freight movements, compared with roads, from 71 per cent in 1992 to 87 per cent in 2012.[64] Although cost of the funding for the maintenance and improvement of the railway system had come from domestic sources, the EBRD had advanced $2.2 billion for the purchase of freight wagons and locomotives.[65] In 2011 the Trans-Siberian railway carried 550,000 TEU containers, but only 40,000 were involved in transit trade.[66] By 2017 that figure has climbed to 415,000 TEU, itself an increase of 60 per cent over the year before.[67] The problem was that the capacity of the railway, and that of the Baikal-Amur railway that ran alongside it for part of the way, was reaching saturation point and the system was in dire need of an upgrade. In August 2018, President Putin announced a major infrastructural investment programme worth $40 billion over the coming six-year term of his presidency which would include both lines and which would boost overall capacity by 50 per cent. By switching mineral and raw materials to the Baikal-Amur line, it was hoped to allow a fourfold increase of container traffic on the main Trans-Siberian line, and to reduce the time of the journey to just seven days.[68]

Before we leave the freight routes travelling through Russia, let us pause to consider the one, head-line scheme that captures all the spirit, ambition and adventure of the new Silk Road. This is the vision of a 7,000 kms HSR dedicated freight line between Moscow and Beijing that could cover the whole distance in only two days.[69] In August 2017, the Russian railway company, RDZ, published a preliminary study for a Eurasia line stretching from Urumqi to Berlin. The total cost of the 9,500 kms line was estimated at $124 billion (7.84 trillion roubles) and could be completed within ten years. The study predicted that by 2050 the line would carry annually 39.9 million passengers and 12.6 million tons of freight (420,000 TEUs) at average speeds of 250 km/h. An expert review conducted by the Ministry of Transport, however, savaged the study for being over-optimistic on the running costs and for providing no information on sources of funding, legal implications or implementation. Essential to the entire plan was the timing. If all the sections of the entire project were not ready at the same time, the consequences for passenger and freight estimates would be disastrous. And the difficulties in realising the Moscow-Kazan section showed how real that danger was.[70]

Figure 4.7 Railway projects in Russia, Ukraine and Belarus

The announcement in 2015 of the construction of a HSR passenger service between Moscow and Kazan (Figure 4.7 route 1) had been canvassed as a pilot project for the whole Moscow-Beijing route. When completed, the 770 kms line would cut the journey time from fourteen hours to three and a half. China agreed to invest $5.2 billion in the project ($4.3 billion as a twenty-year loan and the remainder as equity).[71] In October 2015 the German firm Siemens opened the prospect of funding $2 billion, which would fund the costs of providing equipment and rolling stock.[72] Siemens had already delivered the high-speed trains, (called *Sapsan*, 'peregrine falcon' in Russian) for the Moscow–St Petersburg line which had started operation in December 2009.[73] However, by early 2018 the cost estimates had spiralled. The sums quoted for simply building and electrifying the line had risen to $15 billion, and a further $7.4 billion was quoted for rolling stock and equipment.[74] At the same time, the Russians were pressing for a review of the terms of the Chinese loan agreement which would imply a reduction in the rate of interest (currently fixed at 4 per cent) and an increase in the sums available.[75] In May 2018, however, the Russian-backed Eurasian Development Bank intervened with a commitment to see the line built,[76] and at the China-Russia forum in September 2018, the announcement that the field investigation and design of the line had been completed[77] seemed to suggest that the politics, if not the finances, of the project was still on track. In October RZD agreed to start work on a HSR link between Moscow and Gorokhovets as the first stage of the Moscow-Kazan railway in the form of a public-private partnership between RZD and Chinese backers[78] at a cost of $9.3 billion (621 billion roubles) for 301 kms of line which could allow for speeds of up to 400 km/h. One third for the funding would come from the federal budget, one third from RZD and the rest from investors (Russian and foreign banks). The total cost of the entire Moscow-Kazan line was estimated at $25.3 billion (1.69 trillion roubles).[79] At the time of writing, work on the line has still to commence, and criticism from the Russian Minister of Finance has thrown the whole project into doubt.[80]

Ukraine has never been the first choice route for the final leg of transit freight traffic from China to Europe. Surprisingly however, bilateral rail freight between Ukraine and Russia has continued despite the outbreak of civil war in Ukraine and the annexation of the Crimea by Russia in 2014 (direct flights, however, have been suspended). Nonetheless, Ukraine is still searching for new routes for delivering its goods to the east. One obvious alternative was to use the Trans-Caspian route to China through Georgia and Azerbaijan. In January 2016 Ukraine launched its first pilot block train using the route from its Black Sea port, Illichivsk, but, at that time, a regular service failed to materialise. Four months later, the train made the return journey empty, much to the enjoyment of the Russian press.[81] Nevertheless, Ukraine joined the other countries along the route in simplifying the freight rate structures (and lowering the costs[82]) in an effort to attract traffic. In 2018 Ukraine started its own service over the route and it was joined, later in the year, by the Polish firm FELB in shipping block trains via Odessa in order to export goods embargoed by Russia.[83] Although development of the route is still in its early stages, the EBRD and the EIB have together in July 2017 advanced $300 million of the $367 million project to improve and electrify 254 kms of railway in the south of the country in order to improve the connectivity with Odessa (Figure 4.7 Route 2).[84] In 2019, as part of the Eastern Partnership agreement, the EU envisaged funding a further eight electrification projects to the tune of $565 million in different parts of the country.[85]

All the China-Europe trains from Russia pass through Belarus. Here, China has been the main source of funding for railway improvement, although the sums for specific projects is not large. Since 2010 it has provided $218 million for upgrading and electrifying track between Minsk and the Russian and Lithuanian borders (Figure 4.7, Route 3) and a further $194 million for the purchase of 30 Chinese electric locomotives.[86] From Belarus, most freight trains cross the border into Poland.

Heading East from Europe

Since the fall of the Soviet Union, the EU has been active in improving the transport infrastructure of the former CEE communist states. Chapter Three described the huge funds channelled into the improvement of roads. These amounts far exceeded the support for investment in railways. Initially this was because the region was relatively well-endowed with railways, which had been the favoured means for moving freight in Soviet times. However, railway investment does not last for ever and the existing system was oriented neither to trade with the West nor to the needs of transit trade. Eventually the concentration on roads operated to the detriment of the railways.

The New EU Member States

In Chapter Two we saw how the EU adapted itself to the former socialist economies on its western frontier by reorienting border crossings and by providing financial support. Although the primary focus of this effort was on the provision of roads, railway investment was not entirely neglected. Between 1990 and 2007 the European Investment Bank (EIB) advanced loans worth about $8 billion for the construction and rehabilitation of CEE railways. This was a mere 16 per cent of the amount directed towards the transport sector as a whole, which reflected the priority given to road improvement at the time.[87] Between 2007 and 2014, the EU's ERDF and

Cohesion Funds together invested a further $20 billion in improving the railway network in the CEE member states. This was mostly in the form of grants rather than loans.[88] However, despite the size of the investments, only 22 kms of new railway lines had been built. On the other hand, a further 1,577.2 kms of track had been improved or upgraded (though only 847.2 kms identified as part of the core network in its TEN-T programme).[89] For the period 2014-2020, there has been a major shift in emphasis towards the rail sector, and towards the improvement of designated international routes. The EU, through its European Structural Investment Fund, now envisages spending $19 billion on CEE country railways (76.6 per cent of its total EU spending in the transport sector) with 65 per cent targeted at improving TEN-T railway links.[90] Furthermore the 'Connecting Europe Facility' (a separate fund for pan-European infrastructural investment in transport projects, energy and digital projects) foresaw an expenditure of an additional $13.7 billion. With most of the spending still to take place, at the time of writing, it will be interesting to see how much will be realised.[91]

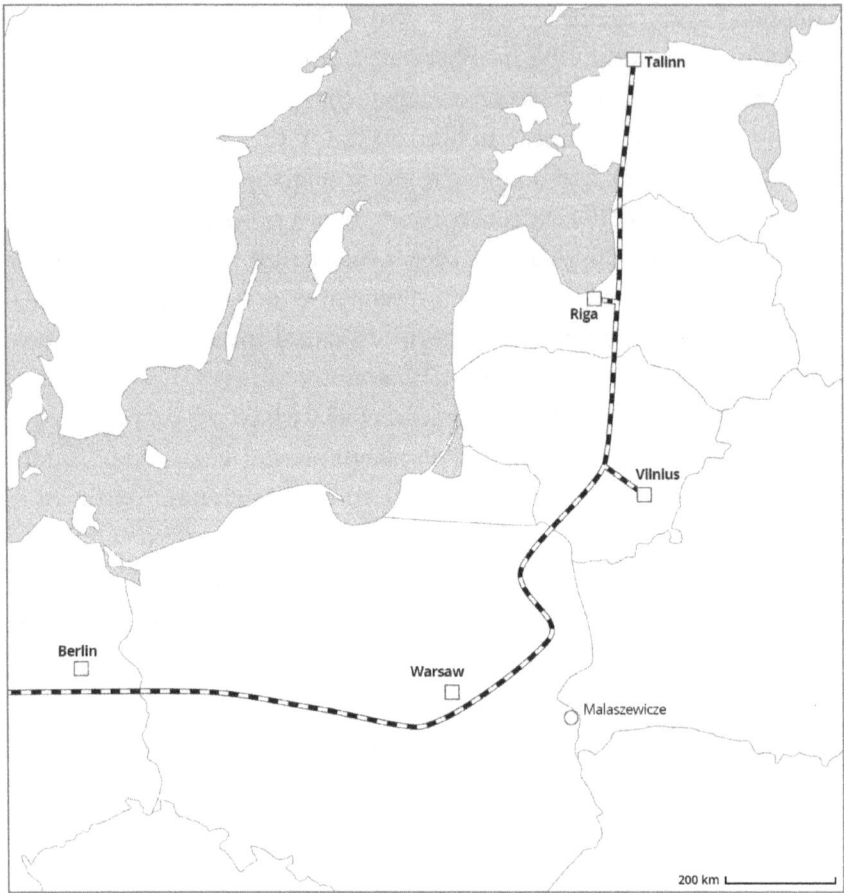

Figure 4.8: Plans for the Rail Baltica Route

Much of the EU's most recent largesse will be directed towards the implementation of the Rail Baltica project (Figure 4.8). This is designed to replace the existing 1,520 mm Soviet gauge line in the Baltic with a new 870 kms HSR line, capable of speeds of 240 kms/h, that will connect the capitals of Tallinn, Riga and Vilnius, and integrate seamlessly into the main EU network.[92] The final cost of the project is estimated at $5.65 billion and the EU will defray 85 per cent of the costs. The assessment by Ernst & Young conceded that the project would not be financially viable without public funding, but that once the investment had been made, running the line itself would be financially sustainable. Moreover the economic benefits such as reduced pollution and increased growth would far outweigh the initial costs.[93] This optimistic assessment quickly came in for criticism. Ernst & Young had seriously overestimated the pollution levels in the absence of the railways, and had not adequately assessed the costs of the inter-modal hubs that would link rail freight to the road network.[94] However, the project has built up quite a head of steam in EU circles[95] and will probably push ahead regardless. Whether the money might not be better spent elsewhere is another question altogether.

Until recently all the China-Europe container freight trains have crossed into Europe through the border crossing at the small Polish town of Malaszewicze. Here there is a delay while all the various documents are checked and the containers are controlled for smuggling and stowaways. However most of the documents have been sent in advance, allowing administrative irregularities to be checked before the train arrives. All that is left is the gauge change. The infrastructure at Malaszewicze has had difficulty in coping with the increased traffic. It can barely reach the fourteen trains a day which it is supposed to process. For each train Khorgos can make the gauge change in less than an hour and Duisburg boasts being able to handle three trains in two hours. At Malazewicze, even at its peak performance, it was common for west-bound trains to take eighteen hours to continue their journey. Since then delays have climbed to two to three days.[96] Part of the problem is that there were only two sets of parallel tracks, but worse still is the fact that these do not even reach the 600 metres to accommodate the train length permissible in Europe, let alone the longer trains originating from Russia. As a result there is much decoupling and shunting around, and the division of containers onto two or more trains to continue their journey.[97] To make matters worse, from March 2018 to April 2019 the capacity of the station will be halved as first one set of tracks and then the other are being repaired. Even after this disruption, there will be no real hike in the station's handling capacity.[98] It is scant consolation, but when, at the end of 2016, a slew of new transport projects supported by $2.1 billion from the EU's 'Connecting Europe Facility' was announced, it contained $3.6 million to fund a study for the improvement of the facilities in Malaszewicze.[99] The capacity at other BCP's is limited, but some trains have started to pass through Kaliningrad and Latvia, where no gauge change is required. There are even trials in sending containers to

Kaliningrad by ship and loading them directly onto Russian-gauge change for the journey, via Dostyk to Chengdu.[100]

Having crossed the border at Malaszewicze, the container trains continue their journey through Poland, Germany and the Benelux countries along (part of) the North-Sea/Baltic corridor. The EU's own Audit Office was seriously concerned whether the EU's investment in transport infrastructure had been worthwhile. Poland was one of the five countries that it visited. The report observed that the share of freight carried by rail had fallen from 42.5 per cent in 2000 to 17 per cent in 2013. The network was in poor condition and transit times were long – the average speed of freight trains was only 22.7 km/h. Access to the tracks was difficult, with few slots available once passenger train schedules had been accommodated. Freight trains were only sixth and seventh in order of priority, having preference only above 'empty passenger trains'. The line-access charges for freight were double those for passenger trains (and far above road-access charges). All of these considerations pushed traffic onto roads, a trend that was compounded by the decision of governments to use EU funding to support road rather than rail construction. Between 2007 and 2013 the EU had provided $29.8 billion for the improvement of Poland's transport infrastructure, but only $7.7 billion had been spent on railways. For the period 2014-2020 the total expenditure envisaged was $27.8 billion, with $8.8 billion intended for railways.[101]

There are other potential routes for freight to enter European markets. In view of the development of the Trans-Caucasus route and the investments in Georgia's Black Sea ports, one could envisage more freight arriving through ports in Romania and Bulgaria. Let us take Constanta as an example. It is the largest of Europe's Black Sea ports. In 2016 it handled both liquid and dry bulk cargo as well as containers and, in 2016, boasted a throughput of over 60 million tons including over 700,000 TEU containers (accounting for 16 per cent of the total).[102] The container terminal is operated by the Dubai-based DP World, which plans to expand the capacity form one- to four million TEUs over the coming years.[103] The problems accumulate when it comes to moving the freight onwards by rail. In 2017, the European Railway Performance Index ranked Romania's railways the worst but one in Europe (just above Bulgaria). Out of a possible score of 10, Romania managed 1.9 (Switzerland, the highest, scored 7.2).[104]

The rail connection to Bucharest cannot carry the EU standard axel load of 22.5 tonnes and cannot comply with EU target for train length of 740 metres.[105] The rehabilitation of this 225 kms stretch between Constanta and Bucharest had been part of a $1 billion contract, but work on this section took six years to complete. It later transpired that the Austrian consortium that had undertaken the work had paid bribes worth $23 million to secure the contract. The then finance minister was possibly one of the recipients and he is currently under investigation. He paid part of his $1 million bail in gold bars.[106] The HSR through to Budapest was originally agreed between Hungary and Romania in 2007, but nothing had been done. In 2014, the Romanian government was speculating that China would finance and build a HSR from Vienna to Constanta, passing through Budapest and Bucharest,[107] but that, too, seems to have fallen through. The reason will become apparent at the end of the next section.

Western Balkans

The collapse of the economies of the Western Balkans, and especially the heavy industries that had characterised their development, had decimated the railways. Freight traffic had fallen by two-thirds between 1990 and 2004, and passenger traffic by almost 75 per cent. As a result the region possessed a railway system with a network density not dissimilar to that of Western Europe, but operating with less than half the traffic and one third of the labour productivity. The system had also been starved of investment and rail operators had adjusted to lower demand by retiring old rolling stock and using, for as long as possible, their newer material.[108] Ironically, the result was that the core railway network was more than sufficient to meet immediate needs and only required modest investment targeting specific bottlenecks. All the forecasts suggested, over the next twenty years, a far greater growth of road traffic than of rail. Nevertheless, the European Commission suggested that the infrastructure needs for the core corridors in the decade to 2015 would be for $14 billion for rail, as opposed to $4.75 billion for roads.[109] It is surely a curious outcome, therefore, that between 2004 and 2012, the EU and national and international partners had invested only $833 million in improving the region's railways and had committed a further $220 million to ongoing and planned projects – only equivalent to 13 per cent and 6 per cent respectively of the comparable figures for roads.[110] Since then, however, a further $3.3 billion has been ploughed into rail improvements, still only slightly over half the sums committed to roads.[111]

It is worth pausing at this juncture to discuss the proposed $2.89 billion 350 km HSR between Belgrade and Budapest. The project was first mooted at a 16+1 meeting in Bucharest in 2013 and, in December 2014, China and the two other parties involved signed a Memorandum of Understanding to jointly develop the project, as part of the TEN-T corridor that would eventually connect to the port of Piraeus, that China is developing into a major hub. The entire line is intended to represent part of China's Belt and Road initiative in Europe. The funding would be provided by the China's EXIM Bank and the construction work would be undertaken by China Railway International Corporation.[112] To be honest, in the short term, it is difficult to see the scheme doing much to boost China's sales in Europe since the southern end of the line (Bucharest) is still 800 kms away from Piraeus. Travelling over the existing tracks, freight trains would take an average of four days to make that journey over the difficult terrain.[113] The problem with the scheme as originally conceived and implemented lay in the 166 kms section running through Hungary. As a member of the EU's single market, Hungary is subject to its rules and regulations. One of those rules is that all public procurements must be submitted for open competitive tender. This is not particularly directed at China, but the measure dates from a period, decades earlier, when the state sector in most Western economies was much larger and when states used public procurement to favour national champions, thereby removing a large sector of the economy from free competition (private investors can do what they like). In February 2017 the EU therefore intervened to examine the nature of the contract and in November the whole procedure was reopened.[114] The lowest bid in the first open tender in May 2018 was $2.53 billion, which was far above the government's $2.11 target. In December the government reopened the tender.[115] At the time of writing, no contract had been awarded.

While this was happening, developments were proceeding apace in Serbia, which is not (yet) a member of the EU and not, therefore, bound by its competition rules. In November 2016 the government signed a contract for its part of a HSR with the China Railway International Group and China Road Communications Construction Company. The specifications of the contract had been reduced to 200 km/h for passenger trains, theoretically still 'high-speed'. Although not as fast the 350-400 km/h originally envisaged, it is considerably cheaper to build.[116] The new 'Brotherhood and Unity' Bridge built to carry the HSR 475 metres over the Danube, was completed in September 2018. The EU contributed $25 million of the $54 million that it cost.[117]

Conclusions

Railways are less flexible than roads, but have a decisive advantage with long-distance freight traffic. They are also far more expensive to build than highways. The ADB has suggested that (measured in 2010 prices) modern (two-track, electrified) railway-lines in Asia cost on average $3.8 million per kilometre to construct.[118] Despite the high costs, across the Eurasian landmass existing railways were upgraded, often with the support of foreign development loans. In Xinjiang, the Chinese government was planning to spend $5 billion in the five years between 2016 and 2020. Most of the railway network in Central Asia was inherited from Soviet times and new construction and most of the improvements seem to have been funded from national resources (railway profits or taxation). Foreign loans were only occasionally involved, as in the case of the new Agren-Pap line and the electrification of lines elsewhere in Uzbekistan. There are other examples, but it is difficult to push the figure for foreign support for railway construction and improvement much above $2-3 billion, which is far lower than the funding made available for road building.

A similar situation prevailed in the Caucasus, where Western development agencies had been initially reluctant to fund projects that might cement the 'frozen border' disputes permanently into place. The recent Eastern Partnership proposals have earmarked just over $1 billion for the electrification of the East-West railway in Georgia and Azerbaijan. In Ukraine, including the recently announced plans by the Eastern Partnership and including investments already committed, the EU foresees expenditure on railway improvement by 2030 of only $850 million.

In Belarus China has provided $400 million in support for the railway industry and the EU a further $150 million. Between 2007 and 2014 the EU invested $20 billion in rail improvements in the new member states, mostly in the form of grants rather than loans, and it envisages spending a further $19 billion by the end of 2020. In the Western Balkans some $1 billion has been spent since between 2002 and 2012 and a further $3 billion has been pledged.

There are only two conclusions to be drawn from this. The first is that despite the hype built up around China's railway building projects, the country has actually helped build very few. The second is that there has been relatively little railway building at all, and what little has occurred, has been in the European countries at the western end of the new Silk Road, and has been built with support of the EU.

It is quite clear that something exciting has been happening on railways. This is the establishment of regular freight container services between Chinese and European cities. In 2006, rail transport had not only been slower than by sea but also twice as expensive. Whilst the price differential has remained, the journey time has been slashed by almost half. Much of the credit for these developments must accrue to logistics providers at both ends of the journey, but especially to the authorities in China. They have actively promoted the development of new routes; they have improved handling facilities at different points along their borders and they have provided subsidies that have helped make the whole operation competitive. China is now starting to reduce the subsidies, but the impact on trade volumes may be compensated by increased competition between the Trans-Siberian railway routes and the new routes being developed through Central Asia and the Caucasus. These new routes may also stimulate the proliferation of similar container freight services among the other countries lying along the new Silk Road.

This chapter also highlights the importance of international borders. No-one has ever denied the problems with border conflicts or even tensions between neighbours but these images are reinforced when railway lines in Uzbekistan and Azerbaijan are built to avoid having to use an existing line across the territory of the neighbouring country. In the railway literature, international borders were also seen as a source of difficulties when it also involved a change in gauge. However these days should be long gone. Nowadays modern container lifting gear can transfer a container in under a minute, meaning that it is possible to transfer an entire train-load in about an hour; the time it would take to clear the documentation. This is not always the case, as was illustrated by the situation before improvements in northern China and, more recently by the crossing into Poland. This confirms what we have always known, if not always affirmed; in a globalised world, geography still matters.

Richard T. Griffiths

1   Statistical Agency of Kazakhstan, *Kazakhstan in Figures*, Astana, 2013. Available at: http://stat.gov.kz/getImg?id=WC16200032251.

2   US Chamber of Commerce, *Land Transport Options between Europe and Asia*, Washington DC, 28-39. Available at: https://www.osce.org/eea/41310? download=true.

3   *Xinhuanet*, 17.3.2019. Available at: http://www.xinhuanet.com/english/2019 -03/17/c_137902322.htm.

4   B. Besharati, Gansakh, F. Liu, X. Zhang and M. Xu, "The Ways to Maintain Sustainable China-Europe Block Train Operation", *Business and Management Studies*, 3, 3, 2017, 28-29. Available at: http://redfame.com/journal/index.php/ bms/article/view/2490/2619.

5   *International Railway Journal*, 16.8.2019. Available at: https://www.railjournal. com/in_depth/can-china-europe-rail-freight-continue-to-prosper-without-chi- nese-subsidies/.

6   E. Gerden, 'Russia considers ending Belt and Road cooperation', JOC.com, 17.8.2017. Available at: https://www.joc.com/rail-intermodal/international-rail/ asia/russia-mulls-ending-belt-and-road-cooperation_20170817.html.

7   C. Rastogi and J-F. Arvis, *The Eurasian Connection. Supply-Chain Efficiency along the Modern Silk Route through Central Asia*, Washington DC. 2014, 40–9. Available at: http://documents.worldbank.org/curated/en/730031468030581540/pdf/ 888910PUB0Box300EPI199120June122014.pdf.

8   JOC.com, 29.10.2018. Available at: https://www.joc.com/rail-intermodal/in- ternational-rail/china-rail-intermodal/china-europe-rail-providers-shrug-full- train-subsidy-rule_20181029.html.

9   National Development and Reform Commission, 中欧班列建设发展规划 （2016—2020 年）(China-Europe Train Construction and Development Plan) Beijing, 2016. Available at: http://www.ndrc.gov.cn/zcfb/zcfbghwb/201610/ P020161017547345656182.pdf.

10 *Trans-Siberian route: development of trans-continental transportations*. Powerpoint Presentation to the Second informal preparatory meeting for the 14th session of the Group of Experts on the Euro-Asian Transport Links 2-3.2.2016. Available at: https://www.unece.org/fileadmin/DAM/trans/doc/2016/wp5-eatl/WP5_ GE2_2nd_informal_session_Mr_Bessonov.pdf.

11 *Peoples Daily*, 7.16.2016. Available at: http://en.people.cn/n3/2016/0607/ c90000-9069339.html.

12 *Freight Week*, 20.9.2017. Available at: https://www.freightweek.org/index.php/en/ latest-news/85-rail/2845-rail-freight-up-19-percent-between-russia-and-china.

13 *Global Times*, 5.11.2017. Available at: http://www.globaltimes.cn/con- tent/1073677.shtml; *Russia Times*, 22.8.2018. Available at: https://www.rt.com/ business/436545-china-russia-railroad-construction/.

14 *Global Times*, 17.3.2019. Available at: http://www.globaltimes.cn/content/1142334.shtml; RT.com, 2.4.2019. Available at https://www.rt.com/business/455328-russia-china-railroad-amur/.

15 E. Gerden, 'Rocketing Asia-Russia container rail volume spurs investment calls', JOC.com, 5.8.2018. Available at: https://www.joc.com/rail-intermodal/track-upgrades-seen-increasing-russia%E2%80%99s-china-europe-rail-volume-growth_20180805.html.

16 *International Railway Journal*, 16.8.2019. See note 5.

17 Xinhua.net, 21.1.2019. Available at: http://www.xinhuanet.com/english/2019-01/21/c_137762280.htm.

18 CAREC, *Corridor Performance Measurement and Monitoring. Annual Report, 2016.* 2018. Available at: https://www.carecprogram.org/uploads/2016-CAREC-CPMM-Annual-Report.pdf.

19 *China Daily*, 21.9.2017. Available at: http://www.chinadaily.com.cn/business/2017-09/21/content_32295740.htm. See also W. Shepard, 'Big Changes In The Gobi: China And Mongolia's Cross-Border Economic Zone Gets Underway', *Forbes Magazine*, 21.9.2016. Available at: https://www.Forbes Magazine.com/sites/wadeshepard/2016/09/21/big-changes-in-the-gobi-china-and-mongolias-cross-border-economic-zone-gets-underway/.

20 *Global Times*, 3.5.2017. Available at: http://www.globaltimes.cn/content/1045206.shtml; Xinhua.net, 2.9.2018. Available at: http://www.xinhuanet.com/english/2018-09/02/c_137438735.htm.

21 *Global Times*, 3.5.2017. See note 19.

22 *UB Post*, 29.6.2016. Available at: http://theubposts.com/over-30-projects-lined-up-for-trilateral-economic-corridor/.

23 Asian Development Bank project database, 48329-001. Available at: https://www.adb.org/projects. Enter the project number to have access to all the relevant documentation. At the time of writing, the only rail project under development in Mongolia was a single track 547 kms line from the Erdenet copper mines to the coal mines of Nurstell and Ovoot to be built by Chinese contractors. A preliminary study estimated the cost at $1.2 billion and, at the time of writing, finance was being sought from the China Development Bank and the Silk Road Fund. *Railway Gazette International*, 10.4.2018. Available at: https://www.railwaygazette.com/news/news/asia/single-view/view/mongolian-railway-draft-feasibility-study-completed.html.

24 CGTV, 9.7.2017. Available at: https://news.cgtn.com/news/3d49444f3259444e/share_p.html. *Railway Gazette International*, 11.7.2017. Available at: https://www.railwaygazette.com/news/high-speed/single-view/view/baoji-lanzhou-opening-completes-high-speed-corridor-to-western-china.html?sword_list[]=Lanzhou&no_cache=1.

25 丝绸之路经济区核心区交通枢纽中心建设规划（2016-2030），2017，45-47. (Silk Road Economic Zone core area transportation hub centre construction plan (2016-2030). Available at: https://www.yidaiyilu.gov.cn/wcm.files/upload/CMSydylgw/201708/201708250626019.pdf. The scheme envisaged two regional integrated networks, in the north and south, a network connecting the two and two links designed to improve the connection of Xinjiang to the East of China and to neighbouring countries (pp 26-28).

26 *Global Times*, 22.8.2018. Available at: https://www.pressreader.com/china/global-times/20180823/textview.

27 CAREC, *Corridor Performance Measurement and Monitoring. Annual Report, 2015*, 2016. Available at: https://www.gica.global/link_click_count?url=http%3A%2F%2Fwww.carecprogram.org%2Fuploads%2F-docs%2FCAREC-Publications%2F2015-CAREC-CPMM-Annual-Report.pdf&nid=2369.

28 This was recognised over ten years ago, and there were plans to move the facilities to a larger site at Aktogai 310 kms away and construct a double track corridor, including one with standard gauge. See K.K. Zhangaskin, 'Trans-Kazakhstan Link will Complete Standard-Gauge Transcontinental Artery', *Railway Gazette*, 1.8.2004. Available at: https://www.railwaygazette.com/news/single-view/view/trans-kazakhstan-link-will-complete-standard-gauge-transcontinental-artery.html.

29 CAREC, *Corridor Performance Measurement Annual Report, 2014*, 2016. Available at: https://www.carecprogram.org/uploads/2014-CAREC-CP-MM-Annual-Report.pdf ; CAREC, *Corridor Performance Measurement Quarterly Report 2015 Q3*.

30 *Journal of Commerce*, 21.6.2016; CrossRoads Today, 6.12.2018. Available at: http://www.cbs8.com/story/39595491/container-traffic-along-titr-surges-in-kazakhstan.

31 Kazakh TV, 24.1.2018. Available at: https://kazakh-tv.kz/en/view/business/page_190401_.

32 M. Parkash, *Connecting Central Asia. A road map for regional cooperation*, Manila 2006, 7-8. Available at: http://unohrlls.org/UserFiles/File/LLDC%20Documents/MTR/ADB%20connecting-CA-roadmap.pdf.. The study did not include Turkmenistan.

33 ADB, *CAREC, Transport and Trade Facilitation Strategy 2020*, Manila 2014. Available at: https://www.adb.org/sites/default/files/institutional-document/34107/files/carec-ttfs-2020.pdf ; ADB, *Central Asia Regional Economic Cooperation Program Twelfth Ministerial Conference*, Astana, Kazakhstan 23–24.10.2013. Available at: https://www.adb.org/sites/default/files/institutional-document/34029/files/in403-13.pdf.

34 ADB, *Unlocking the Potential of Railways. A Railway Strategy for CAREC, 2017-2030*, Manila, 2017. Available at: https://www.adb.org/sites/default/files/institutional-document/227176/carec-railway-strategy-2017-2030.pdf ; CAREC, *Joint Ministerial Statement 15th Ministerial Conference on Central Asia Regional Economic Cooperation Islamabad, Pakistan*, 26 10.2016.

35 *Railway Gazette International*, 15.1.2014; Kazinform 22.8.2014. Available at: https://www.carecprogram.org/uploads/2016-MC-Joint-Ministerial-Statement.pdf

36 W. Shepard, 'A look inside Aktau. Kazakhstan's other hub on the New Silk Road', *Forbes Magazine Magazine*, 15.4.2017. Available at: https://www.Forbes Magazine.com/sites/wadeshepard/2017/04/15/a-look-inside-aktau-kazakhstans-other-hub-on-the-new-silk-road/; EGIS International, *Logistics Processes and Motorways of the Sea II in Armenia, Azerbaijan, Georgia, Kazakhstan, Kyrgyzstan, Moldova, Tajikistan, Turkmenistan, Ukraine, Uzbekistan LOGMOS Master Plan – Annex 3 Part I Maritime Sector Overview*, 2013, 32-39. Available at: http://www.traceca-org.org/fileadmin/fm-dam/TAREP/65ta/Master_Plan/MPA3.1.pdf; *Railway Pro*, 9.12.2015; *ITE Transport and Logistics*, 28.4.2017.

37 *AzerNews*, 28.3.2017. Available at: https://www.azernews.az/business/110654.html; *Astana Times*, 25.10.2017. Available at: https://astanatimes.com/2017/10/one-millionth-tonne-of-cargo-shipped-from-kuryk-port/; *AzerNews*, 12.6.2018. Available at: https://www.azernews.az/region/133389.html; *AzerNews*,14.6.2018. Available at: https://www.azernews.az/nation/133507.html.

38 *Astana Times*, 6.2.2019. Available at: https://astanatimes.com/2019/02/kuryk-seaport-to-boost-shipment-capacity/.

39 *Railway Gazette International*, 1.8.2000. Available at: https://www.railwaygazette.com/news/single-view/view/kyrgyzstan-to-plug-silk-route-gap.html; *Railway Gazette*, 1.4.2001, Available at: https://www.railwaygazette.com/news/single-view/view/silk-road-link-moves-to-engineering-design.html; *Railway Gazette International*, 1.6.2003. Available at: https://www.railwaygazette.com/news/single-view/view/landbridge-planning-moves-ahead.html.

40 World Bank Press Release, 18.6.2012. Available at: http://www.worldbank.org/en/news/press-release/2012/06/18/railway-communications-for-the-development-of-trade-relations-of-kyrgyzstan.

41 J.C.K. Daly, 'China and Kyrgyzstan Discuss Rail Projects', *Eurasia Daily Monitor*, 11, 29, 13.2.2014. Available at: https://jamestown.org/program/china-and-kyrgyzstan-discuss-rail-projects/. *Railway Pro*, 12.1.2015. Available at: https://www.railwaypro.com/wp/kyrgyzstan-to-discuss-again-with-china-about-kyrgyzstan-china-rail-project/ ; *Railway Pro*, 4.3.2015. Available at: https://www.railwaypro.com/wp/kyrgyzstan-offers-china-the-concession-of-china-kyrgyzstan-railway/. C. Putz, 'What Next for the Belt and Road in Central Asia?', *The Diplomat*, 17.5.2017. Available at: https://thediplomat.

com/2017/05/whats-next-for-the-belt-and-road-in-central-asia/. At the Belt and Road Forum in May 2017, the Kyrgyz president made some positive comments, but nothing was been settled.

42 Eurasianet.org, 29.3.2019. Available at: https://eurasianet.org/kyrgyzstan-putin-visit-brings-lavish-deals-and-vows-of-a-bright-future; AzerNews, 2.4.2019. Available at: https://www.azernews.az/region/148192.html.

43 M. Sadykov, 'Uzbekistan: New Ferghana Railway Plan Tweaks Tajikistan', Eurasianet.org, 14.3.2013. Available at: https://eurasianet.org/uzbekistan-new-ferghana-railway-plan-tweaks-tajikistan.

44 World Bank Project Database P146328.; *Implicaton, Status and Results Report*, 13.7.2018; Available at: http://projects.worldbank.org/. Enter the project number to have access to all the relevant documentation. Eurasianet. org, 23.6.2016. Available at: https://eurasianet.org/uzbekistan-china-friends-time-need; *Sputniknews*, 29.11.2013. Available at: https://sputniknews.com/world/20131129185138561-China-to-Provide-Uzbekistan-350M-for-Crucial-Rail-Tunnel/. In November 2017 the ADB agreed to lend a further $80 million to meet 45 per cent of the cost of completing the line's electrification. ADB Project Database, 48025-003. Available at: https://www.adb.org/projects. Enter the project number to have access to all the relevant documentation; *Railway Gazette*, 26.4.2017. Available at: https://www.railwaygazette.com/news/news/asia/single-view/view/adb-loan-for-fergana-valley-electrification.html.

45 JICA Press Release, 27.2.2012 Available at: https://www.jica.go.jp/english/news/press/2011/120227_02.html; *Railway Gazette*, 16.1.2018 Available at: https://www.railwaygazette.com/news/infrastructure/single-view/view/opening-and-electrification-in-uzbekistan.html; ADB Project Database, 45067-005. See note 43.

46 *Railway Gazette*, 6.9.2015, 16.1.2018; *International Railway Journal*, 5.12.2017.

47 EGIS International, *Logistics Processes and Motorways of the Sea*, 39-42; *ITE Transport and Logistics*, 28.4.2017.

48 *Caspian News*, 5.5.2018.

49 *Eurasianet*, 3.5.2018. Available at: https://eurasianet.org/turkmenistans-new-15-billion-port-show-over-substance. The article mocked the regime's over embellishment of its achievements and its pursuit of recognition, even if it was from the Guinness Book of Records. Having won one award for the "largest horse head sculpture" and another for the 705 m² squared carpet mosaic hanging from the roof the new airport, the new harbour added two more to the collection- "largest harbour port below sea level" and having "the largest artificial island below sea level".

50 ADB Project database 43441-013. *Turkmenistan: North–South Railway Project, Completion Report*, July 2018. See note 43.

51 *Today's Zaman*, 27.7.2008 (BTK Project: Dream coming true). The track requiring attention was distributed as follows: 76 kms in Turkey, 29 kms in Georgia and 80 kms in Azerbaijan.

52 *Railway Pro*, 29.8.2017. Available at: https://www.railwaypro.com/wp/azerbaijan-invests-usd-631-million-construction-georgian-btk-section/.

53 *Rail Turkey*, 16.10.2015. Available at: https://railturkey.org/2015/10/16/why-baku-tbilisi-kars-project-stagnated/ ; *Railway Pro*, 21.6.2017; 26.7.2017; 29.8.2017.

54 *Bloomberg*, 30.10.2017. Available at: https://www.bloomberg.com/news/articles/2017-10-30/azerbaijan-to-open-railway-planned-as-new-europe-china-corridor.

55 *Caspian News*, 17.8.2017. Available at: https://caspiannews.com/news-detail/caspian-economy-poised-to-grow-as-azerbaijan-turkey-launch-logistics-center-2017-8-15-21/.

56 *AzerNews*, 7.12.2018. Available at: https://www.azernews.az/business/142249.html.

57 JOC.com, 27.5.2014. Available at: https://www.joc.com/port-news/terminal-operators/apm-terminals/black-sea-growth-spurs-apm-terminals-expansion-georgia%E2%80%99s-poti-sea-port_20140527.html.

58 *Georgia Today*, 16.11.2015. Available at: http://georgiatoday.ge/news/1960/USD-250-million-To-Be-Invested-in-Poti-Mega-Port.

59 Railway Pro, 16.9.2016. Available at: https://www.railwaypro.com/wp/ukraine-and-georgia-sign-agreement-on-direct-ferry-railroad-services/.

60 M. Papidze, 'Project of the century: Georgia starts to build Anaklia Deep Sea Port', *Agenda.ge*, 9.2.2016. Available at: http://agenda.ge/en/article/2016/8 See also N. Gugunishvili, 'Anaklia Deep Sea Port: Reviving Georgia's Transport Potential', *Georgia Today*, 20.11.2017. Available at: http://georgiatoday.ge/news/8250/Anaklia-Deep-Sea-Port%3A-Reviving-Georgia%E2%80%99s-Transport-Potential; *The Economist*, 16.2.2019. Available at: https://www.economist.com/europe/2019/02/16/shrinking-the-black-sea.

61 *Agenda.ge*, 8.2.2018. Available at: http://agenda.ge/en/news/2018/294.

62 *Georgia Today*, 25.3.2019. Available at: http://georgiatoday.ge/news/14977/Investors-List-8-Demands-for-Anaklia-Deep-Sea-Port-Development and http://georgiatoday.ge/news/14979/Anaklia-Development-Consortium-CEO-Responds-to-Rumors.

63 G. Lonsadze, 'Georgian East-West port project mired in controversy', Eurasianet, 28.3.2019. Available at: https://eurasianet.org/georgian-east-west-port-project-mired-in-controversy.

64 EBRD, *The EBRD's projects in the Russian railway sector*, March 2016, 10. Available at: https://www.ecgnet.org/document/ebrds-projects-russian-rail-sector. By contrast the share of railways in passenger transport fell over the same period from 37 per cent to 27 per cent.

65 *Ibidem*, 51. €1.863.

66 *Trans-Siberian route: development of trans-continental transportations*. Powerpoint Presentation to the Second informal preparatory meeting for the 14th session of the Group of Experts on the Euro - Asian Transport Links 2-3.2.2016. Available at: https://www.unece.org/fileadmin/DAM/trans/doc/2016/wp5-eatl/WP5_GE2_2nd_informal_session_Mr_Bessonov.pdf.

67 E. Gerben, 'Rocketing Asia-Russia container rail volumes spurs investment calls', JOC.com, 5.8.2018. Available at: https://dev.joc.com/rail-intermodal/international-rail/analysis-europe-wide-rail-freight-would-be-pro-commerce-green_20180226.html. In the first eight months of 2018, the figure had already exceeded the figure for the whole of 2017 and had risen to 590,000 TEUs. *RailFreight.com*, 2412.2018, Available at: https://www.railfreight.com/specials/2018/12/24/eurasian-rail-traffic-in-2018-heading-to-a-million-teus/.

68 *RTNews*, 23.8.2018. Available at: https://www.rt.com/business/436633-russia-infrastructure-spending-economy/.

69 W. Shepard, '2 Days From China To Europe By Rail? Russia Going For High-Speed Cargo Trains' *Forbes Magazine*, 14.2.2107. Available at: https://www.ForbesMagazine.com/sites/wadeshepard/2017/01/14/2-days-from-china-to-europe-by-rail-russia-going-for-high-speed-cargo-trains/.

70 V. Masirin, 'Минтранс отправил мегапроект РЖД «Евразия» на доработку" RBC, 18.9.2017(Ministry of Transport sent a megaproject of Russian Railways "Eurasia" for revision) https://www.rbc.ru/business/18/09/2017/59bfa4099a7947d3d20ff087. See also N. Trickett, 'The Gordian Rail Tie: Russia's Mythic Belt and Road Cooperation', *The Diplomat*, 20.8.2017. Available at: https://thediplomat.com/2017/10/the-gordian-rail-tie-russias-mythic-belt-and-road-cooperation/.

71 *Russian Times*, 30.3.2015. Available at: https://www.rt.com/business/245125-china-invest-russia-train/.

72 *Russian Times*, 1.9.2015. Available at: https://www.rt.com/business/314003-russia-china-railways-putin/. By November 2016 the sum had risen to $3 billion, with the prospect of a further $0.8 billion later, *Ibid.*, 9.11.2016. Available at: https://www.rt.com/business/366074-kazan-railway-german-consortium/.

73 S. Fischer, *Sapsan: A Parable of Russian Modernisation*, ISS Analysis, December 2010. Available at: https://www.iss.europa.eu/content/sapsan-parable-russian-modernisation.

74 *Construction RU*, 18.11.2016; *TASS*, 28.2.2017. By 2018 the sums quoted had risen to $30.3 billion. https://www.railway-technology.com/projects/moscow-kazan-high-speed-rail-line/.

75 *Russia beyond*, 18.5.2017. Available at: https://www.rbth.com/news/2017/05/18/russia-asks-china-to-boost-moscow-kazan-fast-speed-rail-project-financing_765349.

76 Eurasian Development Bank press announcement, 24.5.2018. Available at: https://eabr.org/en/press/news/the-eurasian-development-bank-and-russian-rail-ways-agree-to-cooperate-on-the-moscow-kazan-high-speed/.

77 *Xinhua.net*, 11.9.2018. Available at: http://www.xinhuanet.com/english/2018-09/11/c_137460976.htm.

78 *Railway Gazette International*, 4.10.2018. Available at: https://www.railway-gazette.com/news/single-view/view/first-section-of-moscow-kazan-high-speed-line-to-open-in-2024.html.

79 Regnum.ru, 5.10.2018 (Строительство ВСМ от Москвы до Гороховца оценили в 621 млрд рублей). Available at: https://regnum.ru/news/2494617.html.

80 *The Epoch Times*, 1.1.2019. Available at: https://www.theepochtimes.com/russian-officials-voice-concerns-about-chinese-funded-rail_2753913.html. He has questioned whether there were sufficient passengers to justify the line and suggested that airlines could complete the journey faster for the same ticket price.

81 *Sputnick*, 22.4.2016. Available at: https://sputniknews.com/business/201604221038432755-ukraine-freight-train-empty/.

82 The cost of a 40-foot equivalent container (FEU) from the Izov station to the border with China (Dostyk) was reduced from $5,559 to $3,980. Centre for Transport Strategies News, 16.5.2017. Available at: https://en.cfts.org.ua/news/ukraine_officially_joined_the_trans_caspian_transport_route.

83 RailFreight.com, 28.9.2018. Available at: https://www.railfreight.com/beltan-droad/2018/09/28/felb-to-introduce-railway-service-for-banned-goods-via-mid-dle-corridor/.

84 EBRD Project database, 45782.. In another loan, agreed the same month, the EBRD advanced $150 million to replace 6,500 open freight wagons, the remaining $90 million raised by the freight company itself. EBRD, Project database, 49039. Available at: https://www.ebrd.com/work-with-us/project-finance/project-summary-documents.html. Enter the project number for details

85 Eastern Partnership, *Indicative TEN-T Investment Action Plan*, 2018. Available at: https://ec.europa.eu/neighbourhood-enlargement/sites/near/files/ten-t_iap_web-dec13.pdf.

86 *Railway Gazette International*, 21.5.2015 Available at: https://www.railwayga-zette.com/news/news/europe/single-view/view/china-to-fund-more-electrifica-tion-in-belarus.html; *Ibid.*, 17.8.2015 Available at: https://www.railwaygazette.com/news/infrastructure/single-view/view/world-rail-infrastructure-market-au-gust-2015.html; *Ibid.*, 20.9.2017. Available at: https://www.railwaygazette.com/news/infrastructure/single-view/view/minsk-vilnius-corridor-electrified.html.

87 EIB, Project Database. Own calculations. Available at: http://www.eib.org/en/projects/index.htm. The sum was €6.5 billion. The transport sector as a whole received €39.7 billion. The EBRD was not particularly active in this area, but

it did advance loans amounting to $480 million for station improvements and in helping to restructure the sector (EBRD, Project Database 1654, 1977, 5955, 7486, 7654, 9366, 12936, 36043). See note 82.

88 European Commission, *Transport, Final report. WORK PACKAGE 5 Ex post evaluation of Cohesion Policy programmes 2007-2013, focusing on the European Regional Development Fund (ERDF) and the Cohesion Fund (CF)*, Brussels, 2016, 28. Available at: https://ec.europa.eu/regional_policy/sources/docgener/evaluation/pdf/expost2013/wp5_final_report_en.pdf. The original figure quoted was €14.8 billion.

89 European Commission, *Ex post evaluation of the ERDF and Cohesion Fund 2007-13*, SWD(2016) 318 final, Brussels, 28. Available at: https://www.espa.gr/elibrary/expost_ERDF_CF_report_en_en.pdf.

90 ESIF Smart Specialisation Platform, Categories 028-034. The ESIF combines five existing EU funding mechanisms. The ERDF and Cohesion Funds. The figure quoted in the text is €14.3 billion.

91 EU, CEF, Project database. https://ec.europa.eu/inea/connecting-europe-facility/cef-transport/projects-by-country. €10.4 billion. Poland (€3.5 billion), Latvia (€2.5billion) Estonia (€1.9 billion) and Romania (€1.1 billion) would be the main beneficiaries.

92 Andžāns, M. and Kristiāns Andžāns, K. 'Rail Baltica – the Railroad Back to Europe' in Sprūds, A., Ščerbinskis, V. and Potjomkina, D.(eds..) *The Centenary of Latvia's Foreign Affairs. Activities and Personalities*, Rīga,, 2017, 251-264. Available at: http://liia.lv/en/publications/the-centenary-of-latvias-foreign-affairs-activities-and-personalities-658.

93 Ernst &Young, *Rail Baltica Global Project Cost-Benefit Analysis. Final Report*, 30.4.2017. Available at: http://www.railbaltica.org/wp-content/uploads/2017/04/RB_CBA_FINAL_REPORT_0405.pdf.

94 See Humal, P., Lambot, K., Paul, I., and Vibo, R., *Major Mistakes in Rail Baltica Cost-Benefit Analysis made by Ernst and Young Baltic*, January 2018. Available at: http://avalikultrailbalticust.ee/PDF/ARB_MMistakesRB_CBA_by_EY.pdf.

95 European Commission, *Core Network Corridors. Progress Report of the European Coordinator*s, 2014, 26-35. Available at: https://www.gica.global/resources/core-network-corridors-progress-report-european-coordinators. European Commission, *North Sea Baltic. Second Work Plan of the European Coordinator*, 2016, 40. Available at: https://ec.europa.eu/transport/sites/transport/files/2nd_workplan_nsb_1.pdf.

96 Participants at the Rail Freight Summit, Wraclow, Poland, 20-21.3.2018. Available at: https://www.railfreight.com/specials/2018/03/20/live-blog-silk-road-poland-gateway-summit-day-1/ and https://www.railfreight.com/beltandroad/2018/03/21/live-blog-silk-road-poland-gateway-summit-day-2/?gdpr=accept.

97   Dziennikwschodni.pl, 21.5.2018. Available at: https://www.dziennikwschodni.pl/biala-podlaska/tylko-20-proc-towarow-z-chin-przechodzi-przez-malaszewicze,n,1000219209.html.

98   DHL Resiliance360, 23.3.2018. Available at: https://www.resilience360.dhl.com/resilienceinsights/europe-china-rail-corridor-repair-works-to-limit-capacity-and-cause-delays/; *International Railway Journal*, 17.1.2018. Available at: https://www.railjournal.com/in_depth/china-europe-rail-freight-in-it-for-the-long-haul.

99   Forsal.pl, 27.11.2016. Available at: https://forsal.pl/artykuly/995114,unia-sypnie-8-miliardow-zlotych-na-inwestycje-infrastrukturalne-w-polsce-lista-projektow.html; *Railway Gazette*, 12.12.2016. Available at: https://www.railwaygazette.com/news/freight/single-view/view/world-rail-freight-news-round-up-12.html.

100 *Railway Gazette*, 26.11.2018. Available at: https://world-rail-freight-news-round-up-829afbd78b.

101 European Court of Auditors, *Rail Freight Transport in the EU. Still not on the right track*. Luxembourg, 2016. Available at: https://www.eca.europa.eu/en/Pages/DocItem.aspx?did=36398.

102 S. Lascu, Constanta Port of the Silk Road, P/P Presentation. Available at: http://www.portofconstantza.com/apmc/portal/static.do?package_id=stiri&x=get&resource=Prezentare_CN_APM_SA_Constanta.pdf.

103 RomanianInsider.com 4.2.2019.Available at: https://www.romania-insider.com/dp-world-renews-concession-contract-constanta-port.

104 BCG, *The 2017 European Railway Performance Index*, 2017. Available at: http://image-src.bcg.com/Images/BCG-The-2017-European-Railway-Performance-Index-Apr-2017-2_tcm9-152164.pdf.

105 European Commission, *Second Work Plan of the European Coordinator*. See note 92.

106 RomanianInsider.com, 18.4.2018. Available at: https://www.romania-insider.com/bribery-investigation-sebastian-vladescu. *Ibid*., 29.5.2018. Available at: https://www.romaniajournal.ro/ex-finmin-vladescu-pays-part-of-the-eur-1-mbail-in-bars-of-gold/. He paid part of his bail money in gold bars.

107 RomanianInsider.com, 20.1.2014. Available at: https://www.romania-insider.com/romanian-transport-ministry-plans-to-complete-high-speed-railway-project-with-chinese-partners-this-year.

108 World Bank, *Railway reform in the Western Balkans*, 2005, 13-16. Available at: http://documents.worldbank.org/curated/en/596211468282880617/Railway-reform-in-the-Western-Balkans.

109 European Commission, *Regional Balkans Infrastructure Study – Transport. Final report*, 2003, 31-32, 50-52, 56-59. Available at: https://wbc-rti.info/object/

document/7232/attach/Rebis_FR_Final.pdf. The sums were €12.4 billion and €4.2 billion respectively.

110 SEETO, *Comprehensive Network Development Plan*, 2013, 19-20. Available at: http://www.seetoint.org/wp-content/uploads/2012/10/bc-facilitation-report-final.pdf. The sums quoted in the text were €737 million and €195 million respectively.

111 SEETO, *Multi -Annual Plan 2018. Common problems- Shared solutions*, 2018, 31-33. Available at: https://www.seetoint.org/seetodocuments/1636. The original sums quoted was €2.9 billion.

112 W. Shepard, 'Another Silk Road Fiasco? China's Belgrade To Budapest High-Speed Rail Line Is Probed By Brussels', *Forbes Magazine*, 25.2.2017. Available at: https://www.Forbes Magazine.com/sites/wadeshepard/2017/02/25/another-silk-road-fiasco-chinas-belgrade-to-budapest-high-speed-rail-line-is-probed-by-brussels/.

113 Z. Vörös, 'Who Benefits From the Chinese-Built Hungary-Serbia Railway?', *The Diplomat*, 4.1.2018. Available at: https://thediplomat.com/2018/01/who-benefits-from-the-chinese-built-hungary-serbia-railway/.

114 *GB Times*, 26.9.2018. Available at: https://gbtimes.com/hungary-to-award-contract-for-chinese-funded-rail-project-by-end-of-year.

115 *Hungary Today*, 19.12.2018. Available at: https://hungarytoday.hu/govt-to-call-new-tender-for-budapest-belgrade-railway-upgrade/.

116 CCCC Company News, 7.11.2016. Available at: http://en.ccccltd.cn/newscentre/companynews/201611/t20161122_50870.html.

117 *World Highways*, 14.9.2018. Available at: http://www.worldhighways.com/categories/road-highway-structures/news/new-zezeljs-bridge-in-novi-sad-symbolises-brotherhood-and-unity/.

118 Asian Development Bank, *Meeting Asia's Infrastructure Needs.*, Manila, 2018, 99. Available at: https://www.adb.org/sites/default/files/publication/227496/special-report-infrastructure.pdf.

CHAPTER FIVE

PIPELINES

The chapter describes the development of oil and gas pipelines along the new Silk Road. It starts by exploring the peculiarities of pipelines as a means of transport, and the power that lies embedded in the patterns of their ownership. The reserves of oil and gas themselves are largely located in Russia, Central Asia and the Caucasus and, aside from some exploitation near the Arctic, with access to the sea in Summer, they require pipelines for at least part of the journey to their markets. This chapter is divided into three sections. The first section discusses the role of pipelines in infrastructure. The second section describes the pipelines extending from the gas and oil fields westwards to Europe. The third section explores the developments of the pipelines that extend eastwards to China. Only the latter appear in China's narrative of the Belt and Road.

The Power of Pipelines

Pipelines are a vital part of our infrastructure, but they remain largely hidden from the public's view. They also have a bad reputation that has grown in direct proportion to the world's increasing aversion to the hydrocarbon fuels that are blamed for much of the global climate change. However, on the Eurasian continent, pipelines represent the backbone of modern society. They shift vast volumes of goods - mostly fuels - over great distances in comparative safety, which otherwise would have to be conveyed over roads and rails at higher cost and greater hazard. Although pipelines allow the rest of the transport network of trains and trucks to operate relatively unencumbered, they have the disadvantage that they cannot freely be used to carry anything, anywhere. Although we think of oil and gas as homogeneous products, differences in chemical composition mean that fuel from different sources cannot simply pass freely through the same pipeline. Moreover, fuel might not be able to pass through a specific pipeline at all. Unlike the situation for railways, there is no international convention that opens national pipelines to traffic from other countries. Nor is there any automatic right that private oil companies can build pipelines that pass through the territory of any country.

Many pipelines are owned by national monopolies that allow the owner to dictate the terms under which fuel can be transported across its territory. The owner might even decide not to allow transit rights at all, but instead offer a contract to buy a fixed supply at a predetermined price. As a monopsonist (a monopolistic purchaser), the pipeline owner would then be in a strong position to dictate the terms, allowing him either to use the gas/oil to supply domestic consumers (possibly to a region far removed from its own supply centres) or, if world prices are higher than the contract price, to sell the supply through to world markets and pocket the difference.

Pipelines are also extremely expensive to construct. The most recent data, compiling the costs of pipelines presently under construction throughout the world, suggest that the average cost of one kilometre of overland pipeline (including pumping and compression stations) varies between $3.65 million and $4.65 million, depending on the diameter of the pipes. Offshore, the price spirals upwards to an eye-watering $13.5 million, although the higher price for laying off-shore pipelines can be partly compensated by the higher speed of construction. Offshore pipelines also allow the oil and gas to be pumped through the system at far higher pressures, enabling the transport of greater volumes and removing the need for interim pumping and compression stations that have to be placed every 50-150 kms along the route.[1]

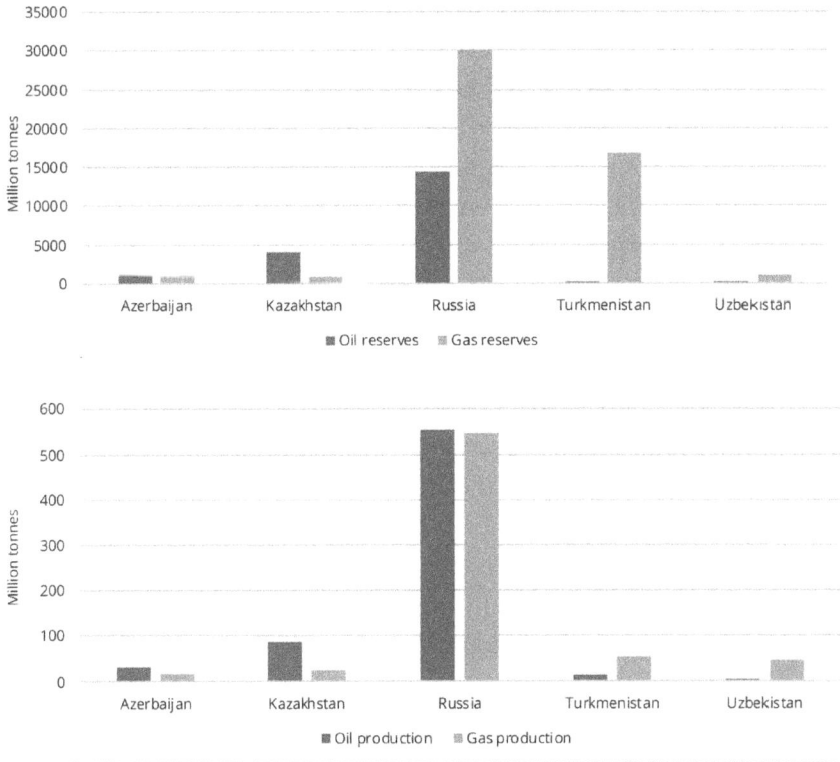

Figure 5.1 Gas and oil reserves and production
in Russia and Central Asia (end 2017)

Measured at the end of 2017, Russia and Central Asia have 8.5 per cent of the world's proven oil reserves, but account for 15.3 per cent of its output. For natural gas the percentages are 30 per cent and 21.6 per cent respectively. Russia dominates the picture in both reserves and production of oil and gas. Of the Central Asian countries, Kazakhstan has the largest proven reserves of oil and is also the largest producer. Turkmenistan and Uzbekistan each have smaller oil reserves and their production is mostly for the domestic market. On the other hand, Turkmenistan has huge reserves of natural gas and is the region's largest producer, narrowly followed by Uzbekistan, whose reserves, however, are much smaller. [2]

Pipelines are particularly important in questions of infrastructure and trade facilitation along the new Silk Road. The first reserves of oil and gas were located in and around the Caspian Sea and, under the Soviet regime deliveries were mostly directed northwards and inland, towards the more populated areas of western Russia and East-Central Europe. Although the successor states discovered plentiful new oil and gas reserves in the neighbourhood of the Caspian Sea, Russia's new discoveries lay in the less populated centre of the country and in the icy wastes near the Arctic Circle, far away from potential markets. In 2017 Russia and Central Asia exported 318.9 million tonnes of crude oil to each other, and to China and Europe, in addition to 103 million tonnes of oil products (mostly gasoline) and 214.91 million tonnes (oil equivalent) of natural gas. Almost this entire total of 636.8 million tonnes was moved by pipeline, often over vast distances.[3] If we consider that the average China-Europe Express train carries 82 TEU (twenty foot equivalent) containers and that each container carries, on average, 20 tonnes, then the volume carried on pipelines would be equivalent to 338,000 fully loaded trains each and every year. Compare this with the 11,000 China-Europe trains that have made their journey since the whole initiative began seven years ago, and one can appreciate the contribution of pipelines to the development of long-distance trade.

From Russia and Central Asia to Europe

For countries with easy access to the sea, the most evident means of transport is the tanker. However, the Central Asian energy producers are land-locked countries and the favoured alternative for shifting large volumes over long distances is through pipelines. Before the end of the Cold War, there was no discussion that the energy was destined mainly for the urban centres of the Soviet Union and for the Western markets. This was reflected in the direction of the main trunk pipelines. When the Soviet Union collapsed, the new countries regained control over the extractive side of their operations as well as the feeder and local pipelines. However, the main international pipeline network remained in the hands of Russian companies, which were later consolidated into a monopoly company, known as Transneft.[4] This left the countries of Central Asia dependent on Russia for their access to foreign markets and for the means of transportation. Once they had become independent, Transneft had neither the requirement, nor the incentive, to afford them equality of treatment.

Faced with a monopsonistic buyer, these countries were continuously searching for alternative outlets but they faced a critical dilemma. Lack of guaranteed access to international pipelines reduced the incentive to invest in increasing output. Equally, without a guaranteed throughput of the energy, there was little point in expanding capacity.

Kazakh Oil

In 1979 the Tengiz oil field was discovered in the north-west banks of the Caspian Sea, but it was only after Kazakh independence, in 1993, that a consortium of international oil companies was created to exploit it. Tengizchevroil was initially led by Chevron (50 per cent), Exxon Mobil and Kazakhstan Petroleum (each with 25 per cent).[5] In order to transport the oil a second group, the Caspian Pipeline Consortium (CPC), was formed. Half the shares were held by the Kazakh, Russian and Omani governments, and half were in the hands of eight oil companies, led by Chevron and Exxon Mobil. Initially Turkey attempted to thwart the pipeline by attempting to limit the number of ships passing into the Black Sea, and therefore the means for the oil to reach third markets. Already the maximum size of vessels able to access the Black Sea, meant that oil cargos had to be trans-shipped onto larger vessels before reaching more distant destinations.[6] Nevertheless, in 2001 the Consortium opened the 1,510 kms $2.67 billion pipeline from the Tengiz field to the Russian port of Novorossiysk on the shores of the Black Sea (Figure 5.2). From there the oil could be loaded onto tankers and shipped to world markets.[7] Despite the fact that the pipeline runs through Russian territory, Russia does not hold a controlling share of the Consortium. Neither, for that matter, does Kazakhstan.[8]

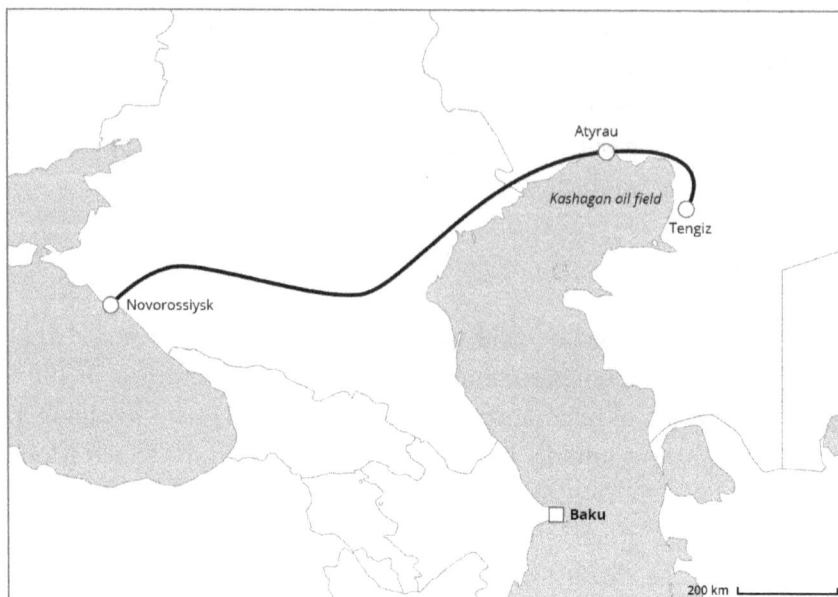

Figure 5.2: The Caspian Pipeline Consortium Pipeline

The Consortium members also enjoyed guaranteed and preferential access to the pipeline. This means that they have a clear interest in keeping the oil flowing and even expanding capacity. By contrast, it was in Russia's interest to slow it down, as it competed with its own supplies. Moreover, had the oil been destined for transfer through Transneft's network, it would probably need to be mixed with lower quality Urals crude, which would reduce the price that it could fetch on world markets. [9]

Pipelines, like roads and railways are not static. They need to adapt and expand. The original capacity of the CPC pipeline was 17.7 million tonnes annually and over the years it has gradually been enlarged. In 2014 the Consortium completed a major $5.4 billion upgrade to double the pipeline's capacity. This involved laying larger diameter pipes over 88 kms of its length, creating six new reservoirs, upgrading the five existing pumping stations and adding ten others.[10] It is now capable of transporting 70.2 million tonnes per annum and it carries over 70 per cent of Kazakhstan's total oil exports. The other side of the equation involved securing extra oil supplies for transportation. This was made possible because many of the same production companies operating the Tengiz field are also participating in the exploitation of the nearby giant Kashagan oil field, which at the time of its discovery in 2000, was heralded as the largest single discovery in the previous thirty years. This allowed the companies to claim their share of access in the ever expanding CPC pipeline. The exploitation of the Kashagan field itself was plagued by delays caused by the extreme depths of the field, the high pressure of the wells and the problems caused by the sea freezing in winter. The costs had spiralled to over $50 billion before the oil eventually started to flow from the project in September 2013. Unfortunately, production had to be halted again after discovering that gas had been leaking from the pipeline bringing the oil to shore.[11] It was only in October 2016 that oil production finally resumed.[12] In November 2018 the pipeline celebrated delivering 500 million tonnes of oil over the seventeen years of its operation.[13]

Turkmen Oil and Gas

The 'shippers' pipeline', that the CPC represented, allowed Kazakhstan to find an independent outlet for its oil and to free it from its previous dependence on Russia. By contrast, the tale of Turkmen gas reveals the darker side of dependence on single pipeline outlets. Turkmenistan had begun supplying gas to the other parts of the former Soviet Union during the 1960s, when the first phase of the Central Asia-Centre gas transmission system was brought into operation. Much of the gas supplied to Russia was then sold through, at a profit, to Europe (Figure 5.3, Route 1). Russia was able to do this because Transneft held the monopoly of the transit route to third markets and refused Turkmenistan direct access. In some ways Turkmenistan was its own worst enemy in that it was reluctant to allow international companies into the exploitation of its oil and gas fields. So the situation that had occurred in Kazakhstan, where the oil companies constructed their own pipeline to bypass the Russian monopoly, was not ever an option.[14] In 1997 the pressure was somewhat relieved when Iran financed and built the 190 kms Korpeje-Kordkuy pipeline, including a 135 kms section through Turkmenistan to supply gas to the north of its country (Figure 5.3, Route 2). This was to be repaid through gas deliveries.[15]

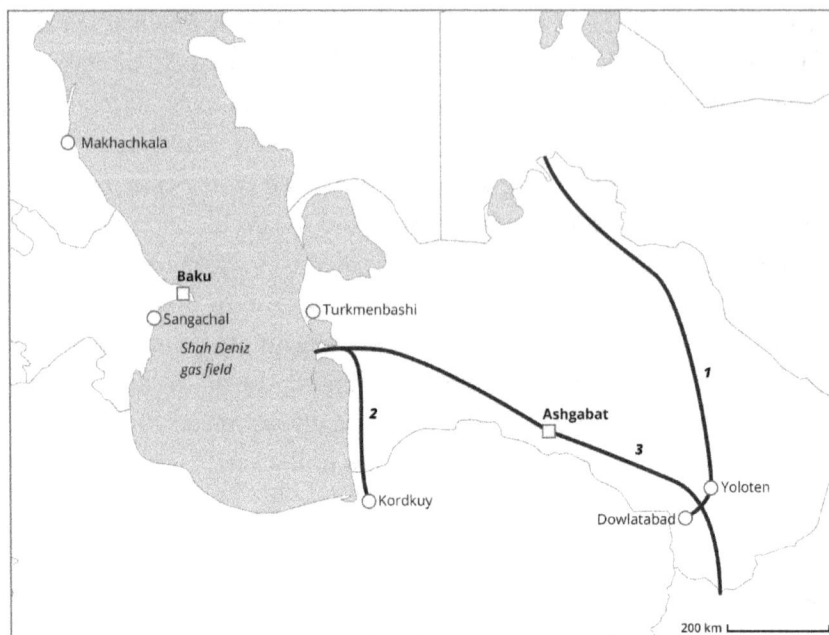

Figure 5.3: The Turkmen Gas Network

In April 2009 Turkmenistan was rocked by developments which highlighted the dangers of not having diversified its markets earlier. An explosion in the gas pipeline to Russia (Figure 5.3, Route 1), just over the border with Uzbekistan, disrupted exports. What happened next was a little more interesting. Since Gazprom[16] had been the main customer and the only available pipelines had run to Russia, Gazprom had been buying gas cheaply from Turkmenistan and selling it through, with high oil-indexed margins, to customers in the former Soviet Union and later to western markets. When the global economic downturn began in 2009, Gazprom had no need for supplies from Turkmenistan and so the timing of the 'accident' (and the duration of the repairs) was extremely fortunate. When deliveries were resumed in 2010 they were on a 'take-or-pay' basis, but only with a volume 25 per cent of the previous level. Again, in 2014, when energy prices were again sagging, Gazprom unilaterally broke the contract, but eventually agreed to take Turkmen gas, although at an even lower volume and at an even more disadvantageous base for calculating prices.[17] Finally, after yet another price dispute, in 2016 Russia stopped purchases of Turkmen gas altogether.[18]

Meanwhile, back in May 2010 Turkmenistan had announced that it would independently build an internal East-West gas pipeline allowing the transfer of gas from the biggest deposits in Turkmenistan (Dowlatabad and Yolotan) to the coast of the Caspian Sea (Figure 5.3, Route 3). The 733 kms pipeline was eventually completed in December 2015 at a cost of $2.5 billion. But having reached the Sea, the question was where next?[19] It could divert gas southwards towards Iran, and eventually to Afghanistan, Pakistan and India but that project, although agreed on paper, was unlikely ever to become reality.[20] Turkmenistan could expand its gas deliveries to Iran were it not for the fact that it had been in a stand-off with Iran since 2007/8 over the settlement of a disputed account of $1.8 billion. In January 2017 Iran announced its own plans for a 170 kms gas pipeline to supply the region directly and dispense with imports altogether, a development which Turkmenistan seems to have pre-empted in August 2017 by announcing its own suspension of deliveries to Iran.[21] With options blocked to the north and the south, Turkmenistan has offered to reopen the troubled talks with Azerbaijan for a Trans-Caspian pipeline, despite its hefty price tag on $11 billion.[22]

This project would involve laying a pipeline for 300 kms across the Caspian Sea, from Turkmenbashi to the Sangachal terminal, south of Baku. The project had been conceived as long ago as 1996 but it had stalled because of fierce resistance from Russia and Iran. Later, when the Shah Deniz gas field was discovered, Azerbaijan lost interest in the project in favour of developing its own supplies. Besides wanting to forestall an alternative transit route for Turkmen gas, Russia also raised environmental objections and insisted that since the integrity of the Caspian Sea was at risk, the pipeline should be agreed by all five littoral nations. The EU was also querying whether, with current low energy prices and the probability of new supplies coming on stream nearer to home, there would be sufficient demand to make the entire project viable.[23] At the centre of the dispute lay the question whether the Caspian Sea was a sea or a lake.

If the Caspian Sea were indeed a sea, it would be covered by the law of the sea. If it were a lake, the five parties would have to agree a solu-tion. In August 2018 the five states signed a Convention that established off-shore territorial rights (rather like a sea) but which fudged the issue of the exploitation of undersea resources. Pipelines were a concern only for the states through whose territories it would pass, making it a pure Azerbaijan-Turkmen issue, but environmental questions were assigned to the common decision-making domain.[24] Following the summit in Ashgabat the two countries signed a memorandum to cooperate on energy transportation. This breakthrough revived European interest and the EU labelled the project one 'of common interest', making it eligible for European funding. On the other hand, Turkmenistan wants to export 30-40 bcm (which is the capacity of the pipelines on its territory) and therefore needs an undertaking that the links carrying the gas to Europe would be sufficient.[25] Although it makes the question of undersea pipelines a bilateral issue, Russia's invocation of environmental concerns pushed the decision back to all five littoral states.[26] Ironically, as this option was crystallising, Gazprom offered to negotiate a new contract for the purchase of Turkmen gas[27] and the Turkmen government also decided to switch deliveries of oil from government-owned fields from Azerbaijan to Russia via the Russian Black Sea port of Makhachkala. To what extent these decisions were linked, or were a response to changes in transit charges in unclear. However, the change was not without its difficulties. The oil had previously been shipped to Baku in Azerbaijan in tankers owned by the Azerbaijani state company SOCAR (State Oil Company of Azerbaijan Republic) and then transferred to the Baku-Kars-Ceyhan pipeline. SOCAR controlled most of the Caspian tanker fleet. The new contract was with a Swiss company, Vitol, which would have to charter the necessary oil tankers. Not surprisingly, SOCAR proved reluctant to cooperate. As a result the deliveries could not be made and the unsold oil began to fill the available storage tanks.[28] At the time of writing, no resolution was in sight.

Finally, for the sake of completion of the alternatives open to Turkmenistan, the country has recently pushed Pakistan to renew the TAPI pipeline. The $7-10 billion pipeline would pass through Afghanistan and Pakistan, and eventually reach into India. Therein lies an even more difficult problem; that of building a pipeline through 800 kms of Afghan territory.[29]

Azerbaijan Oil and Gas

At the other side of the Caspian Sea, Azerbaijan had already started planning for an oil pipeline to markets in Turkey and Europe immediately after independence. The first to open, in 1997, was a 1,330 kms pipeline from Baku to the Russian Black Sea port of Novorossiysk with an annual capacity of 5.2 million tonnes (Figure 5.4, Route 1). However, in 2007, following a dispute with the Russian authorities, Azerbaijan suspended deliveries through the pipeline. Although supplies resumed a year later, volumes never recovered.[30] In 1999 a second 833 kms oil pipeline, running from Baku to the Georgian Black sea port of Supsa was opened (Figure 5.4, Route 2), with an annual capacity of 7.2 million tonnes.[31] Finally, in 2006 the 1,776 kms oil pipeline from Baku, passing Georgia and ending at the Turkish Mediterranean port of Ceyhan was opened (Figure 5.4, Route 3). The pipeline cost $3.9 billion to construct and had an annual capacity of 50 million tonnes.[32]

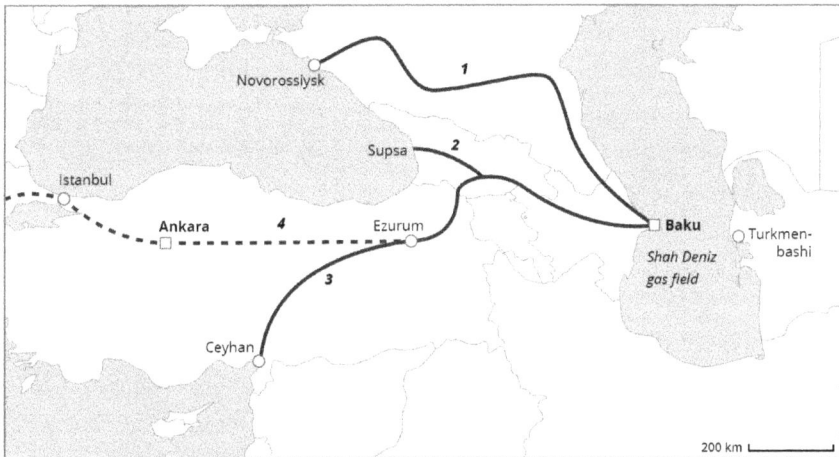

Figure 5.4: The Azerbaijani Gas Pipeline

In 2006 the South Caucasus Pipeline Company[33] opened a 980 kms gas pipeline from Baku to the Turkish city of Erzurum, with an initial annual capacity of 15 million tonnes (oil equivalent). Since the pipeline runs through Georgian territory, the country is entitled to five per cent of the volume (instead of a transit fee) and the right to purchase a further 3 million tonnes (oil equivalent) at a special rate.[34] From the start, there were plans to extend the pipeline to serve European consumers which would entail an upgrade of the pipeline to reach 36 million tonnes annually by 2023. This would be made possible by a more intensive exploitation of the Shah Deniz field and allow for 10 million tonnes to be supplied to Turkish consumers and 7.5 million tonnes (oil equivalent) to be supplied to Europe.[35]

The pipeline was planned to be extended through Ankara and Istanbul onwards to the border with Europe (Figure 5.4, Route 4). Both the EU and the USA backed the scheme since it would diversify energy supply routes to Europe, and, more especially, reduce the reliance on Russian supplies.[36] Work on the 1, 841 kms Trans-Anatolian Pipeline (TANAP) started in 2015 and was completed in June 2018 at an estimated cost of $8.5 billion. The pipeline finished at the border with Greece where it was supposed to join the Trans-Adriatic pipeline (TAP) carrying the gas through Greece, Bulgaria, Hungary and the rest of Europe. The project was finished in June 2018 and deliveries to Greece were expected to start a year later.[37] The 878 kms Trans-Adriatic pipeline would carry the gas through Greece (550 kms) and Albania (215 kms) before passing under the Adriatic Sea (105 kms) and coming onshore in Italy (8 kms). The $4.5 billion project is run by a consortium of leading energy producers[38] and is expected to start deliveries in 2020.[39]

Russian Gas

While the EU Commission is concerned to reduce its dependence on Russian gas, several member states are engaged in constructing a new gas pipeline in order to reduce potential disruption of supplies that were traditionally routed through Ukraine. Despite the underlying conflict between Russia and Ukraine, Russian gas had continued to be delivered through the pipelines crossing Ukraine, but there is no guarantee that the contract will be renewed when it expires at the end of 2019. Even before the flare-up of civil war in Ukraine, the transit of both oil and gas through the former Soviet Republics had proved problematic. Russia accused Ukraine of illegally tapping gas for domestic consumption and of delays in making payments. Although Russia still supplies oil through the pipeline network established in Soviet times[40] and upgraded since those times, the most ambitious new routes involve supplies of natural gas.

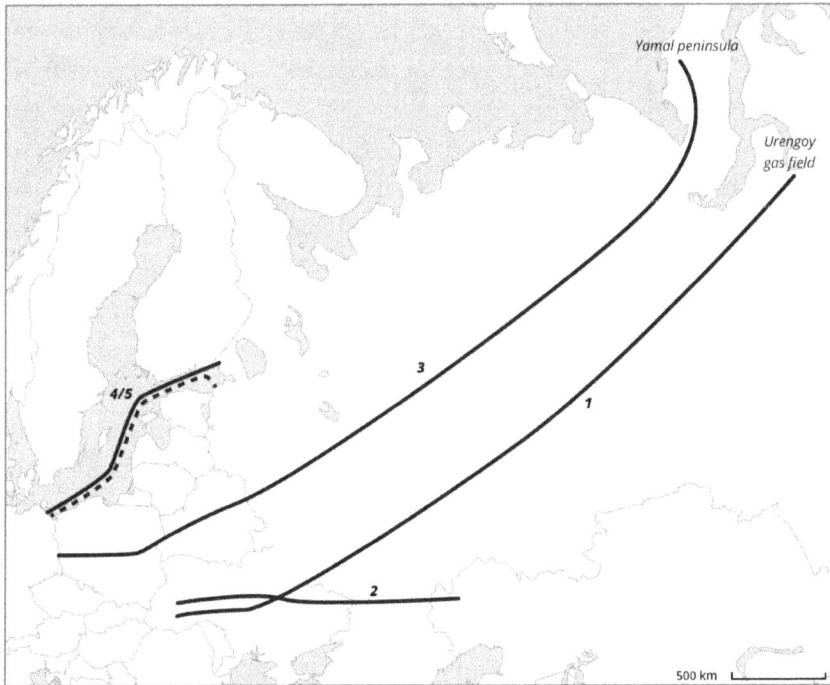

Figure 5.5: Russia's Main Western Gas Pipelines (actual and planned)

The Bratstvo (brotherhood) pipeline was built in the early 1980s to carry gas from the Urengoy field through Ukraine to Western Europe (Figure 5.5, Route 1). It is supplemented by the smaller Soyuz pipeline that carries Russian and Central Asian gas, and runs parallel for the last part of the way (Figure 5.5, Route 2). The gas from the vast fields in the Yamal peninsula began to flow in 1996 through Belarus before reaching Western European destinations (Figure 5.5, Route 3). Slowly but surely Europe was becoming more dependent on Russia for its supplies of natural gas.[41] However, the fact that most of the natural gas reached Western Europe through the same pipelines that transit countries used for their own supplies, made the security of supply always vulnerable to disputes. To reduce their risks, some Western countries proposed constructing a direct pipeline that would cut out the transit countries. The American administration, which considered that Europe was dangerously increasing its strategic dependence on Russia for its energy needs, opposed this development and it forbade any American cooperation in the operation.

Transporting gas directly to the main markets in Germany and the Netherlands posed serious technical challenges. It involved constructing the pipeline for 1,222 kms under the Baltic Sea and it also necessitated keeping the gas at the correct pressure without employing any of the usual intermediary compression stations (Figure 5.5, Route 4). The 'Nord Stream' project[42] was completed at the cost of $9 billion in 2012 and was capable of delivering annually 40 million tonnes oil equivalent.[43] After the direct line had opened, Germany built a 470 kms pipeline to connect it to the Central European distribution network. However its operation was initially blocked by a legal challenge by the Polish government, which also opposed any extra gas deals with Russia, on the grounds that the pipeline constituted a monopoly and an impediment to free competition. In May 2017 the dispute appeared to have been resolved. Meanwhile, the Ukraine crisis in 2014 further undermined the predictability of supply routes, and Western European companies conceived of Nord Stream II, a pipeline of identical capacity to run parallel with the original (Figure 5.5 Route 5).[44]

The project carries an estimated price tag of $10.6 billion. It will be owned by Gazprom, but financed largely by Austrian, German and Dutch backers. However, if the Ukraine crisis had prompted the new initiative, it also made its realisation more difficult. The sanctions imposed on Russia had targeted the transfer of energy technology, and had made it virtually impossible for Western oil companies to assist in the exploitation of Russia's Arctic oil and gas fields. Moreover, in 2017 the new Trump administration had threatened to increase sanctions by penalising Western firms engaged in the finance of major Russian companies, which would place the entire investment package at risk. The European Commission also opposed the pipeline since Ukraine would risk losing the revenues from transit fees, but it resisted the temptation to block its construction.[45] Despite the widespread resistance to the project, at the time of writing construction of the new pipeline was forging ahead.[46]

In the Caucuses, the war between Armenia and Azerbaijan in 1993 had led to both Turkey and Azerbaijan closing their borders with Armenia. This forced Russia to seek a direct route for transporting its gas to Turkey. A joint $3.2 billion venture was agreed between Gazprom, the Turkish energy company BOTAŞ and the Italian energy giant ENI. This involved laying a pipeline for 373 kms on Russian territory, a 396 kms off-shore section under the Black Sea and a last 444 kms section carrying the gas to Ankara. The pipeline has an annual capacity of 12 million tonnes (oil equivalent). Gas started to flow through the new pipeline, named 'Blue Stream' (Figure 5.6, Route 1) in 2003.[47]

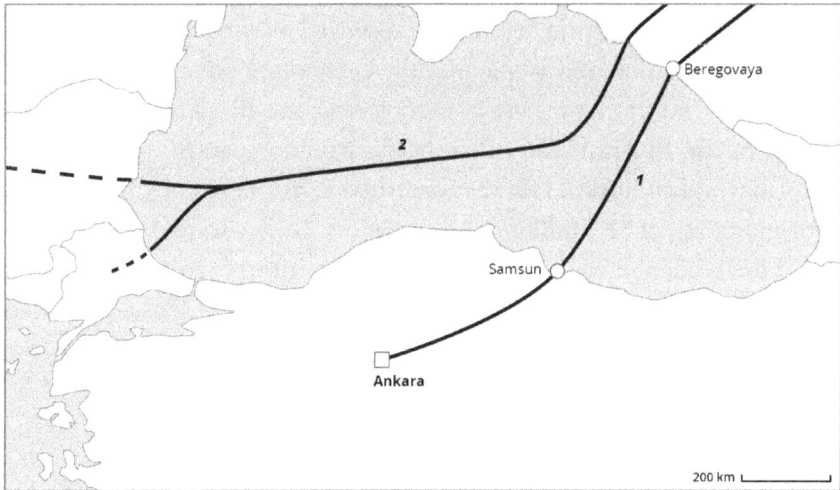

Figure 5.6: Blue Stream, South Stream and Turk Stream

The success of Blue Stream led to the development of more schemes for augmenting a direct connection with Russia, all under different names and with different end destinations. Difficulties in agreeing pipeline routes, the waxing and waning of bilateral Turkey-Russia relations, legal squabbles with the EU and continued American resistance all contributed to stymying further progress. However, at the time of writing, the realisation of a new project seemed closer than ever. The original 'South Stream' envisaged laying a 931 kms pipeline under the Black Sea to Bulgaria and from there to Greece and Italy in the west and as far as Austria in the north. Gazprom dropped the project in 2014 after legal difficulties from the EU's anti-trust legislation, leaving decisions on whether to continue (as well as the financing and construction) in the hands of the customer countries.[48] However interest in the project soon revived. In 2016 the Russian and Turkish governments agreed to a new route for two parallel pipelines, renamed Turk Stream (Figure 5.6, Route 2) with a combined annual capacity of 23 million tonnes bringing gas directly to the west of the country. One pipeline would serve Turkish demand and the future of the other was initially left open. The total cost of the project was $12.5 billion and the Turkish and Russian underwater sections were finally joined in March 2019.[49] At the time of writing, plans were being made to start routing Russian gas through the second pipeline to Bulgaria and into the Balkan network. Bulgaria has already approved starting construction of a gas receiving station and employing the current gas pipeline, that brings gas into the country, in reverse to carry it from the Black Sea to countries further north. In April it awarded the construction contract to the Saudi Arabian firm Saudi Akrad for the construction of a new 474 kms pipeline, with a price tag of $1.5 billion.[50] In December Turkey started work on laying of the section of the pipeline crossing its territory.[51] In addition, work on a new 403 kms Serbian section is scheduled to start in March 2019 and to be completed a year later, at the cost of $2 billion.[52]

From the West to China

China's rapid industrial growth has contributed to a voracious appetite for oil and gas. Over the 20 years from 1997, its consumption of oil has risen from 195 million tonnes to 608 million. Over the same period, its consumption of natural gas has spiralled from 17 million tonnes (oil equivalent) to 207 million.[53] In both cases demand has outstripped supply by some considerable margin. Russia and Central Asia have become increasingly important in filling the gap. Moreover, since they are not vulnerable to maritime blockade, they also offer relatively secure sources of supply

Kazakh Oil

China's interest in Kazakh oil started in 1997 when the China National Petroleum Corporation (CNPC) spent $9 billion acquiring control in two Kazak oil concerns on the Caspian Sea, with estimated reserves of 2.5 billion barrels (341 million tonnes). Since, at the time, China was reluctant to become dependent on Russian pipelines for its transport of oil, it immediately started a feasibility study to link the fields via a 2,230 kms pipeline directly to Western China, at an estimated cost of $3.5 billion (Figure 5.7, Route 1). A fall in oil prices helped delay the start of the pipeline's construction, but in 2004 the two governments agreed to revive the project, which was eventually completed in 2009.[54] Today, China takes about 25 per cent of the oil extracted in Kazakhstan but owing to the delays in exploiting the oil fields, the pipeline operates at 50 per cent of its capacity, sometimes less.[55]

Central Asian Gas

As far as natural gas was concerned, the main fields lay in Turkmenistan and Uzbekistan. The Central Asia-China pipeline started life as a plan to construct a gas pipeline parallel with the existing oil pipeline in Kazakhstan. In 2006 China agreed to explore the idea of taking the pipeline south to connect to gas fields in Turkmenistan and, the following year, both Uzbekistan and Kazakhstan also agreed to the pipeline project. Stroytransgaz, a subsidiary of Gazprom, started work on the 188 kms Turkmen section in August 2007.[56] The construction of the first phase of the pipeline in the other two countries was undertaken by joint ventures involving the CNPC and their respective national energy companies. The Uzbek section was some 530 kms in length and that running through Kazakhstan was 1,100 kms. The whole project was estimated to have cost $7.2 billion, with Chinese corporations, led by CNPC, contributing $4.4 billion.[57] The first pipeline (A) became operational in December 2009. The parallel line (B) was finished nine months later (Figure 5.7, Route 2).[58] The original dispute with Gazprom meant that Turkmenistan welcomed the possibility of diversifying its markets that the Central Asia-China pipeline created and the government needed no prompting in agreeing to the construction of Line C (also Figure 5.7, Route 2) as part of the Central Asia-China route with a designed capacity of 25 billion cubic metres per annum. The line would eventually become fully operational in 2015.[59]

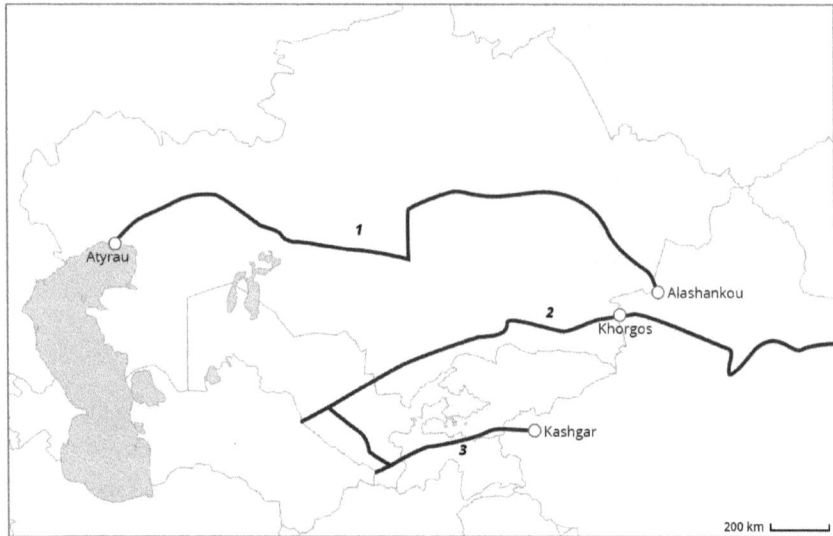

Figure 5.7: Main Oil and Gas Pipelines in Central Asia

In 2013 China signed an agreement with Uzbekistan, Kyrgyzstan and Tajikistan for a fourth line (Line D) of the Central Asia-China pipeline intended to route Turkmen gas through their countries to Kashgar (Figure 5.7, Route 3). The pipeline would be 1,000 kms long, with 840 kms outside China, and it would have an annual capacity of 22 million tonnes (oil equivalent). Joint companies were formed between CNPC and Uzbekniftegaz and Tajiktransgaz to undertake the work.[60] Although its route would be considerably shorter than the other routes and although its capacity would be greater than the existing pipelines, this was always a strange construction since 'it would bind Uzbekistan to two countries with whom it is currently barely on speaking terms - Kyrgyzstan and Tajikistan.' Uzbekistan had recently cut supplies of its own natural gas to both countries at different points in time. In addition Uzbek and Kyrgyz troops had engaged in a firefight near the two countries' disputed border and Tajik and Uzbek leaders were still locked in a battle over Dushanbe's plans to build the world's tallest hydroelectric dam upstream. Uzbekistan's relations with Turkmenistan were also frosty.[61] At the beginning of 2016, against a backdrop of sagging energy prices, the Uzbek government unilaterally suspended work on its section of the project for 'technical reasons'.[62] This was followed in May 2016 by an announcement by the Kyrgyzstan economics minister of the indefinite postponement of its part of the project, citing the escalation of the cost projections owing to the mountainous terrain and uncertainties over the conditions attached to Chinese finance.[63] By contrast, in January 2018 work on building the 400 kms passing through Tajikistan was reported to have resumed, with China providing the necessary funds and equipment,[64] These postponements are unlikely to have much immediate impact on China, where energy demand has dropped, but they will rob Kyrgyzstan and Tajikistan of their share of transit fees. They will also stymie Turkmenistan's intentions of further increasing gas sales in the future, leaving it to service the large loans from China but without the underlying income to support this.[65] However, the fact that even before the onset of winter in 2018 the remaining three pipelines appeared to be running at near their capacity levels, might still revive interest in completing the route.[66]

Russian Gas

An alternative source of gas for China lies in Russia. Its western fields are too distant to be of great interest but new discoveries in the east have changed the equation. The small Russian population in the Far East are unlikely ever to justify the expense of exploiting the vast reserves that lie within the Arctic Circle, and Russia's own population in the west would involve a huge expense in pipeline construction. On the other hand, the seemingly insatiable demand of the far larger neighbouring Chinese population could lead both parties to conclude a mutually beneficial commercial arrangement.[67]

Figure 5.8: Russia's Eastern Oil and Gas Pipelines (actual and planned)

In 2003 the Russian government decided on a twin project to bring oil from the Sakhalin field to the coastal port of Kozmino (near Nakhodka) for transport to Japanese and Korean markets. At the same time, it was agreed to build a side-shoot to Daqing in China. For its part, China agreed to pre-pay for twenty years of deliveries in the form of a $25 billion loan to Transneft and Rosneft for further development of the oil fields and pipeline network. The Chinese section, which required a short 40 kms pipeline to the Amur River and then a 992 kms section to refineries in Daqing, was built by CNPC and the whole project was completed in 2012 (Figure 5.8, Route 1).[68]

In 2013 Gazprom and CNPC signed a memorandum of understanding for a far more ambitious project, namely to build a natural gas pipeline capable of delivering annually 45 million tonnes (oil equivalent, 61 billion cubic metres) from the Eastern Siberian gas fields to China.[69] Memoranda of understanding do not always produce results but, during the State visit to Beijing in May 2014, President Xi and President Putin gave the deal their official sanction. The deal involved an undertaking over a thirty-year period to supply China with gas worth $400 billion. Annual deliveries of 28 million tonnes (oil equivalent, 38 bcm) would start in 2020, by which time China (through pre-payment) would have funded $80 billion worth of new production and pipeline infrastructure.[70] It was Gazprom's largest contract ever and the Russians committed themselves to $55 billion in pipeline construction costs while China would pay $22 billion.[71] An indication of how tough the negotiations were is afforded by the fact that the section carrying gas eastwards is constructed on the Russian side of the border. Gazprom, which accounts for more than 10 per cent of Russia's export revenues, was hoping that the project to supply gas to China would reduce Russia's dependence on exports to Europe.[72] There were to be two routes: a 3,000 kms eastern route to China from the Chayanda gas field, known as Power of Siberia (Figure 5.8, Route 2), and a 3,200 kms western route reaching from the West Siberian fields to Xinjiang, known as the Power of Siberia-2 (Figure 5.8, Route 3). China consented to the Russians issuing an open tender for the project, with the intention of winning it itself. However such hopes were dashed when a Gazprom director reportedly stated, 'we do not need Chinese men and equipment here, we never did and never will'.[73] In addition, the agreement included the option of an overland pipeline from China to the Russia's Sakhalin fields.[74] Almost a year later China officially started work on the construction of its side of the Power of Siberia, which would stretch from the border town of Heihi to Shanghai. It was anticipated that most of the pipe-laying on the Russian side would be completed by the end of 2018.[75] However, in July 2015 work on the Power of Siberia-2 was suspended indefinitely because of low energy prices and the slow-down in the Chinese economy.[76] Another sign that not all was well was the announcement by Gazprom, in November 2018, of a reduction of the Power of Siberia-1 pipeline's capacity to 48bcm. If China's demand remained at 38bcm, this would only leave 10 bcm for domestic consumption.[77]

At this stage, Russia was suffering serious liquidity problems since it had been denied access to Western capital markets by sanctions imposed in the wake of the Ukrainian crisis. China agreed in late 2015 to increase its stake in a $27 billion liquefied natural gas project in the Arctic that was blocked from dollar financing. In March 2016 the Bank of China granted Gazprom a five-year $2.17 billion loan. Russia's second largest gas producer, OAO Novatek (on the US sanctions list), was also looking to conclude a deal with China for financing its Arctic LNG plant, which would start deliveries to Asia in 2017.[78] In December 2016, China's Silk Road Fund pumped $1.3 billion into acquiring a ten percent stake in the Sibur Group, Russia's largest LPG and petrochemical processing firm (in addition to the ten per cent acquired by Sinopec in 2014). Despite the pre-payments for supplies and the injections of capital, the Power of Siberia pipeline is running behind schedule and costs are spiralling. The costs of the contracts on the Russian side have grown from $7.8 billion in 2015 to $9.7 billion in 2018 and the completion dates have shifted to December 2019.[79] Meanwhile, China's rising demand for natural gas, caused in part by the authorities' desire to reduce air pollution in the cities, is reviving interest in implementing the Power of Siberia-2 pipeline. At the time of writing it is still too early to say if, or when, such plans will leave the drawing board and start to become a reality.[80]

Conclusions

Pipelines are indispensable for the distribution of primary energy along the new Silk Road. They are also highly expensive to build. For example, it cost the Caspian Pipeline Consortium $2.7 billion for the 1,500 kms pipeline it opened to the Black Sea in 2001, and a further $5.4 billion to double its capacity in 2014. Turkmenistan paid $2.5 billion for its 730 kms gas pipeline to the Caspian Sea, only to confront a veto on extending it to the other shore, because of a dispute over the Sea's legal status. Gazprom's western backers have spent $9 billion to build one gas pipeline under the Baltic Sea to Germany, and a further $10.6 billion to fund a second. The first oil pipeline carrying oil from Chinese owned-fields in Kazakhstan to China cost an estimated $5.3 billion. Parallel gas pipelines carrying natural gas from Central Asia cost $7.7 billion. Crowning all of these projects is the 'Power of Siberia' pipeline carrying Russian gas from the Arctic to Eastern China with a total price tag of $77 billion. These are but some examples of the vast expenditures that are currently transforming the energy markets of the new Silk Road.

What is interesting in the development of energy pipeline is that the driving force of much of the activity is the need for diversification, experienced differently by producers and consumers. Russia, facing sanctions in the West, looks to diversify its markets towards China by initiating a huge pipeline project it can scarcely afford. At the same time, it strives to keep its markets in Europe with new pipelines in the Baltic Sea and, in response to the prospect of competition from Azerbaijani pipelines, also the Black Sea. Turkmenistan, having tried and failed to reduce its dependence on Russia by turning to China, finds itself courting Russia once more. Western Europe, in its turn, wishes to insure its transit routes against the uncertainty in Russian-Ukrainian relations by encouraging the expansion of the Baltic routes. It is not just geography that matters, politics does as well.

1   *Pipeline and Gas Journal*, 2.4.2018. Available at: https://www.ogj.com/articles/print/volume-116/issue-2/special-report-worldwide-pipeline-construction/near-term-pipeline-plans-nearly-double-future-slows.html. An earlier study of pipelines in the United States calculated the average cost of one kilometre of pipeline to be around $2.5 million, *Pipeline and Gas Journal*, 1.9.2014. Available at: https://www.ogj.com/articles/print/volume-112/issue-9/special-report-pipeline-economics/crude-oil-pipeline-growth-revenues-surge-construction-costs-mount.html.

2   *BP Statistical Review of World Energy*, 2018. Available at: https://www.bp.com/content/dam/bp/business-sites/en/global/corporate/pdfs/energy-economics/statistical-review/bp-stats-review-2018-full-report.pdf.

3   Data obtained from BP, *Statistical Review of World Energy,* 2018. For gas, billion m^3 were converted to million tonnes of oil equivalent by multiplying the figures by 0.86.

4   Transneft is a state owned enterprise, established in 1993, with a national monopoly on oil and gas pipelines.

5   *Azernews*, 13.2.2018. Available at: https://www.azernews.az/region/127122.html. Output in 2017 reached 28.7 million tonnes or 229 million barrels. Recently the Russian company Lukoil bought into the Consortium for 5 per cent).

6   M. Alexandrov, *Uneasy Alliance. Relations between Russia and Kazakhstan in the Post-Soviet era, 1992-1997*, Westport, Conn, 1999.

7   *New York Times*, 27.3.2001. Available at: https://www.nytimes.com/2001/03/27/business/oil-begins-flowing-through-kazakh-pipeline.html.

8   *Georgia Today*, 2.4.2018. Available at: http://georgiatoday.ge/news/9737/Transneft-Receives-Russian-Share-in-the-Caspian-Pipeline-Consortium. The CPC's shareholders are the Russian Federation (24% for Transneft, 7% for CPC Company), 31% for Kazakhstan (20.75%), Chevron Caspian Pipeline Consortium Company (15%), Lukoilco B.V. (12.5%), Mobil Caspian Pipeline Company (7.5%), Rosneft-Shell Caspian Ventures Ltd (7.5%), BG Overseas Holding Ltd (2%), Eni International N.A. N.V. (2%) and Oryx Caspian Pipeline LLC (1.75%). In 2018 the Russian government transferred its shares to Transneft.

9   A. Dellecker, *Caspian Pipeline Consortium, Bellweather of Russia's investment Climate*, IFRI, Russi.Nei.Visions 31, 2008. Available at: https://www.ifri.org/sites/default/files/atoms/files/ifrirnvdelleckercpcengjuin2008.pdf.

10 *Oil and Gas News*, 10.4.2014; Reuters, 12.4.2017. Available at: https://www.reuters.com/article/russia-cpc-oil/update-1-caspian-oil-pipeline-eyes-massive-expansion-thanks-to-new-oilfields-idUSL8N1IE3HB; *Latin American Herald Tribune*, 19.4.2018.

11 *Australian Business Review*, 2.7.2014. Available at: https://www.theaustralian.com.au/business/mining-energy/pipeline-problems-cloud-kashagan-oil-outlook/news-story/a6683e7c2ac13caa51d929cae6f86620.

12 *Bloomberg*, 14.10.2016. Available at: https://www.bloomberg.com/news/articles/2016-10-14/oil-from-50-billion-kashagan-field-starts-flowing-for-export. The share ownership is KazMunaiGas 16.88%; Eni, Total, Royal Dutch Shell and Exxon Mobil each with 16.81%. CNPC 8.33% and Inpex 7.56%.

13 *Port News*, 19.11.2018. Available at: https://www.neweurope.eu/article/half-a-billion-tonnes-of-kazakh-oil-loaded-from-cpc-marine-terminal/.

14 E.C. Chouw and L.E. Hendrix, *Central Asia's Pipelines: Field of Dreams and Reality*, NBR Special Report 33, 2010, 32-33. Available at: https://csis-prod.s3.amazonaws.com/s3fs-public/legacy_files/files/publication/1009_EChow_LHendrix_CentralAsia.pdf.

15 Robert M. Cutler Blog 8.7.2010. Available at: http://www.robertcutler.org/blog/2010/07/turkmenistan_diversifies_gas_e.html. *Gas and Oil Connections*, 6.6.2000. Available at: http://www.gasandoil.com/news/central_asia/c7a24e58ca53a419bb2a7b95b4b4e2eb.

16 Gazprom had been a Soviet state monopoly oil and gas producer until it was privatised in 1992. In 2005 the government decided to rein in its activities and renationalised the company.

17 M. Vladimirov, 'Gazprom putting the Squeeze on Turkmenistan', *Oil Price.com*, 28.7.2015. Available at: https://oilprice.com/Energy/Gas-Prices/Gazprom-Putting-The-Squeeze-On-Turkmenistan.html. By now annual deliveries were 4 bcms compared with 40 bcms before 2009.

18 *BBC*, 29.12. 1997. Available at: http://news.bbc.co.uk/2/hi/world/monitoring/43226.stm.

19 C. Putz, 'Turkmenistan Completes East-West Pipeline: What's Next?', *The Diplomat*, 29.12.2015. Available at: https://thediplomat.com/2015/12/turkmenistan-completes-east-west-pipeline-whats-next/.

20 *Dawn*, 14.11.2018. Available at: https://www.dawn.com/news/1445485; *Pipeline Technology Journal*, 22.11.2018. Available at: https://www.pipeline-journal.net/news/tapi-pipeline-sees-light-end-tunnel. For a critical reflection see B. Pannier, 'TAPI And Other Turkmen Tales', *Radio Liberty*, 1.12.2018. Available at: https://www.rferl.org/a/tapi-turkmen-tales-pipeline-qishloq-ovozi-pannier/29632356.html.

21 D. Cancarini, 'Il mare di gas degli "stan" post-sovietici che nessuno vuole', *EastWestEU*, 11.1.2018. Available at: https://eastwest.eu/it/opinioni/open-doors/energia-gas-asia-centrale-post-sovietica-iran-russia-cina.

22 *Caspian News*, 23.8.2017. Available at: https://caspiannews.com/news-detail/turkmenistan-turns-to-europe-as-iran-russia-shut-off-their-gas-markets-2017-8-18-8/.

23 R.M Cutler, 'Commentary: U.S. Push Could Revive Turkmen Gas Hopes', *Radio Free Europe*, 23.1.2018. Available at: https://www.rferl.org/a/commentary-turkmenistan-gas-hopes/28990352.html.

24 S. Pritchin, 'What comes after the Caspian sea deal?', *The Diplomat*, 5.12.2018. Available at: https://thediplomat.com/2018/12/what-comes-after-the-caspian-sea-deal/.

25 Cutler, 'Commentary: U.S. Push Could Revive Turkmen Gas Hopes'. See note 23.

26 P. Karle 'Caspian agreement: Many issues still to be settled', *Observer Research Foundation*, 15.10.2018. Available at: https://www.orfonline.org/expert-speak/caspian-agreement-many-issues-still-to-be-settled-44871/.

27 *AzerNews*, 11.2.2019. Available at: https://www.azernews.az/region/145421.html. See also Eurasia.net, 4.2.2019. Available at: https://eurasianet.org/are-turkmenistans-economic-fortunes-changing.

28 Reuters, 14.2.2019. Available at: https://www.reuters.com/article/us-oil-caspian/as-traders-tussle-over-tankers-turkmenistan-slashes-oil-exports-idUSKCN-1Q823W. R. Rahimov, 'Turkmenistan redirects its oil exports from Azebaijan to Russia', *Eurasian Daily Monitor*, 25.2.2019. Available at: https://jamestown.org/program/turkmenistan-redirects-its-oil-exports-from-azerbaijan-to-russia/.

29 *Business Recorder*, 30.1.2019. Available at: https://www.brecorder.com/2019/01/30/469979/pakistan-turkmenistan-discuss-tapi-gas-pipeline-project/; *Pakistan Observer*, 12.2.2019, Available at: https://pakobserver.net/tapi-most-important-project-in-region/.

30 In 2017 the pipeline carried 1.49 million tonnes, less than 30% pf the pipeline's capacity. *AzerNews*, 31.1.2018. Available at: https://www.azernews.az/oil_and_gas/126358.html.

31 *Georgia Today*, 17.5.2016.

32 Its maximum oil transported, however, was 39 million tonnes that it carried in 2010. *Daily Sabah*, 8.7.2018. Available at: https://www.dailysabah.com/energy/2018/07/09/baku-tbilisi-ceyhan-pipeline-carried-nearly-3b-barrels-of-oil-to-global-markets-over-12-years.

33 The pipeline is owned by BP (28.8%) the Turkish TPAO (19%) Azerbaijan's SOCAR (16.7%) Malaysia's Petronas (15.5%) Russia's Lukoil and Iran's Naftiran Intertrade (10% each).

34 BP Azerbaijan Webpage. Available at https://www.bp.com/en_az/caspian/aboutus.html; *AzerNews*, 30.1.2018. Available at: https://www.azernews.az/oil_and_gas/126332.html.

35 *AzerNews* 11.11.2018. Available at: https://www.azernews.az/oil_and_gas/140688.html.

36 For a while there were two alternative routes: the Trans-Adriatic route and an overland route ending in Vienna, named the Nabucco pipeline. The latter was

eventually cancelled in 2013. For some background on the 'competition' between the two see P.K. Baev and I. Øverland, 'The South Stream versus Nabucco pipeline race: geopolitical and economic (ir)rationales and political stakes in mega-projects', *International Affairs*, 86, 5, 2010, 1075-1090.

37 *Daily Sabah*, 12.6.2018. Available at: https://www.dailysabah.com/energy/2018/06/12/dubbed-the-silk-road-of-energy-tanap-begins-gas-delivery.

38 TAP's shareholders are BP (20%) Azerbaijan's, Socar (20%) Italy's Snam (20%), Belgium's Fluxys (19%), Spain's Enagás (16%) and Switzerland's Axpo (5%).

39 *Energy Reporters*,14.11.2018. Available at: https://www.energy-reporters.com/production/trans-adriatic-pipeline-82-complete-consortium/.

40 There are four main Western oil pipelines that are devoted mainly to exports. The oldest and largest of these is the Druzhba (friendship) pipeline which carries oil from western Siberia and the Volga-Urals fields and branches into both Belarus and Ukraine, before splitting further to serve various East-Central European markets or to access their seaports. Since the Ukraine crisis, Ukraine has suspended its own purchases via the pipeline but that has not stopped it from continuing to be used for transit. Another pipeline connecting the oil from the southern fields around Baku to the Black Sea port of Novorossiysk was completed in 1996. The first Baltic Pipeline System carries oil from the Timan-Pechora to the port of Primorsk, while the second moves oil to the Ust-Luga port, both in the gulf of Finland.

41 P. Högselius, *Red Gas: Russia and the Origins of European Energy Dependence*, New York, 2013.

42 The project is owned by Gazprom (51%) German gas importers, E.ON Ruhrgas AG and BASF SE/Wintershall Holding GmbH (16% each), the Dutch NV Nederlandse Gasunie and the French GDF Suez AG (9% each).

43 *Secure Energy for Europe. The Nord Stream Pipeline Project*, 2014. Available at: https://www.nord-stream.com/media/documents/pdf/en/2014/04/secure-energy-for-europe-full-version.pdf.

44 *New Europe*, 2.8.2017. Available at: https://www.neweurope.eu/article/ban-lift-german-opal-line-will-let-russian-gas-flow/.

45 K. Rapoza, 'European Partners In Russia's Nord Stream II Pipeline Stumble On Sanctions', *Forbes Magazine Magazine*, 14.9.2017. Available at: https://www.Forbes Magazine.com/sites/kenrapoza/2017/09/14/european-partners-in-russias-nord-stream-ii-pipeline-stumble-on-sanctions/.

46 *Deutsche Welle*, 4.2.2019. Available at: https://www.dw.com/en/nord-stream-2-pipeline-row-highlights-germanys-energy-dependence-on-russia/a-47344788. By April 2019 915 kms of off-shore pipeline had already been laid in German, Finnish and international waters. SputnickNews, 1.4.2019. Available at: https://sputniknews.com/business/201904011073735516-nord-stream-gazprom/. At the time of writing the Danish authorities had asked for a new environmental

assessment of the pipeline route. Whether this is a presage for further complications, time will tell.

47 Gazprom Press Release, 28.2.2018. Available at: http://www.gazprom.com/press/news/2018/february/article408339/.

48 T. Marzec-Manser, 'The silent return of the South Stream gas pipe', *ICIS News*, 4.4.2018. Available at: https://www.icis.com/explore/resources/news/2018/04/04/10208849/icis-view-the-silent-return-of-the-south-stream-gas-pipe/.

49 RT.com   19.3.2019.   Available   at: https://www.rt.com/business/454195-turkish-stream-pipeline-connected/.   *Offshore   Energy Today*,   20.3.2019.   Available   at: https://www.offshoreenergytoday.com/gazprom-completes-pipeline-system-for-turkstream-project/.

50 *Daily Sabah*, 5.2.2019. Available at: https://www.dailysabah.com/energy/2019/02/05/bulgaria-to-build-pipeline-to-transport-russian-gas;   M. Assenova, 'The Balkan Gas Hub: A European Gas Trading Platform or South Stream Lite?', *Eurasian Daily Monitor*, 15, 172, 6.12.2018. Available at: https://jamestown.org/program/the-balkan-gas-hub-a-european-gas-trading-platform-or-south-stream-lite/. Reuters, 7.3.3019. Available at: https://www.reuters.com/article/us-bulgaria-gas/three-groups-bid-to-build-16-billion-gas-pipeline-in-bulgaria-idUSKCN1QO1A7. Bloomberg.com, 3.4.2019. Available at: https://www.bloomberg.com/news/articles/2019-04-03/a-saudi-company-may-build-gazprom-s-new-way-through-east-europe.

51 *Sputnik International*, 13.12.2018. Available at: https://fr.sputniknews.com/economie/201812131039291536-gaz-turkish-stream-turquie-construction/.

52 IBNA Newsroom, 10.12.2018. Available at: https://www.balkaneu.com/expansion-of-turkish-stream-to-serbia/. *Russian Times*, 8.3.2019. Available at: https://www.rt.com/business/453316-serbia-approves-turkish-stream/.

53 BP Energy database. Available at: https://www.bp.com/content/dam/bp/business-sites/en/global/corporate/xlsx/energy-economics/statistical-review/bp-stats-review-2018-all-data.xlsx.

54 M. Meidan, *The Structure of China's Oil Industry: Past Trends and Future Prospects*, OIES Working Paper 66, 2016: 24–5, 42. Available at: https://www.oxfordenergy.org/wpcms/wp-content/uploads/2016/05/The-structure-of-Chinas-oil-industry-past-trends-and-future-prospects-WPM-66.pdf.

55 L. Parkhomchik, 'Energy Relations between China and the Caspian Littoral States', *Eurasian Research Institute Weekly e-Bulletin*, 48, 29.12.2015–4.1.2016. Available at: http://www.ayu.edu.tr/static/aae_haftalik/aae_bulten_en_48.pdf. In March 2019, the Kazakh enegy ministry announced cutting oil exports to China from 1.38 million tonnes in 2018 to 0.5 million tonnes for 2019, while maintaining the volume of oil flows to the West. *Financial Tribune*, 3.3.2019. Available at: https://financialtribune.com/articles/energy/96982/kazakhstan-to-cut-oil-exports.

56   On the territory of Turkmenistan the gas pipeline has two branches. The 184.5 kms Malay-Bagtiyarlyk pipeline is operated by the state concern, Turkmengaz. A second branch of the pipeline (76kms), connecting to the Samandepe field, is operated by the Chinese National Petroleum Corporation (CNPC).

57   Reuters, 19.2.2008. Available at: http://uk.reuters.com/article/oilRpt/idUKL194546920080219.

58   S. Blank, 'The Strategic Implications of the Turkmenistan-China Pipeline Project', *China Brief*, 10, 3, 2010. Available at: https://jamestown.org/program/the-strategic-implications-of-the-turkmenistan-china-pipeline-project/.

59   Reuters, 14.12.2009. Available at: http://uk.reuters.com/article/oilRpt/idUKL194546920080219. *Pipelines International,* March 2012. Available at: https://web.archive.org/web/20141112042852/http://pipelinesinternational.com/news/construction on third line begins for central asia-china gas pipeline/066998.

60   Aiddata: http://china.aiddata.org/projects/39955?iframe=y.

61   C. Rickleton 'Central Asia: Can Chinese Cash Glue the Region Together?', *Eurasianet*, 10.10.2013. Available at: https://www.eurasianet.org/s/central-asia-can-chinese-cash-glue-the-region-together.

62   C. Michel 'Can China Really Save Central Asian Economies?', *The Diplomat*, 13.2.2016. Available at: https://thediplomat.com/2016/02/can-china-really-save-central-asian-economies/.

63   *Press Club New Agency*, 25.5.2016.

64   Eurasianet, 31.1.2018. Available at: https://eurasianet.org/tajikistan-resumes-building-turkmenistan-china-pipeline.

65   C. Michel 'Line D of the Central Asia-China Gas Pipeline Delayed', *The Diplomat*, 31.5.2016. Available at: https://thediplomat.com/2016/05/line-d-of-the-central-asia-china-gas-pipeline-delayed/. At the time of writing the project was still stalled. C. Michel, 'The Central-Asia Gas Pipeline Network: Line D(ead)', *The Diplomat*, 21.3.2017. Available at: https://thediplomat.com/2017/03/the-central-asia-china-gas-pipeline-network-line-dead/; B. Pannier, 'The End Of The (Gas Pipe-) Line For Turkmenistan', Radio Free Europe, 6.3.2017. Available at: https://www.rferl.org/a/turkmenistan-gas-pipeline-china-berdymukhammedov-iran-russia/28353522.html.

66   *Intefax Global Energy*, 12.11.2018.

67   L. Goodrich and M. Lanthemann, 'The Past, Present and Future of Russian Energy Strategy', *Geoploitical Weekly,* 12.2.2013. Available at: https://worldview.stratfor.com/article/past-present-and-future-russian-energy-strategy.

68   *China Daily*, 29.5.2003. Available at: http://www.chinadaily.com.cn/en/doc/2003-05/29/content_166888.htm. E. Wilson Rose, 'Regional Influence in Oil and Gas Development: A Case Study of Sakhalin' in Russian Analytical Digest, 33/08, 1008, 18-21. Available at: http://www.css.ethz.ch/content/dam/ethz/special-interest/gess/cis/center-for-securities-studies/pdfs/RAD-33.pdf.

69　*Pipelines International*, 27.3.2013. Available at: https://www.pipelinesinterna-tional.com/2013/03/27/gazprom-and-cnpc-sign-mou-on-gas-supplies-via-east-ern-route/.

70　J. Koch-Weser and C. Murray, *The China–Russia Gas Deal: Background and Implications for the Broader Relationship*, U.S.–China Economic and Security Review Commission Staff Research Backgrounder, 9.6.2014. https://www.uscc.gov/sites/default/files/Research/China%20Russia%20gas%20deal_Staffbackgrounder.pdf; E. Wishnick, *The "Power of Siberia" No Longer a Pipe Dream*, PONARS Eurasia Policy Memo No. 332, August 2014. Available at: http://www.ponarseurasia.org/memo/%E2%80%9Cpower-siberia%E2%80%9D-no-longer-pipe-dream.

71　*The Guardian*, 21.5.2014. Available at: https://www.theguardian.com/world/2014/may/21/russia-30-year-400bn-gas-deal-china.

72　J. Marson and A. Ostroukh, 'Gazprom Secures $2.17 Billion Loan From Bank of China', *Wall Street Journal*, 3.3.2016. Available at: https://www.wsj.com/articles/gazprom-secures-2-17-billion-loan-from-bank-of-china-1457017070.

73　Economist Intelligence Unit (2016)*'One Belt, One Road': An Economic Roadmap*, London, 61-62. Available at: https://www.eiu.com/public/topical_report.aspx?campaignid=OBORSept2016.

74　*Foreign Brief*, 23.8.2016. Available at: https://www.foreignbrief.com/asia-pacific/china/risky-business-china-standard-obor-financing-model-unpacked/.

75　UPI News, 21.11.2018. Available at:" https://www.upi.com/Energy-News/2018/11/21/Gazprom-to-soon-complete-bulk-of-pipeline-work-to-ship-gas-to-China/9931542808081/.

76　*Russian Times*, 22.7.2015. Available at: https://www.rt.com/business/310451-gazprom-cnpc-gas-deal/.

77　Reuters, 12.11.2018. Available at: https://af.reuters.com/article/commoditiesNews/idAFL8N1XN3X2.

78　Marson and Ostroukh, 'Gazprom' (see note 71). See also J. Henderson and T. Mitrova, *Energy Relations between Russia and China: Playing Chess with the Dragon,* Oxford Institute for Energy Studies, Working Paper 67, 2016.Available at: https://www.oxfordenergy.org/wpcms/wp-content/uploads/2016/08/Energy-Relations-between-Russia-and-China-Playing-Chess-with-the-Dragon-WPM-67.pdf.

79　*Moscow Times*, 27.3.2018. Available at: https://themoscowtimes.com/news/cost-of-russias-power-of-siberia-gas-pipeline-to-china-balloons-to-97-bln-60949.

80　Oil Price.com 17.9.2018. Available at: https://oilprice.com/Energy/Energy-General/The-Altay-Pipeline-A-Geopolitical-Game-Changer.html; *Petroleum Economist*, 15.2.2019. Available at: https://www.petro-leum-economist.com/articles/politics-economics/europe-eurasia/2019/russia-s-hunger-for-second-eastern-gas-outlet-grows.

FINAL REFLECTIONS

The story told in this book starts almost thirty years ago with a shattered Eurasian trading bloc and it stops in Spring 2019, just over five years into China's Belt and Road initiative. Of course the story does not stop here. There are still many challenges to be overcome if the vision of an open and prosperous new Silk Road is ever to be realised. What has the book demonstrated?

First, the end of the Cold War has been too long simplified as a 'victory' of one system over another and the discussion of its effects have been homogenised over the countries most affected. The end of the Cold War has to be recognised as a major disruption of the existing economic network encompassing the 20th century Silk Road. Both the existing states, released from Soviet tutelage, and new countries emerging from the wreckage of the Soviet Union reassessed their priorities and opportunities, and framed the results into new national laws and regulations. The new national frontiers allowed new discriminations to emerge. The effects of that initial economic implosion still scar the economic landscape of the new Silk Road.

Second, at the western end of the new Silk Road, the reintegration of the newly independent states into each other, and into the richer markets of Western Europe, should be recognised as a major contribution to the creation of the new Silk Road. What was, in effect, Europe's 'Belt and Road' differed in design from that of China. Its three overlapping stages began with help for administration reform, moved through the gradual elimination of all frontier barriers to trade and ended with support for infrastructural investment.

Third, borders do matter. This globalising world is often described as though distance no longer matters, as though connectivity has made national lines on a map redundant, and as though liberalisation has made tariffs and quotas irrelevant. In many parts of the world, and certainly along the new Silk Road, when goods try to cross a national frontier the process of crossing the border imposes costs. When aggregated, these costs depress the level of transactions and reduce potential GDP. There are very real welfare gains to be harvested by improved cross-border cooperation.

Fourth, the reconstruction of the new Silk Road involves many more players than China alone. The international development banks, the European Union and private companies have also contributed to the task. Any analysis of the BRI should acknowledge and include this contribution if it is to reflect reality. China's narrative is very effective. It conjures a vision of peace and prosperity, and reserves for itself the role of a friend who, having experiences similar problems, extends a helping hand to others now in a comparable situation. As a piece of branding, it is superb, but it does have the effect of alienating other partners.

Last, but not least, this book contests the one-sided focus of much commentary in the West, since 2013, on the geopolitical rivalry between China and the West. This focus is to the detriment of the very real regional and economic cooperation that is occurring in the world, and that is helping to improve the lives of the majority of its citizens. The story of the new Silk Road is a shining example of this process in action, if only either 'side' in these discussions could be bothered to embrace it.

Having highlighted the contributions of this book to the debates on the nature and intention of China's Belt and Road initiative, I would like to offer four policy recommendations for the EU:

First, the national European statesmen and EU representatives and officials should adopt a more positive attitude to the BRI and promote the contribution that Europe, in collaboration with other Western agencies, has already made to the creation of the new Silk Road. National leaders should start shedding their annoying tendency of claiming the credit for everything positive stemming from the EU whilst blaming 'Brussels' for everything that goes wrong. The reintegration of the western end of the new Silk Road into the regional and global economy is a massive achievement of which Europeans can be proud. The support of the Eastern Partnership (January 2019) for vital infrastructural investment will be an important contribution to the region's prosperous future. It also represents a significant extension of the geographical range of European ambitions in this field and, as such, it should have been announced with a degree of aplomb and not with a whimper.

Second, the EU should realise that it is a geo-political player. Its *EU-China Strategic Outlook* document (March 2019) in seeing China simultaneously as a partner, a competitor and a rival, depending on the field of activity is a timely recognition of this fact. Its international credibility now relies on it acting accordingly. The EU is not a moral crusade. It does not need to preface every initiative with a reference to the 'norms and values' that supposedly underpin its existence. The general EU concerns with the direction of China's domestic and foreign policy are best addressed at the appropriate time and in the appropriate fora.

Third, the EU should realise that its businesses operate in a global market place and that rules made for the sanctity of free markets within the European Single Market may not be appropriate for meeting competition outside its jurisdiction. For example, if European business is excluded from government contracts financed by Chinese development banks, it is worth considering the option of reserving European-funded infrastructure projects for European firms (just as happens with armaments contracts). Again, it makes little sense in applying EU competition rules forbidding mergers, such as the Alstom-Siemens merger, on the basis of the relative weight in the European market when firms have to face competition for international contracts from massive Chinese state-enterprises such as the CRRC. In such situations, domestic market interests can better be guaranteed by improved supervision and regulation.

Last, but not least, the EU should pay more attention to the operation of its own infrastructural program. It should recognise that the differences in rules governing the proportion of national government contributions towards projects receiving EU grants is creating perverse incentives and leading to the sub-optimal use of funds. The EU should either tighten central management of its international priority transport corridors or adjust the rules on national contributions that govern EU subsidies and grants in this policy area.

Finally, for the Chinese government, I have one request and one recommendation.

First, my request. Please start providing more clarity of the BRI projects, especially when providing aggregate data. For a start, it would be useful to know which countries are included in the GDP and population aggregates. For example, it is difficult to envisage the coverage to reach 60 per cent of the world's population without including India. However India certainly does not consider itself part of the BRI. When aggregated figures for the growth of foreign trade are released we do not know whether the number of countries is constant over the time-span or whether extra countries are added as they join. When the trillions of dollars are paraded in the investment figures, we do not know whether they cover only new infrastructural investment or whether they include investments in on-going projects or even mergers and take-overs. We do even not know whether the data refers only to infrastructure or if it also includes mining, mineral processing or even manufacturing. If it includes 'everything', we do not know when BRI stops and simple FDI begins. Without more clarity, it is impossible to properly assess the impact of China's BRI or to compare it to the performance of other countries.

Finally, China should recognise that the BRI is already a multilateral effort, albeit one in which China is making its own unique and important contribution. One does not need to have signed an MoU with China to contribute to building the new Silk Road. A road, railway or pipeline will facilitate the movement of goods regardless of by whom it has been constructed. Western development banks may well impose tiresome conditions of authoritarian regimes, but for China to deal 'neutrally' with such national governments bypasses the fact that authoritarian regimes do not necessarily reflect the real 'needs' of their citizens. It would benefit China's narrative if it recognised and incorporated the efforts and achievements of other foreign participants, without carping at their intentions. China's BRI has the potential to change the lives of millions of people on the Eurasian continent. Broadening its scope and anchoring it within a more multilateral framework will help engender the trust that is necessary for it to succeed.

ABOUT THE AUTHOR

Richard T. Griffiths is emeritus professor of economic history and of international studies at Leiden University. He directs the 'New Silk Road' research project at the International Institute for Asian Studies (Leiden University). He is the author of the book *Revitalising the Silk Road. China's Belt and Road Initiative* (2017).

CONTENTS

Introducción   1

Capítulo 1: Instagram para empresas   3

Capítulo 2: Tipos de publicaciones en Instagram   15

Capítulo 3: Crear una estrategia de marketing de contenidos   28

Capítulo 4: Aumentar el número de seguidores   40

Capítulo 5: Análisis de Instagram   48

Capítulo 6: Publicidad en Instagram   53

Conclusión   59

INTRODUCCIÓN

Las redes sociales han crecido a pasos agigantados en los últimos diez años, revolucionando tanto la comunicación personal como la empresarial. Todo el mundo utiliza las redes sociales por diversas razones, y es difícil imaginar a alguien que no tenga unas cuantas aplicaciones de redes sociales o más en sus dispositivos personales en los tiempos que corren. De entre todas las más populares, Instagram se ha convertido en una de las más potentes entre la plétora de aplicaciones para compartir fotos y vídeos, y durante mucho tiempo ha sido el estándar de facto en esta categoría. La aplicación ha recorrido un largo camino desde que irrumpió en escena en 2010. Por aquel entonces, no era más que otra plataforma social que te permitía compartir fotos de tus mascotas, comida y viajes a destinos exóticos, e incluso propició el resurgimiento de la moda de los "selfies".

En 2022, Instagram ha pasado de ser una simple aplicación para compartir fotos a convertirse en una herramienta de marketing muy utilizada por empresas, marcas y personas influyentes. Tradicionalmente, antes de que las redes sociales empezaran a tomar el relevo, la única forma en que una empresa podía iniciar su actividad de marketing digital y en línea era mediante el desarrollo y mantenimiento de un sitio web alojado en un dominio. Tanto si tenías un medio de comunicación, un blog, un producto o un servicio, era necesario tener un sitio web para atraer tráfico de clientes y hacer crecer el negocio. Hoy en día, tener un sitio web es una buena idea para la mayoría de las empresas, pero dista mucho de ser necesario. Instagram y las plataformas de medios sociales han empezado a cambiar el marketing digital y en línea tal y como lo conocemos.

Con más de dos mil millones de usuarios activos, Instagram es sin duda la plataforma socialmente más activa del mundo en la actualidad. Según SendPulse, "la media de tiempo que pasan los usuarios en la plataforma es de 53 minutos cada día y al menos el 90% de los usuarios siguen al menos a una empresa o marca." Sea cual sea el sector al que pertenezcas, la comercialización de tus servicios o productos en Instagram nunca ha sido tan fácil y, desde luego, no tiene desperdicio. Con métodos estratégicos y análisis perspicaces, una marca puede ampliar fácilmente su negocio en la plataforma.

El marketing como proceso sigue necesitando mucho esfuerzo para comprender a tu audiencia y la plataforma en la que operas. Afortunadamente, Instagram simplifica este proceso para las empresas con sus funciones de análisis integradas, que pueden ayudar a realizar un seguimiento de varias métricas y KPI relacionados con el tráfico y la participación de los clientes. Las empresas y las marcas también pueden medir el rendimiento de sus publicaciones en función de la interacción con los clientes, por lo que es esencial que todas las marcas interactúen con sus seguidores y los conviertan en clientes potenciales. Tener la capacidad no sólo de dirigir el tráfico de clientes existentes a los canales adecuados desde la plataforma, sino también de hacer crecer la audiencia y atraer nuevos seguidores a través de la publicidad es igualmente importante. Con la estrategia publicitaria adecuada y enlaces en los que se puede hacer clic, la plataforma ofrece a todas las marcas y empresas la oportunidad de dirigirse a los clientes adecuados e interactuar con ellos a través del tipo de contenido que buscan.

Tanto si eres propietario de una pequeña empresa como si eres una persona influyente en las redes sociales, esta guía te llevará a través de todo el proceso, desde la creación de tu cuenta de empresa hasta la publicidad en la plataforma, y te equipará con toda la información que necesitas para ayudarte a hacer crecer y escalar tu marca con el marketing en Instagram.

CAPÍTULO 1: INSTAGRAM PARA EMPRESAS

A medida que seguimos creciendo y avanzando en la era de las redes sociales, es de vital importancia que las empresas y las marcas continúen evolucionando, adaptándose y acogiendo todas las oportunidades promocionales que las plataformas de redes sociales pueden aportar. Comercializar tus productos o servicios en Instagram requiere mucha estrategia y coherencia con el contenido y el compromiso con tus seguidores. En esta sección se tratarán las ventajas de la comercialización en Instagram, la creación de una cuenta de empresa y el establecimiento de objetivos.

Crear y mantener un perfil excelente es el primer factor clave para convertir a los visitantes curiosos en fieles seguidores que puedan interactuar y comprometerse con el contenido que usted crea. El compromiso con el contenido es lo que inicia el proceso de construcción de esa relación fundacional con tus seguidores. De ahí que sea imperativo para las empresas y marcas tener un feed de Instagram que sea tan bueno como la página de inicio de su sitio web, ya que cada vez más personas están empezando a buscar empresas en Instagram antes de buscarlas en Google.

Importancia de tener una cuenta de empresa

Hay una diferencia entre tener una cuenta personal clásica y una cuenta de negocio profesional en Instagram. Al principio, si eres una pequeña empresa, una marca o una persona influyente, está bien empezar con una cuenta personal si lo que quieres es publicar contenido decente de forma regular. Sin embargo, a medida que tu marca empieza a crecer y a ganar popularidad, puede ser difícil seguir el ritmo de crecimiento utilizando una cuenta personal. Puede que no entiendas lo que tu audiencia está buscando, puede que no publiques suficiente contenido para que el algoritmo de Instagram promueva tu perfil a más gente, etc. Esto puede llevar a un estancamiento de tu crecimiento en la plataforma e incluso puede decaer si no se analiza detenidamente el problema. Actualizar a una cuenta de negocios te da más características que puedes usar a tu favor para impulsar una mejor experiencia de usuario para tus seguidores. En esta sección, echaremos un vistazo de cerca a cómo puedes configurar fácilmente tu perfil de Instagram para que esté listo para los negocios.

Si bien es posible crear una marca y comercializar tus servicios o productos con una cuenta personal clásica si eres un influencer, tienes la opción de cambiar a un perfil empresarial que desbloqueará un montón de funciones avanzadas como:

- Análisis de la información: los análisis te dirán qué publicaciones están funcionando bien, cuántos seguidores han reaccionado a ellas, etc.

- Botón de contacto y respuesta rápida: los clientes pueden llamarle o enviarle un correo electrónico directamente con el botón de contacto, y las respuestas rápidas enviarán mensajes preescritos a los clientes para las preguntas más habituales.

- Promocionar publicaciones: impulsar o promocionar tus publicaciones con anuncios puede ampliar tu alcance y atraer a más público objetivo.

- Función Swipe up: después de superar los 10.000 seguidores, puedes incluir enlaces en tus historias de Instagram para redirigir el tráfico a un sitio web, una tienda online, servicios y recursos, etc.

- Instagram Shopping - Esta es una gran característica para las tiendas minoristas en línea y marcas de comercio electrónico, lo que permite una cuenta de negocio para activar la pestaña de la tienda que redirige el tráfico de clientes a la tienda en línea para completar la compra de un servicio o producto.

Configuración de su cuenta de empresa

Una cuenta de empresa bien configurada crea una gran primera impresión, irradia profesionalidad y atraerá la atención de tus seguidores potenciales. Las marcas más populares de sus respectivos sectores entienden la importancia de tener un perfil impecable que ofrezca a sus seguidores una experiencia de usuario ordenada y sobresaliente.

Por otro lado, descuidar una configuración profesional o no optimizar la experiencia del usuario en su perfil podría llevarle a perder seguidores en favor de la competencia, incluso si la marca es líder en el sector correspondiente.

Para empezar a configurar tu perfil para empresas, puedes hacerlo de varias maneras. Si ya tienes una cuenta personal clásica y ahora quieres cambiar a una cuenta de empresa, puedes seguir estos pasos:

1. Accede a tu cuenta de Instagram

2. Seleccione la opción de menú en la esquina superior derecha de su perfil

3. Seleccionar ajustes

4. Seleccionar cuenta

5. Pulse "Cambiar a cuenta profesional".

6. Pulse "Continuar".

7. Seleccione entre las opciones de "Lo que mejor le describe"

8. Seleccione "Empresa" entre las opciones de "¿Es usted un creador?

9. Añade el correo electrónico, el teléfono y la dirección de tu empresa

10. Pulsa el botón para mostrar tus datos de contacto o selecciona "No utilizar mis datos de contacto" para ocultarlos.

11. Pulsa "Iniciar sesión en Facebook" para conectarte con tu página de empresa de Facebook o salta

12. Pulse "OK" para completar el cambio

Si aún no tienes una cuenta personal en Instagram o, por el contrario, quieres crear una nueva cuenta específica para tu empresa, es muy recomendable que primero crees una página de empresa en Facebook y la optimices para obtener la mejor experiencia de usuario. También puedes utilizar las siguientes instrucciones para crear una nueva página de empresa de Facebook y vincularla a tu perfil de empresa de Instagram. Para crear una página de empresa, sigue estos pasos:

1. Accede a tu cuenta de Facebook

2. Seleccione el icono de menú en la esquina superior derecha junto al icono de su perfil

3. Seleccione "Página" y accederá a la pantalla "Crear una página".

4. Añada el nombre de su página

5. Seleccione la categoría de su empresa

6. Añade una breve descripción de la empresa

7. Pulse "Crear página".

8. Añadir una imagen de perfil y una foto de portada

9. Pulse "Guardar".

Puedes optimizar aún más tu página de empresa de Facebook creando un nombre de usuario, añadiendo y quitando botones para dirigir el tráfico de clientes, optimizando para anuncios y reseñas de Facebook, añadiendo datos de contacto y ubicación, horarios de atención, tipos de servicios y rangos de precios, etc.

Es importante optimizar cuidadosamente tu página de empresa de Facebook para crear la mejor experiencia de usuario para tus clientes y visitantes que intenten buscarte en Facebook. Una vez que hayas terminado de configurar tu página de empresa de Facebook, inicia sesión en Instagram a través de tus datos de Facebook y sigue los pasos anteriores para configurar un perfil de empresa en Instagram. Una vez que hayas configurado tu página de empresa y tu perfil en ambas plataformas, podrás publicar constantemente el mismo contenido para aumentar la participación de los clientes en ambas plataformas a la vez.

Optimizar la configuración de la cuenta

Ahora que hemos repasado cómo configurar correctamente tu perfil de empresa en Instagram y también hemos repasado brevemente cómo crear una página de empresa en Facebook y vincularla a tu perfil de empresa en Instagram, vamos a empezar a optimizar tu perfil de empresa.

Nombre y usuario

nombre

Es muy recomendable que utilices el nombre real de tu empresa en la sección "Nombre" para que sea fácil y reconocible para los visitantes y seguidores existentes, ya que este será tu nombre para mostrar justo debajo de tu foto de perfil. Lo mejor es que sea sencillo, ya que hay un límite de 30 caracteres y debes tenerlo en cuenta si tienes un nombre de empresa largo. Si eres una persona influyente, puedes utilizar tu nombre real si estás construyendo tu marca y creando contenido centrado en ti y en tu estilo de vida.

El nombre de usuario es un nombre único para tu perfil, específico para la plataforma. Puedes ser creativo con esto, pero en general, es mejor mantenerlo simple, fácil de encontrar y reconocible para los visitantes y seguidores existentes si quieren interactuar contigo. Este es el nombre que utilizarás cuando interactúes con tus seguidores y colabores con otras cuentas de Instagram. Tu nombre de usuario debe ser un reflejo de tu presencia en la plataforma, así que asegúrate de elegir uno que resuene con tu marca y por lo que quieres ser conocido.

Foto de perfil

Tu foto de perfil debe ser relevante para tu negocio o marca. Por ejemplo, si tienes una pequeña empresa y ya tienes un logotipo que define tu marca, puedes utilizarlo como foto de perfil. Si eres una persona influyente y promueves un determinado tipo de contenido en torno a un servicio o producto, podrías tener una foto personal que resuene con la visión y el mensaje general de tu marca. Una buena foto de perfil dejará una imagen duradera en la mente de tus seguidores, así que ten siempre una imagen que sea coherente con tu marca. Asegúrate de dejar un poco de espacio alrededor de las esquinas de tu imagen, ya que Instagram recortará tu foto de perfil en un círculo.

Bio

Tu biografía de Instagram es como tu primera presentación al mundo, al estilo de un discurso de ascensor. Es tu oportunidad para mostrar tu personalidad y hacer que la gente sepa quién eres y por qué deberían seguirte. También debe ser lo suficientemente concisa como para que tus seguidores potenciales se hagan una idea del tipo de contenido que pueden esperar de ti.

Instagram tiene un límite de 150 caracteres para tu biografía, por lo que debes ser lo más creativo y conciso posible.

Tu biografía de Instagram es también el único lugar donde puedes incluir un enlace en el que se pueda hacer clic para dirigir tráfico a otro sitio web o página. Utiliza un acortador de enlaces para acortar el enlace y que no ocupe demasiados caracteres, y un creador de enlaces si tienes más de uno.

Si eres una persona influyente y quieres destacar por una profesión, afición, habilidad o interés específico, también puedes describir estos detalles en tu biografía. Puedes utilizar palabras clave específicas que describan con precisión lo que haces sin ocupar demasiado espacio. El uso de palabras clave no tendrá ningún efecto en su capacidad de búsqueda, pero se centrará más en el tipo de contenido con el que desea que resuenen sus seguidores. También puedes incluir un enlace de hashtag de marca para redirigirles a otro perfil que destaque el tipo de contenido que puede interesar a tus seguidores.

Ajustes adicionales

Una vez que te hayas ocupado de la estética de tu cuenta, también es importante que optimices algunos ajustes del backend para mantener una experiencia de usuario fluida para tus seguidores. Dado que eres una marca o figura pública, es importante que te asegures de que la privacidad de tu cuenta está configurada como pública y no privada. Esto es importante porque quieres que la gente te busque, vea tus publicaciones y te siga sin obstáculos. Una vez que vincules tu página de empresa de Facebook a tu cuenta de empresa de Instagram, la configuración debería cambiar automáticamente a "cuenta pública" si antes eras una cuenta privada, pero siempre es bueno comprobar y ver cuál es la configuración de privacidad cuando creas tu cuenta. Para ello, puedes ir a la opción de menú de tu cuenta > Seleccionar Privacidad > Seleccionar Cuenta > Desactivar "Cuenta privada".

Otra función que puede interesarte es ocultar los comentarios ofensivos que puedan perjudicar a tu marca y ofender a otros seguidores. Para ello, puedes ir a la opción de menú de la configuración de tu cuenta > Seleccionar Privacidad > Seleccionar Comentarios > Activar "Ocultar comentarios ofensivos".

A medida que tu marca crece y amplías tu alcance a más seguidores, es posible que desees que otras personas te ayuden a gestionar tus redes sociales y tu marketing en Instagram, y puedes hacerlo añadiendo hasta cinco cuentas más a tu cuenta de empresa. Para ello, ve a la opción de menú de la configuración de tu cuenta > Selecciona "Añadir cuenta" en la parte inferior > Introduce el nombre de usuario y la contraseña de la persona que vas a añadir a tu cuenta de empresa. De este modo, la persona que te ayude podrá alternar entre su propia cuenta y tu cuenta profesional sin tener que entrar y salir de ambas cuentas.

Metas y objetivos

Ahora que ya tienes configurada tu cuenta de empresa, vamos a ver qué quieres conseguir exactamente con ella. Definir metas y objetivos para tu cuenta de empresa en línea con tu marca y tu mensaje es directamente proporcional a cómo comercializas tus productos o servicios en la plataforma.

Utilice las siguientes preguntas como marco básico e intente redactar respuestas detalladas y específicas para definir metas y objetivos claros:

- ¿Qué quiere conseguir con sus contenidos?

- ¿Su contenido va a educar y sensibilizar a sus seguidores?

- ¿Qué tipo de contenidos va a publicar y con qué frecuencia?

- ¿Quién es su público objetivo y le resultan útiles sus contenidos actuales?

- ¿Cómo y qué va a hacer para mantener el interés de su público?

- ¿Cómo se ve progresando cada año en la plataforma?

- ¿Qué métricas le interesa seguir para analizar el crecimiento?

- ¿Cuánto tiempo y recursos puede dedicar al marketing y la publicidad?

Una vez que hayas escrito y definido unas metas y unos objetivos claros, echa un vistazo a los perfiles de tus competidores y evalúa qué están haciendo que quizá podrías adoptar o evitar. Estudia el tipo de contenido que publican y la frecuencia con la que lo hacen, qué hacen de forma diferente para interactuar con sus seguidores, qué aspecto tienen sus anuncios, si los tienen, y cómo te anunciarías tú de forma diferente, etc.

Una vez que haya determinado lo que hacen sus competidores, analice detenidamente su perfil y vea cómo puede diferenciarse de la competencia. Analice su contenido actual y vea cómo puede mejorarlo. Tal vez desee archivar algunas publicaciones antiguas que contienen información que ha quedado obsoleta y que probablemente necesite volver a publicar con información más relevante. Tal vez quiera empezar a publicar con más frecuencia. Construye un sistema que te ayude a auditar continuamente tu propia cuenta y tus publicaciones para asegurarte de que la calidad está a la altura de tus seguidores.

Ventajas del marketing en Instagram

Según Social Pilot, "Instagram tiene más de dos mil millones de usuarios activos y más del 64% de los usuarios son menores de 34 años." Esa es la ventaja añadida de hacer marketing en Instagram. Ahora que tienes una cuenta de empresa y has definido metas y objetivos claros para ella, vamos a entender los beneficios y ventajas de comercializar tus productos y servicios en la plataforma.

Atractivo visual

Las personas son seres visuales. Si el feed de tu perfil de Instagram tiene un gran contenido y una combinación de colores coherente, es más probable que los visitantes te sigan solo por tu capacidad de ofrecer un atractivo visual relajante. La gente está más dispuesta a interactuar con contenidos visuales que son a la vez concisos e informativos, lo que es esencial si quieres captar la atención de tus seguidores y visitantes mientras se desplazan a través de interminables cantidades de contenido en la plataforma.

Pequeñas empresas

Instagram ha sido capaz de ayudar a las pequeñas empresas sin capital de marketing a aumentar su presencia simplemente con la publicación constante de contenidos. La plataforma también permite a los visitantes y usuarios encontrar estas pequeñas empresas a través de enlaces y búsquedas de hashtags. Incluso si no tienes un gran presupuesto de marketing para anunciar tus servicios o productos, con una configuración profesional, publicar contenido coherente y relevante puede hacer que el algoritmo de Instagram trabaje a tu favor. Destinar tu presupuesto de marketing a hacer que tus publicaciones llamen la atención de los visitantes ocasionales puede ayudarte a aumentar tu audiencia, especialmente si eres una persona influyente.

Notoriedad de marca

Según SendPulse, "el 74% de los usuarios de la plataforma consideran que las marcas que tienen un perfil de Instagram o presencia en las redes sociales son dignas de confianza y relevantes." Los usuarios no solo admiten conocer nuevas marcas y personas influyentes en la plataforma, sino que también se alejan de las empresas que no tienen una huella en las redes sociales. Las redes sociales solían ser algo bonito para una empresa, pero ahora son imprescindibles para todas las empresas en 2022.

Mejor compromiso

Tener presencia en las redes sociales, y especialmente en Instagram, es la mejor manera de generar confianza y establecer una relación con los clientes. Curiosamente, una publicación en Instagram obtiene de media un 23 % más de interacción que en Facebook, a pesar de que Facebook tiene más usuarios activos. Esto dice mucho de cómo y dónde quieren interactuar con usted sus seguidores.

Aumento de las ventas

Una de las mayores ventajas de hacer marketing en Instagram es que el público suele tomar decisiones de compra mucho más rápido que en cualquier otra plataforma de redes sociales o sitio web. Esto sin duda ayuda si empiezas a anunciarte en Instagram. Afortunadamente, Instagram ayuda tanto a las marcas como a las empresas en este sentido haciendo que su plataforma esté optimizada para la compra impulsiva con diversas herramientas que llevan al cliente directamente de la aplicación a la tienda.

Nutrición de la audiencia

Instagram te ayuda a ampliar tu alcance al permitirte identificar con precisión a tu público objetivo. Con el gestor de anuncios de Instagram, puedes atraer hacia ti al público adecuado en función de su información demográfica, comportamiento de compra, intereses y otras métricas. Si un visitante muestra interés haciendo clic en tus anuncios, o bien seguirá adelante y realizará una compra o bien se quedará inseguro y decidirá volver más tarde. En esta situación, el gestor de anuncios ofrece fuertes alternativas de retargeting para ayudar a animar al visitante a seguir adelante con su interés inicial en su producto o servicio.

CAPÍTULO 2: TIPOS DE PUBLICACIONES EN INSTAGRAM

Ahora tienes una cuenta de empresa, has establecido metas y objetivos para tu crecimiento y has optimizado la cuenta para el éxito. Observemos en detalle los diferentes tipos de publicaciones que puedes hacer en Instagram y los beneficios de cada una.

Imágenes

Las imágenes normales son fácilmente la publicación más común en la plataforma por muchas razones. Puedes publicar una gran variedad de imágenes versátiles que aumenten la participación, despierten el interés y despierten la curiosidad. Ser creativo y diverso con la publicación de imágenes es importante y no debe sentirse como una constante publicidad abierta a tus seguidores, sino que más bien quieres parecer genuino y real a tus seguidores al publicar contenido con contexto.

Instagram tiene un diseño muy sencillo y sin complicaciones. Aunque el diseño no ha cambiado mucho desde su creación, se han introducido mejoras en la plataforma para competir con otras.

La plataforma sigue permitiendo publicar fotos en formato horizontal y vertical; sin embargo, todas las imágenes que publiques aparecerán por defecto cuadradas en tu perfil. Evidentemente, es más importante centrarse en la calidad de las imágenes teniendo en cuenta la resolución, las dimensiones y el tamaño. Quieres que tu público se sienta inspirado y cautivado por tu contenido, por lo que siempre debes publicar imágenes de alta resolución en tu feed.

Dado que todas tus imágenes se recortarán a una imagen cuadrada en tu feed, el tamaño estándar para imágenes cuadradas es de 1080px por 1080px con una relación de aspecto de 1:1. Para las publicaciones apaisadas, el tamaño ideal es de 1080px por 566px con una relación de aspecto de 1,91:1, y para los retratos, el tamaño ideal es de 1080px por 1350px con una relación de aspecto de 4:5. Teniendo en cuenta estas proporciones de imagen, siempre debes tratar de editar tus imágenes en torno a esas dimensiones para mantener la coherencia con tus otras publicaciones de imágenes.

Tomar una foto realmente buena puede llegar muy lejos, y esto se consigue con práctica y habilidad. La tecnología de las cámaras ha avanzado mucho en los últimos años, sobre todo con los smartphones, que pueden competir con las caras cámaras DSLR. Con una cámara de teléfono impresionante, tú también puedes hacer fotos espectaculares de alta calidad con tu smartphone. Exploremos los siguientes consejos para ayudarte a hacer fotos impresionantes que llamen la atención de tus seguidores.

Luz natural y hora dorada

Comprender la luz es uno de los aspectos más importantes de la fotografía. Si hay demasiada luz, la imagen parecerá descolorida y cansará la vista; si hay muy poca, se crearán sombras oscuras no deseadas alrededor de las zonas claras de la imagen. La mejor manera de contrarrestar este problema es entender la luz en cada momento del día y qué zonas de tu entorno reflejan la mejor luz en esos momentos del día.

Haz varias fotos de un objeto en el mismo lugar, ángulo y escena a lo largo del día para comprender los distintos matices de la luz natural.

Aprenda a aprovechar el poder de hacer fotos durante la hora dorada del día. La primera hora después del amanecer y la primera hora antes del atardecer son codiciadas por los fotógrafos y se conocen comúnmente como la "hora dorada". La razón por la que todo el mundo adora las fotos tomadas durante la hora dorada es que son estéticamente más naturales e impactantes. No se necesitan filtros.

Regla de los tercios y espacio

La regla de los tercios es un principio popular y muy practicado entre los fotógrafos. Se trata de la composición y se aplica a la disposición y el equilibrio de todos los elementos que componen las imágenes, como las formas, las texturas, el fondo, los colores y mucho más. Un buen truco para entender cómo utilizarlo para mejorar la calidad de tus imágenes sería utilizar el ajuste de líneas de cuadrícula de la cámara de tu teléfono y practicar aprendiendo a alinear tus imágenes. Divide el marco de tu imagen en tres líneas verticales espaciadas uniformemente y tres líneas horizontales espaciadas uniformemente que formarán una cuadrícula de 3x3 o nueve partes. En la intersección de las líneas es donde debe centrarse la atención de tu producto.

Negativo o blanco es el espacio vacío alrededor de su producto que está aislado en el marco de la imagen, esto le permite atraer el foco y centrar la atención en el producto. Combinar el uso del espacio en blanco y la regla de los tercios puede crear una imagen potente y de alta calidad.

Profundidad y capas

Hemos visto cómo el uso de la regla de los tercios y los espacios puede aislar y centrar la atención únicamente en el sujeto; del mismo modo, añadir capas y profundidad a tus imágenes también puede ser interesante de forma natural. Las capas pueden comenzar con el enfoque de un sujeto, seguido de otro sujeto detrás ligeramente desenfocado, seguido de otro en el fondo ligeramente más desenfocado de nuevo. Es importante no exagerar ni subestimar la estratificación, sino experimentar con ella y probar cómo se puede resaltar el enfoque en el sujeto principal mientras se difumina ligeramente el resto.

Ángulos y puntos de vista

¿Alguna vez has hecho una foto con tu smartphone o cámara y la has colocado instintivamente a la altura de los ojos antes de hacerla? Para nosotros es muy natural hacer fotos con este punto de vista, pero intenta mezclarlo y ver cómo puedes hacer fotos con diferentes puntos de vista, tal vez a vista de pájaro, que está muy por encima del suelo, o a vista de gusano, que está cerca de la superficie del suelo, etc.

Utilizar las líneas de cuadrícula en los ajustes de tu cámara te ayudará a enfocar y a equilibrar cuando hagas las fotos desde distintos ángulos. Si tienes varios sujetos, intenta alinearlos y experimenta con los ángulos y comprueba lo bien que puedes retratarlos en tus imágenes en vertical, horizontal e incluso en diagonal si queda bien y el ángulo tiene sentido.

Simetría y patrones

Al ojo humano le fascinan las composiciones simétricas, que realzan un tema que, de otro modo, podría no resultar interesante. La simetría puede ayudar a atraer la mirada hacia los detalles sencillos de la imagen si resulta agradable a la vista. Si la simetría es buena para los ojos, los patrones son buenos para el cerebro. Nuestro cerebro es una máquina natural de reconocer patrones y experimentar con ellos puede mejorar la calidad de las imágenes.

Fotos espontáneas, de acción y de detalle

Capturar una imagen con el sujeto en movimiento es una habilidad en sí misma, pero puede dar lugar a tomas increíbles. No tiene por qué ser perfecta, incluso un poco de movimiento y un toque de desenfoque dan lugar a una imagen casi artística. Una buena forma de conseguir un buen número de fotos es asegurarse primero de que el sujeto está en el encuadre de la composición y con buena luz natural, después activar el modo ráfaga del smartphone para capturar un montón de imágenes en poco tiempo y, finalmente, cuando las revises, puede que encuentres una que sea lo suficientemente "cándida" como para colgarla en tu feed.

Vibrante y con humor

Los colores brillantes tienden a hacernos sentir cálidos, felices y nos dan energía, por lo que a veces tener esa explosión de colores ricos y brillantes puede tener un gran impacto en la calidad de tus imágenes. Encontrar el equilibrio adecuado entre colores vibrantes y neutros moderados puede ser refrescante para tu feed. Con el mismo espíritu de añadir un poco de vitalidad, mantener la diversión y añadir comedia a tus imágenes también añadirá un toque más real y personal que puede resonar con tus seguidores.

Edición de imágenes

Cuando echas un vistazo a algunos perfiles de Instagram realmente buenos y te preguntas por qué sus feeds de imágenes tienen tan buen aspecto, no es solo porque las fotos se hayan tomado de forma profesional. También es gracias al proceso de edición. La edición por sí sola no puede hacer que una mala foto se vea bien, así que asegúrate de que estás siguiendo los pasos anteriores y de que estás tomando fotos de alta calidad para empezar. En lo que respecta a la edición, hay una gran cantidad de aplicaciones y programas que puedes utilizar para editar tus imágenes. La mayoría de ellos deberían incluir los siguientes elementos esenciales de edición.

Cultivos

Recortar la foto elimina cualquier detalle que distraiga o sea innecesario y que no quieras que aparezca en la imagen final.

Balance de blancos

El balance de blancos te ayuda a ajustar los niveles de color y las condiciones de iluminación de la foto si no estás satisfecho con la toma original, y la mayoría de las aplicaciones de edición tienen modos preestablecidos entre los que puedes elegir.

Contraste

El contraste es la gama de tonos oscuros a claros que ayudan a que ciertos elementos de tu imagen destaquen; demasiado bajo y podrías tener una imagen plana sin nada que destaque, o demasiado alto y tendrás todos los tonos sin importar los colores que destaquen, así que intenta encontrar un equilibrio evitando los extremos.

Exposición

La exposición te ayuda a hacer la foto tan brillante u oscura como quieras dependiendo del brillo de la imagen original. Evita hacerla demasiado brillante o demasiado oscura y ajusta la exposición moderadamente.

Saturación

La saturación ayuda a aumentar la intensidad de los colores en tus imágenes, haciéndolas más brillantes y añadiendo un aspecto dramático a tu imagen final. El aumento de la saturación hace que la imagen "salte" de intensidad.

Limpieza de manchas

La mayoría de las aplicaciones de edición deberían tener una función de limpieza de manchas que puede ayudar a minimizar o eliminar elementos polvorientos o arenosos de la imagen final, así que examina cuidadosamente la imagen final para ver si hay alguna mancha que quieras reducir o eliminar.

Filtros y carga

Una vez que hayas completado toda la edición en otra aplicación de tu elección, es el momento de seguir adelante y subir tu imagen final a tu feed de Instagram. Cuando subas una imagen editada, se recortará automáticamente en un cuadrado si aún no lo has hecho, y después de esto, tendrás algunas opciones de filtro para elegir. Si has editado la imagen a tu gusto, puedes omitir totalmente la adición de filtros adicionales.

Conviene comprobar siempre la imagen final antes de publicarla y escribir un pie de foto que añada contexto y significado a la imagen.

Vídeos

Instagram también te permite publicar vídeos. Los siguientes consejos te ayudarán a optimizar tus vídeos para que tengan éxito en el marketing. También hay una gran cantidad de aplicaciones de edición de vídeo que te ayudarán a mejorar la calidad de tus vídeos antes de publicarlos y siempre debes ser consciente de publicar vídeos que sirvan a un propósito y se alineen con la voz y el mensaje general de tu marca.

Miniaturas

Como con todo lo demás, captar la atención de tu audiencia incluso con los vídeos es importante, por lo que debes ser estratégico a la hora de elegir una buena imagen en miniatura que excluya el contenido del vídeo. Esto ayudará a crear intriga y dará a tus seguidores una idea de lo que pueden esperar del vídeo.

Sonido

La aplicación tiende a reproducir automáticamente los vídeos sin sonido, por lo que para que el público escuche el sonido con el vídeo, tendrá que pulsar sobre él. Por lo tanto, es un buen consejo a tener en cuenta a la hora de crear tus vídeos para no depender del sonido, ya que quieres que tus seguidores entiendan el contenido de tu vídeo sin tener que pulsar sobre él. Añadir subtítulos es una gran idea si el vídeo es de alguien hablando.

Hyperlapse

Instagram te permite "hyperlapse" tus vídeos de larga duración o, en otras palabras, condensar la duración total en un vídeo más corto de un minuto. Hyperlapse es una aplicación propia de Instagram que te ayuda a crear vídeos time-lapse de forma fácil y sin esfuerzo, y también te permite elegir la velocidad de reproducción. Puedes experimentar con la duración de tus vídeos y ver qué resulta cómodo para tu audiencia y qué consigue más engagement.

Boomerangs

Los boomerangs son vídeos en bucle de tres segundos que se reproducen hacia delante y luego hacia atrás, y que pueden resultar divertidos y entretenidos para el público, como momentos divertidos entre bastidores o brindis de celebración con copas de vino, etc.

Instagram Reels

Con el fin de mantenerse al día con la competencia de otras aplicaciones con contenido de vídeo de formato corto, la nueva función de la plataforma llamada

Instagram Reels te permite crear entretenidos clips de vídeo de entre 15 y 30 segundos para casi cualquier propósito, como vídeos informativos y tutoriales rápi-
dos. Tienen su propia sección en la plataforma, así que cuando crees contenido
para comercializar tu producto, aprovechar los Reels es una gran oportunidad
para aumentar la tracción y el compromiso con tus seguidores. Cada día se ven al
menos 100 millones de Reels. Los siguientes pasos deberían ayudarte a publicar
Instagram Reels:

1. Pulse el icono más en la parte superior de la pantalla y seleccione Carrete

2. En consecuencia, ajuste su configuración:

- Timing - elige si es un Reel de 15 o 30 segundos

- Música - escriba en la barra de búsqueda la música que desea utilizar

- Velocidad: elige si quieres acelerar o ralentizar el ritmo.

- Efectos - seleccione los efectos aplicables si es necesario

- Temporizador: establece un temporizador o una cuenta atrás antes de
  que el carrete empiece a grabar

3. Graba tu Carrete y, en consecuencia, pausa o reanuda la grabación si necesitas
cambiar a una nueva escena vigilando la barra de progreso en la parte superior de
la pantalla.

4. Revisa la grabación y vuelve a editarla si no estás satisfecho. Si estás satisfecho,
pulsa el icono "Compartir en" en la parte inferior derecha de la pantalla para
compartir en Reels o en Stories.

Al compartir el clip en Reels, aparecerá automáticamente en la página separada
de Instagram Reels y también tendrás la opción de compartirlo en tu feed, entre
otros ajustes adicionales como etiquetar a otras personas o recortar la imagen

de visualización del Reel. Si aún no estás listo para publicarlo, también puedes guardarlo en tu borrador para publicarlo más tarde.

Cuando seleccionas la opción Historias, puedes compartirlo en tus historias de Instagram o solo con amigos cercanos.

Historias de Instagram

Las historias de Instagram son otra función en la que puedes publicar imágenes y vídeos mucho más reales y auténticos que no están tan pulidos como tu feed de perfil. Estas publicaciones duran solo 24 horas, tras las cuales desaparecen. A diferencia de tu feed principal, puedes experimentar con las Historias y mostrar el lado real y genuino de tu marca o negocio publicando contenido menos pulido. Este es un gran lugar para compartir detrás de las escenas de su negocio. Las Historias de Instagram también son una gran manera para que las empresas sean descubiertas cuando se combinan con las capacidades de búsqueda de la plataforma. A continuación te explicamos cómo empezar a publicar en tus Historias de Instagram:

1. Toca el icono más en la parte superior de la pantalla y selecciona "Historia".

2. Seleccione la foto o el vídeo que desea cargar

3. Añade funciones adicionales como ubicación, texto, filtros, encuestas, música, etc.

4. Pulsa el botón "Enviar a" y publica tu historia

Otra gran característica de la plataforma es que Instagram te permite guardar las mejores y más destacadas historias como Instagram Highlights desde tus Instagram Stories. Las imágenes y los vídeos no se pueden añadir directamente a los destacados y tendrían que publicarse primero como Historias. Los destacados de Instagram son una excelente forma de añadir más detalles sobre tu marca o negocio que quieras segregar de tu biografía y feed principal, como tu horario de trabajo, testimonios o diversos servicios. Normalmente aparecen justo debajo de tu biografía y son una forma estupenda de hacer permanente el contenido temporal. Hay dos formas de añadir historias a los destacados: desde las historias actuales o desde tu archivo.

A continuación te explicamos cómo añadir historias actuales a los destacados:

1. Abra una historia publicada o actual y haga clic en el icono del corazón situado en la parte inferior de la pantalla.

2. Añade la historia a un Destacado existente o crea uno nuevo si aún no tienes ninguno.

3. Una vez que la historia se ha publicado en el destacado, puede editar la imagen de portada o elegir un nuevo nombre para el destacado.

A continuación te explicamos cómo añadir historias de tu archivo a destacados:

1. Accede a tu archivo en la parte superior derecha de tu perfil. El archivo contendrá las historias que caducaron después de su límite de 24 horas y cualquier otra publicación que hayas eliminado en el pasado.

2. Seleccione la historia y, a continuación, haga clic en resaltar en la parte inferior del menú y seleccione a qué resaltado desea añadirla.

Instagram en directo

Mientras que las Historias son una gran manera de mostrar contenido pregrabado con fecha de caducidad, Instagram Live es otra función que te permite interactuar con tu audiencia en tiempo real. Puede resultar intimidante para muchas marcas en crecimiento y prometedoras aventurarse en el espacio en directo. Siempre ayuda prepararse con antelación y tener una agenda si planeas utilizar Instagram Live. El directo es una forma estupenda de interactuar con tu audiencia en tiempo real a través de debates y preguntas y respuestas.

Cuando haces un directo en Instagram, tienes la opción de retransmitirlo a tus Instagram Stories para que los usuarios actuales de la plataforma sepan que estás en directo e incluso enviar una notificación a los usuarios offline para que vengan a pasar el rato. Puedes invitar a personas a tus retransmisiones en directo para que colaboren, lo que abre la puerta a muchas otras posibilidades de marketing.

CAPÍTULO 3: CREAR UNA ESTRATEGIA DE MARKETING DE CONTENIDOS

Todo negocio en línea necesita un canal de marketing táctico sólido con una estrategia bien pensada. Desarrollar una estrategia de marketing no debería ser complicado, pero la atención al detalle, la paciencia y la coherencia sin duda verán un retorno significativo de la inversión con el tiempo. En esta sección se describe todo lo que debes tener en cuenta a la hora de desarrollar tu estrategia de marketing en Instagram.

Fijar objetivos

Al desarrollar cualquier estrategia empresarial o de marketing, no es de extrañar que establecer objetivos sea siempre la primera tarea que hay que emprender. La fijación de objetivos de marketing en Instagram debe comenzar siempre por preguntarse por qué se está en la plataforma y qué se pretende conseguir promocionando el negocio o la marca en ella. Hay muchas razones y pueden ser las siguientes:

- Puede que ya sea una marca o empresa consolidada y quiera atraer a más seguidores de diversos grupos demográficos.

- Busca aumentar la notoriedad de su marca y su reputación en su sector.

- Tal vez desee conocer mejor un mercado y un público mientras pone a prueba una nueva empresa o idea.

- Podrías estar buscando construir una comunidad con tus seguidores y proporcionar conocimientos sobre ciertos productos y servicios que no se satisfacen en otros lugares.

- Probablemente quiera impulsar las ventas y aumentar los ingresos con campañas promocionales.

Independientemente de los objetivos que defina para construir el marco general de su estrategia de marketing, es importante alinearlos siempre con la estrategia SMART: Específicos, Mensurables, Alcanzables, Relevantes y Oportunos.

Definir el público destinatario

Determinar su público objetivo es un paso crucial para que su estrategia de marketing tenga éxito. En pocas palabras, lo ideal es aumentar la audiencia con personas que estén realmente interesadas en sus productos o servicios, ya que hay más posibilidades de que participen. Dirigirse al público equivocado socavará drásticamente su estrategia de marketing.

Una de las formas habituales de evitarlo es crear un personaje o avatar de comprador y conocer sus datos demográficos e intereses. Utiliza métodos basados en datos para conocer primero a tu audiencia y aprender sobre su edad, género, ubicación, ocupación, capacidad de ingresos y más. Cuanto más específico y detallado sea, mejor los conocerá.

Otra forma es buscar hashtags relacionados con su negocio, marca, mercado o industria y buscar los perfiles que participan con estos hashtags para aprender sobre su comportamiento, puntos de dolor, preocupaciones y deseos.

Análisis de la competencia

Analizar lo que hacen sus competidores es una medida inteligente. Siempre es mejor comprender las condiciones generales del mercado y encontrar oportunidades en las que pueda destacarse de la competencia. Si sabes quiénes son los principales competidores de tu sector o mercado, puedes buscar sus perfiles y anotar detalles sobre su contenido, participación, crecimiento y otras métricas. Repite este proceso hasta que tengas suficientes datos recopilados de al menos los cinco o diez perfiles principales y, a continuación, empieza a analizar todos los datos recopilados en busca de puntos en común y patrones. Una vez que hayas terminado con el análisis, deberías tener una buena idea del tipo de contenido que publican tus competidores y de qué publicaciones consiguen más participación. También es una buena idea revisar sus secciones de comentarios para conocer la opinión de sus clientes. Esta es una buena forma de medir el grado de satisfacción y descontento de los clientes. Con esta información, puedes identificar oportunidades perdidas y lagunas que podrías aprovechar.

Diseñar contenidos de calidad

En capítulos anteriores hemos analizado los distintos tipos de contenido que puedes publicar en Instagram, y no hace falta decir que, como marca o empresa, quieres que tu contenido sea atractivo y agradable a la vista. El contenido es, sin duda, el rey en todas las plataformas de redes sociales, y el contenido de calidad es lo que separa el mejor perfil de la media. Tu contenido puede centrarse en la promoción de tus productos y servicios, en mensajes de motivación o en la cultura de tu marca o empresa. Pero si el contenido no está a la altura, sus seguidores podrían pasarse a sus competidores, que podrían estar publicando contenidos de mejor calidad. Por tanto, invertir en el diseño de contenidos de calidad es fundamental para el éxito del marketing en la plataforma.

Estética coherente

Tener una estética desorganizada en torno a tus contenidos no sólo puede hacer que tu marketing fracase, sino también que pierdas seguidores. Tanto si atraes a nuevos seguidores como si conservas a los que ya tienes, es importante entender que en la mente de la audiencia de una plataforma visual te reconocen y te segregan mentalmente del contenido de los demás.

Seguir la estética de tu marca con coherencia es muy importante. Los elementos visuales de tu perfil y tu feed deben estar en consonancia con la personalidad de tu marca. Mantener un tema o un concepto visual coherente en todas tus redes sociales, incluida Instagram, te ayudará a establecerte como marca a los ojos de tus seguidores.

Esbozar un calendario editorial

No es ningún secreto que para crecer en cualquier plataforma de medios sociales es necesario ofrecer contenidos de forma constante. De media, las marcas con más éxito publican algún tipo de contenido al menos dos veces al día. Ahora bien, como nueva marca o empresa que acaba de comenzar su incursión en el mundo del marketing digital y en línea, esto puede o no parecer una responsabilidad monumental al principio, pero con el tiempo se encontrará con un obstáculo. Puede que te quedes sin ideas, te sientas agotado o pierdas la coherencia.

La forma más sencilla de mantener la eficacia y la coherencia es crear un calendario de programación en el que se describa la difusión de contenidos durante un periodo de tiempo determinado. Existen multitud de herramientas y aplicaciones que pueden ayudarte a planificar con antelación las horas de publicación, así como el contenido, los pies de foto y los hashtags. También puedes utilizar estas herramientas para automatizar la publicación y obtener datos analíticos para obtener más información sobre tus publicaciones.

Convierta a sus seguidores en clientes

No debemos olvidar que, al fin y al cabo, el objetivo general del marketing en Instagram es hacer crecer tu marca o tu negocio llevando a tus clientes desde la plataforma a comprar tus productos o servicios. La participación en la plataforma por sí sola no es suficiente para aumentar los ingresos, por lo tanto, al ejecutar campañas promocionales, siempre trata de incluir una llamada a la acción (CTA) en tus pies de foto indicando a tus seguidores que hagan clic en el enlace en tu biografía, ya que tu biografía es el único lugar donde puedes incluir enlaces.

Poner en práctica su estrategia de contenidos

Ahora que entiendes la importancia de crear una estrategia de marketing de contenidos en la plataforma, veamos cómo podemos poner el plan en marcha. Ya hemos repasado los distintos tipos de publicaciones que puedes utilizar en la plataforma en forma de imágenes, vídeos, historias y directos. Esta sección debería darte una idea de los métodos y variaciones de esas publicaciones que puedes utilizar en tu estrategia de marketing.

Imágenes

Hay muchas variaciones diferentes de publicaciones con imágenes que puedes utilizar en tu estrategia, e incluso se te pueden ocurrir tus propias variaciones, así que sé siempre creativo y no tengas miedo de probar o experimentar con nuevas ideas. También es importante que estas publicaciones parezcan reales y auténticas y que no estén escenificadas de ninguna manera que pueda hacer que tu audiencia sienta que estás haciendo mucha publicidad para una llamada a la acción.

Entre bastidores

Estas publicaciones son una forma estupenda de ofrecer a su público una visión desde detrás de las cortinas de cualquier ocasión, evento o trabajo que esté realizando.

Puestos educativos

Estas publicaciones tienen un gran historial de éxito, sobre todo si tu audiencia te sigue en busca de orientación sobre determinados temas de los que tienen menos conocimientos. Este tipo de publicaciones te ayudan a establecerte como una autoridad.

Influencer Posts

Trabajar con una persona influyente en las redes sociales que tenga muchos seguidores promocionando y hablando de tu producto o servicio es una forma estupenda de abrir tu marca y tu negocio a un público sin explotar.

Mensajes de motivación

Las publicaciones motivadoras son una forma estupenda de transmitir el mensaje y los valores de tu marca a tu audiencia, dependiendo del tipo de negocio o marca que dirijas.

Contenidos generados por los usuarios (CGU)

Si bien es importante centrarse en la creación de contenido original para su audiencia, también se puede sacar mucho provecho del contenido generado por los usuarios o del contenido en el que sus seguidores le etiqueten o publiquen con el hashtag de su marca. Siempre que la publicación esté en consonancia con tu mensaje y se dé crédito a la persona, es una forma estupenda de presentar a tu propio público en la plataforma e incluso de demostrar que realmente te preocupas por ellos.

Puestos de vacaciones

Hay casi una festividad para cada ocasión y acontecimiento en todo el mundo y, a medida que tu marca crece en Internet y llega a muchos en todo el planeta, participar o celebrar la festividad con un post no sólo puede ser una forma estupenda de estrechar lazos con tu audiencia, que te lo agradecerá, sino también de llegar a más seguidores potenciales en ese grupo demográfico.

Compras

Estas publicaciones son sin duda la mejor forma de impulsar las ventas y aumentar los ingresos, siempre que se publiquen con moderación y no se anuncien constantemente. Las publicaciones de compras deben tener tus productos o servicios etiquetados en la publicación, lo que facilita a tus seguidores pulsar en el cuadro de información que les redirigirá a tu tienda y les ayudará a completar su compra.

Carrusel de entradas

Con las publicaciones en carrusel, puedes publicar hasta 10 imágenes o vídeos en una única publicación en carrusel y en el mismo formato. Son una forma creativa de promocionar nuevos productos o servicios y puedes ser realmente creativo con ellos proporcionando más contexto sobre el producto o servicio, testimonios de clientes, secuencias del antes y el después y cualquier evento que hayas organizado para el producto o servicio.

Vídeos

Ya hemos establecido que el contenido de vídeo tiende a tener más tracción que las publicaciones de imágenes, por lo que incluir vídeos de alta calidad y bien editados debería formar parte de tu estrategia de marketing, ya que realmente no hay límite a lo que se puede hacer con vídeos de Instagram de un minuto. Según HubSpot, el 64% de los consumidores son más propensos a comprar un producto después de ver primero un vídeo del mismo. Por lo tanto, es muy importante tener en cuenta las siguientes indicaciones a la hora de crear contenido de vídeo convincente.

Promocione sus productos

Cuando empiece a crear su mensaje en vídeo, es importante que promocione su producto de la forma correcta para destacar entre la competencia sin lanzar al mercado vídeos insípidos sin mensaje. Enfócate siempre en dar valor y haz que tu audiencia sepa primero cómo el producto va a beneficiarles.

Eduque a su público

Dependiendo de sus productos o servicios, es posible que desee educar a la audiencia sobre lo que el producto o servicio proporciona exactamente, y por qué eso puede beneficiarles.

Genere confianza entre sus seguidores

Como siempre, es importante establecer una relación de confianza con tus seguidores. Si te aseguras de comunicar tu mensaje de vídeo en consonancia con la cultura y los valores que defiende tu marca, tu público siempre te admirará y te respetará.

Historias de Instagram

Como hemos mencionado antes, las Stories son una forma estupenda de interactuar con tu audiencia y atraer a nuevos seguidores. Las empresas y las marcas están empezando a ver el valor de publicar contenido breve, que no tiene por qué ser completamente profesional. A continuación te explicamos algunas de las mejores formas de utilizar las Stories.

¿Con qué frecuencia publicar historias?

Esto es muy importante cuando se empieza a elaborar una estrategia de marketing. Las historias consumen mucho tiempo y usted, como marca o empresa, tendrá que decidir con qué frecuencia desea publicarlas. Si publicas demasiado, puede que tus seguidores dejen de prestarte atención. Si publicas menos, puede que tus competidores te adelanten o que pierdas seguidores por falta de interacción. Encontrar el punto medio óptimo para tu negocio que se ajuste a tu marca y a tu mensaje es clave, porque lo que puede funcionar para otra persona no tiene por qué funcionar para ti. Básicamente, ¡prueba lo que te conviene y lo que consigue el mayor nivel de compromiso de tu audiencia particular!

¿Cuándo publicar historias?

En el caso de las publicaciones regulares, es importante publicar cuando tus seguidores están en su momento de mayor interacción. Sin embargo, en el caso de las historias, como tienen una ventana de 24 horas a menos que las añadas a destacados, tienes la flexibilidad de publicar en cualquier momento del día sin problemas.

¿Qué historias publicar?

La plataforma te lo ha puesto realmente fácil y cuenta con un montón de herramientas creativas que puedes utilizar para publicar grandes historias. Como hemos comentado antes, no tiene por qué ser todo profesional y empresarial; puedes aportar un lado divertido y cómico a tu marca o negocio. Analizar las historias que tienen más engagement debería decirte todo lo que necesitas saber sobre el tipo de contenido con el que a tus seguidores les gusta interactuar.

Funciones de Instagram Stories

Estas son algunas características con las que puedes jugar al publicar Instagram Stories que no solo ayudarán a aumentar los comentarios de tus seguidores existentes, sino que también pueden hacer que los visitantes ocasionales se interesen al tocar tu foto de perfil.

Ubicación

Desde que la plataforma introdujo los stickers, se han convertido en un gran medio de interacción y puede ser muy divertido jugar con ellos. Por ejemplo, si estás en un restaurante y etiquetas la ubicación de ese restaurante con un sticker, aparecerás en las historias de esa ubicación.

Hashtags

Lo mismo ocurre con las pegatinas de hashtags: si publicas una historia y añades ese hashtag como pegatina, aparecerá en la página del hashtag, y cualquier visitante casual de la página del hashtag podrá ir a ver tu perfil si le interesa tu contenido.

Enlaces

Este es un gran negocio para todas las marcas, negocios e influencers, ya que Stories es el único lugar donde puedes agregar enlaces clicables aparte de la biografía, y un bono sería si guardas esa historia como destacada para futuras referencias para tu audiencia. Tener la capacidad de dirigir tráfico desde tu perfil de Instagram a enlaces externos es fundamental para tu marketing en la plataforma.

Colaboraciones

A medida que trabajes y colabores con otros perfiles y personas influyentes, etiquetarlas sería una forma estupenda de impulsar la participación y ganar más seguidores, ya que todas las partes aprovechan los seguidores de las demás.

Encuestas, preguntas y deslizadores

Esta es otra gran característica para las marcas y las empresas, ya que es una oportunidad directa para comprometerse con la audiencia mediante encuestas sobre ideas, sus productos, servicios y mucho más. Incluso puedes ser bastante directo con esta función y encuestar directamente a tu audiencia sobre qué tipo de contenidos prefieren.

Cuenta atrás

Se trata de una función muy útil, sobre todo si quieres animar a tu público con motivo de una venta, un lanzamiento o cualquier otro acontecimiento después de una cuenta atrás.

Regalos y memes

Estos nunca envejecerán, y siempre es divertido añadir una expresiva personalidad cómica a tu marca. Además, Instagram te permite encontrarlos y añadirlos fácilmente desde una biblioteca.

Instagram en directo

Instagram Live es una gran manera de hacer que tu audiencia participe contigo, y definitivamente deberías usar esta función como parte de tu estrategia de marketing general.

Provocar algo

Últimamente, muchas marcas y empresas utilizan Live para anunciar o hablar del lanzamiento de un nuevo producto, servicio o evento. Es una forma estupenda de crear expectación e intrigar a la audiencia sobre lo que se va a lanzar o dejar caer. Evidentemente, no hay que desvelar todos los detalles, por lo que bromear sobre lo que se va a hacer y establecer expectativas sobre la fecha y la hora es una buena forma de obtener resultados positivos.

Preguntas y respuestas, tutoriales y talleres

Esta es otra forma estupenda de relacionarte con tu público, sobre todo si eres alguien a quien acuden en busca de ayuda y consejo.

Promocione sus campañas

Promocionar tu campaña es una buena forma de utilizar la función Live e incluso puedes ser creativo con ella mientras generas una sensación de urgencia entre tus seguidores. Dejar caer códigos de descuento y ofertas promocionales únicas para los seguidores que estén en directo contigo puede aumentar enormemente la audiencia y la participación.

CAPÍTULO 4: AUMENTAR EL NÚMERO DE SEGUIDORES

En los capítulos anteriores, has leído sobre la importancia del marketing en Instagram, los distintos tipos de publicaciones y cómo crear una estrategia de contenidos con ellas. En esta sección, veremos cómo optimizar tu estrategia de contenidos para aumentar tus seguidores. Tu perfil de Instagram es más que tus seguidores, es tu comunidad online. Comprar seguidores nunca es una buena opción ya que nunca conseguirás engagement de ellos, ni tu contenido será de valor para ellos. Tus recursos deben invertirse siempre en aumentar el número de seguidores y hacer que se conviertan en clientes a largo plazo. La única forma de aumentar el número de seguidores orgánicos es crear contenidos atractivos de alta calidad y optimizarlos para que lleguen al mayor número posible de nuevos seguidores. Esta sección entrará en detalle sobre algunas formas muy útiles para hacer crecer orgánicamente su audiencia sin comprarlos o usar bots de spam.

Conservación de perfiles

La razón por la que es importante conservar tu perfil es que los seres humanos somos ante todo seres visuales. Crear una buena primera impresión para tus visitantes es importante si quieres que te sigan. Mantener una estética de color y un tema coherentes para su perfil que resuene con su marca en general puede mejorar el atractivo visual y el ambiente de su perfil, dando una sensación y un aspecto profesionales.

Utilizar carretes

Ya has leído y entendido qué son los reels, su importancia y lo importantes que son en la estrategia de marketing actual. Aprovechar el poder de los reels puede ayudarte a aumentar tu audiencia si se hace bien, porque los reels son, con diferencia, el tipo de contenido más atractivo de Instagram. Puede que pienses que usar reels no tiene sentido con la estrategia de marketing general de tu marca o negocio, pero la creatividad no tiene límites. Tus seguidores siempre te apreciarán por tu originalidad y si te esfuerzas en crear contenido de alta calidad para ellos.

Optimice sus pies de foto

Este es un gran consejo o "truco" para cualquiera que quiera aumentar sus seguidores: Optimizar los pies de foto de tus posts para la búsqueda o, en otras palabras, la optimización para motores de búsqueda (SEO). La optimización para motores de búsqueda es una estrategia en sí misma, e implementar una estrategia que optimice todas tus publicaciones es la forma más sencilla de conseguir más visitantes ocasionales a tu perfil. La propia plataforma es un motor de búsqueda gigante y utiliza el aprendizaje automático para encontrar contenido de alta calidad que sea relevante para ti en función de tus criterios de búsqueda. Esto es importante, ya que muchos usuarios de la plataforma encuentran contenido escribiendo palabras clave en la barra de búsqueda, lo que les ofrece una gran cantidad de opciones, desde hashtags hasta perfiles que consultar. Hay muchos factores detrás del algoritmo que conforman los criterios para seleccionar el mejor contenido y, aunque tener las palabras clave adecuadas es importante, también es esencial tener publicaciones de alta calidad con pies de foto bien escritos.

Estrategias Hashtag

Invertir en una estrategia de hashtags es otro gran consejo y "truco" que, si se pone en práctica de la manera correcta, producirá un ROI significativamente alto. Según SocialPilot, "Los posts con al menos un hashtag consiguen un 12% más de engagement y de media cada post contiene al menos diez hashtags". Usar los hashtags correctos y relevantes que tengan sentido y se alineen con el mensaje general de tu publicación es fundamental, ya que esto atraerá a más seguidores que utilicen la función de búsqueda.

Hay muchos hashtags populares que pueden parecer saturados y congestionados con demasiadas publicaciones irrelevantes. Para contrarrestar esto, siempre es importante analizar los hashtags que tu audiencia, competidores y líderes de la industria utilizan y que tienen un gran nivel de participación. Aquí es donde puedes concentrarte en hashtags más específicos y menos competitivos.

Regalos

¿A quién no le gustan los sorteos? Los sorteos son una gran táctica de marketing para hacer crecer tu audiencia y, si se hacen bien y con la estrategia adecuada, tienes el potencial de atraer a muchos más seguidores. Establecer expectativas y criterios de participación claros es crucial, y hay muchas opciones, como publicar en las historias o etiquetar a un amigo, que pueden ampliar tu alcance.

Influenciadores y marcas

Asociarse con influencers y marcas para atraer a sus audiencias con el fin de promocionar tus productos o servicios es una gran estrategia de marketing y puede beneficiar a todas las partes implicadas. Según SendPulse, "las marcas tienden a obtener cinco veces más ROI de la cantidad gastada en marketing de influencers y asociaciones con marcas." Esto es lo que hace que esta estrategia de marketing sea una obviedad. Sin embargo, es esencial asegurarse de trabajar con el influencer y la marca adecuados. Lo ideal es trabajar con una persona influyente que se identifique con tu producto o servicio, de modo que le resulte más fácil promocionarte en sus redes sociales para llamar la atención y atraer a sus seguidores hacia ti. Del mismo modo, cuando trabajes con una marca, debes encontrar la forma de que tu producto o servicio encaje bien con el suyo. Siempre debes hacer una rápida revisión de los antecedentes del influencer o de la marca con la que quieres trabajar para evaluar cómo interactúan con su público y cuánta participación puedes esperar de ellos. Otro elemento importante de esta estrategia es determinar si su interacción es genuina, auténtica y si no se trata de bots.

Invitados

Se trata de un truco de marketing poco ortodoxo y sin explotar que, si se hace bien, puede hacer crecer el número de seguidores. Contar con un invitado (un empleado, una persona influyente, un famoso o simplemente alguien que no sea usted y que esté detrás de la marca y que todo el mundo esté acostumbrado a ver todos los días) puede ser una forma estupenda de captar el interés de su público y sus seguidores. Puedes anunciar con antelación que tu invitado se hará cargo de las historias en un formato de preguntas y respuestas o AMA (Ask me Anything).

Contenidos compartibles

En los capítulos anteriores se ha hablado de lo importante que es crear contenidos de alta calidad, y la razón por la que se ha hecho hincapié en ello es que favorece enormemente su marketing en términos de compartibilidad. La creación de contenido de alta calidad no sólo inspira a su audiencia y puede llevarles a una llamada a la acción, sino que también puede animarles a compartirlo con sus propios seguidores. El contenido no tiene por qué ser del todo serio, a veces incluso un meme o un gif que se alinee con tu marca puede ser un poco divertido y podría ser enorme si ya es tendencia en la cultura pop. Cuanto más le gusten a su público las publicaciones divertidas no relacionadas con la empresa, más probable será que compartan su contenido.

Interacción entrante

Otro gran consejo para aumentar el compromiso con tus seguidores es hacer que interactúen contigo a través de AMA y preguntas y respuestas, a las que puedes responder en una secuencia de Instagram Stories. Esto es muy útil si eres un experto en algún tema y puedes ofrecer consejos y conocimientos a tus seguidores, que también pueden compartirlos con sus conocidos, lo que a su vez atraerá más visitas a tu página. Este proceso de interacción inbound es una forma estupenda de establecer la confianza y no sólo ayuda a aumentar tu audiencia, sino también su interés y lealtad hacia tu marca y tu negocio. Otro gran consejo para la interacción inbound es tomarse el tiempo necesario para responder y reaccionar a todos los comentarios que recibas de tus seguidores en tus publicaciones, especialmente si se trata de comentarios o de cualquier idea que tengan para ti.

Propuesta de valor

Es importante tener un esquema de expectativas sobre lo que sus clientes van a obtener al seguirle. Imagínese que entra en un restaurante o en una cadena de comida y no sabe qué tipo de comida preparan. Probablemente no sería la mejor experiencia, y usted daría la vuelta e iría a un lugar del que sabe qué esperar. Su perfil y su marca siguen exactamente los mismos principios. Una propuesta de valor clara del tipo de contenido que ha creado es fundamental para convertir a los visitantes en seguidores y, finalmente, en clientes.

Promoción cruzada

Al comercializar en Instagram, también es importante tener en cuenta que la plataforma es sólo un canal de comercialización y como negocio, usted debe aprovechar tantas plataformas sociales altamente atractivas como sea posible como TikTok, Facebook y YouTube. También tienes la opción de vincular tu página de empresa de Facebook, como ya comentamos en un capítulo anterior.

Desafíos

Uno de los retos más populares de las redes sociales que se hizo viral y que casi todo el mundo conoce es el reto del cubo de hielo de 2014. Los retos en redes sociales han experimentado un gran auge recientemente y son una forma estupenda de aumentar la audiencia y crear nuevas tendencias. Esta es también una gran manera de interactuar con tus seguidores y tiene el potencial de llegar a millones de usuarios haciendo que acepten el reto y te etiqueten con un hashtag de marca. Haz que los retos sean sencillos y fáciles de realizar, y agradece siempre a tu público que se tome el tiempo de interactuar contigo a través de ellos.

UGC

Hablando de apreciar a su público, una de las mejores maneras de hacerlo es utilizando el contenido generado a través de hashtags de marca, o en otras palabras, contenido generado por el usuario. Hay muchas maneras de utilizar el contenido generado por los usuarios, además de la estrategia de crear contenido original. Puedes organizar un reto y hacer que tus seguidores te etiqueten con el reto en el hashtag de la marca, y cuando selecciones el contenido, puedes añadir una publicación en carrusel con los cinco mejores envíos, por ejemplo. Esta es una gran manera de destacar a tu audiencia en el feed principal de tu perfil y podría motivar al resto de la audiencia a querer participar de nuevo la próxima vez. Es una forma estupenda de crear un vínculo con tu comunidad y aumentar la participación de forma orgánica.

Accesibilidad

Hacer que tus contenidos sean accesibles a todo el mundo es extremadamente importante y sin duda contribuirá en gran medida a demostrar que te preocupas por todos tus seguidores. Cosas tan sencillas como añadir subtítulos o superposiciones de texto, escribir todas las palabras en mayúsculas de forma adecuada en los subtítulos, garantizar una gran calidad de sonido en las publicaciones de audio y vídeo, y describir los elementos visuales en detalle si es posible, son algunas de las mejores formas de hacer que tu contenido sea accesible e inclusivo para algunos de tus seguidores con dificultades auditivas o problemas de visión.

Coherencia

En cualquier tipo de marketing en redes sociales, el contenido es el rey y la coherencia es la clave. Ya has leído lo importante que es publicar contenido de alta calidad de forma constante. Hay muchas maneras de mantener tu estrategia de marketing de contenidos en Instagram funcionando sobre las cuatro ruedas. Algunas de ellas son invertir en aplicaciones y herramientas de programación; encontrarás muchas de ellas en internet, así que investiga y sopesa siempre las diferencias entre las gratuitas y las de pago y decántate siempre por la opción que te aporte más beneficios que reduzcan tu tiempo. También puedes contratar a un asistente virtual o a un gestor de marketing en redes sociales para que lleve un horario ajustado con las publicaciones en tu cuenta siguiendo los pasos mencionados en capítulos anteriores vinculando sus cuentas con el perfil de tu empresa. Otro consejo profesional es analizar los momentos de mayor actividad y participación de tu audiencia a lo largo de la semana en cada día para saber cuáles son los mejores momentos para publicar en la plataforma. Si quieres maximizar tu capacidad de llegar a más seguidores y visitantes ocasionales durante las horas de mayor actividad, tendrás más posibilidades de aumentar el número de seguidores.

CAPÍTULO 5: ANÁLISIS DE INSTAGRAM

Cuando reúna todos los elementos de su estrategia de marketing y empiece a aplicarla, se dará cuenta de la necesidad de saber si su estrategia está dando resultados. Cualquier estrategia de marketing, después de una cierta duración, requerirá algún tipo de análisis de datos para comprender su rendimiento. La mejor ventaja de actualizar su perfil a una cuenta de empresa es que tendrá acceso a Insights, una herramienta utilizada para este tipo de análisis.

La analítica es la mejor manera de obtener información sobre el tipo de contenido que le gusta a su público y cuándo está más activo durante el día. Es importante conocer esta información para que tu estrategia de marketing tenga éxito. Es importante elegir las métricas adecuadas para realizar un seguimiento, ya que hay una gran cantidad de ellas, y lo más probable es que desee realizar un seguimiento de las métricas que se curan específicamente para su estrategia de marketing. Dado que cada empresa y cada marca son diferentes, su estrategia de marketing y sus análisis serán igualmente diferentes entre sí.

En este capítulo, comprenderás todo lo que necesitas saber sobre las analíticas de Instagram y sobre cómo hacer crecer tu cuenta, mejorar tu estrategia de marketing y llegar al público objetivo. También veremos la importancia del crecimiento de la audiencia y varias analíticas de publicaciones basadas en las métricas con las que viene cada publicación.

Análisis de la audiencia de Instagram

Independientemente de las métricas en torno a las que se diseñe su estrategia de marketing, siempre debe analizar y estudiar los datos sobre su audiencia porque, al fin y al cabo, toda estrategia de marketing en redes sociales requiere hacer crecer una audiencia, cultivar nuevos seguidores y convertirlos en futuros clientes. Algunas métricas clave de audiencia que siempre debes tener en cuenta son las siguientes:

- **Ubicación** - Querrás saber en qué parte del mundo, país y ciudad se encuentran la mayoría de tus seguidores para ayudarte a determinar cuál podría ser la mejor hora para publicar según su zona horaria y durante sus horas más activas.

- **Edad** - También querrá analizar y ver qué grupo de edad resuena con su contenido para decidir en consecuencia la frecuencia de sus tiempos de publicación, ya que los seguidores más jóvenes tienden a pasar más tiempo en las redes sociales.

- **Género** - Una importante métrica demográfica para determinar qué género resuena más con tu contenido, y esto debería ayudarte a curar más contenido específicamente para ellos.

Otra métrica clave a la que debes prestar atención es la de seguidores y no seguidores, que te dirá cuántos seguidores pierdes y ganas cada día. Obviamente, querrás minimizar los seguidores no seguidos y aumentar los seguidos. Por lo tanto, no pierdas de vista esta métrica a medida que publicas en tu perfil y observa cualquier pico irregular que pueda indicarte si el contenido ha sido bien recibido o no.

Feed Post Analytics

Ya hemos hablado de la importancia de crear tu feed principal y de utilizar una combinación estratégica de contenidos de vídeo e imágenes. A medida que continúas publicando contenido de calidad en tu feed principal, es esencial analizarlo a lo largo del tiempo para determinar qué tan bien están funcionando tus publicaciones. Eso te dará una idea de si tu contenido encaja bien con el algoritmo de Instagram y si está ayudando a que tu contenido llegue a más ojos. Las métricas de rendimiento importantes para rastrear son likes, comentarios, shares, saves y clics. Analizar estas métricas debería darte una buena idea del número de interacciones que han tenido lugar en esa publicación y a cuántas cuentas llegó el contenido. Incluso puedes animar a tus seguidores a guardar y compartir tu contenido si les resulta útil. Este es un gran consejo, especialmente si se trata de contenido de vídeo, ya que esto aumentará continuamente la participación pasiva con el tiempo a medida que tus seguidores vuelven a ver la publicación. Animar a tus seguidores a compartir tu contenido con alguien que puedan conocer también es una forma estupenda de atraer a nuevos seguidores afines y crear una comunidad sólida.

Historias Analíticas

Ya leíste sobre Instagram Stories anteriormente en el capítulo dos y también descubriste lo fácil que puedes ser con los distintos tipos de publicaciones que puedes compartir en Stories. Instagram te ayuda a saber si el contenido de tus Historias ha sido bien recibido por tu audiencia o no con las siguientes métricas:

- Volver

- Adelante

- Emocionado

- Siguiente historia

- Enlaces

- Impresiones

- Perfil Visitas

- Pulsaciones de botones de texto

- Deslizar hacia arriba

Revisar cada una de estas métricas puede indicarte cómo ha navegado tu audiencia por tus historias: Si hicieron clic en los enlaces o cuadros de texto que añadiste, si reaccionaron a tu historia y si visitaron tu perfil desde la historia. Otras métricas clave que puedes seguir son la tasa de seguimiento y la tasa de finalización por historia. La tasa de seguimiento calcula el porcentaje de espectadores que vieron tus historias de principio a fin y la tasa de finalización calcula el porcentaje de espectadores que vieron la longitud completa de cada diapositiva de tus historias. Analizar estas dos métricas junto con las demás puede darte una idea clara de lo que funciona y lo que puedes mejorar en función del contenido que publiques en las historias.

Carretes y análisis en directo

Hemos repasado la importancia de usar Instagram Reels y Live y también hemos leído sobre lo cruciales que son para tu estrategia de marketing de contenidos. Algunas métricas clave que verás tanto para los directos como para los reels son cuántas veces se reprodujeron, el número de interacciones en el post del reel, el número de cuentas a las que llegó el reel y otras métricas de engagement como comentarios, guardados y likes. Reels es actualmente el mejor post de la plataforma y aprovecharlo puede ayudarte a aumentar tu alcance. Con Instagram Live, verás comentarios, reacciones y el número total de espectadores que estuvieron presentes durante el Live, entre otras métricas. Es una información realmente útil para cuando planees organizar más Lives en el futuro.

Análisis de compras

Anteriormente hemos revisado cómo puedes optimizar tu cuenta para integrar tu tienda online y también cómo puedes crear publicaciones de compras con enlaces externos etiquetados en la publicación. Otra función que querrás activar es Instagram Checkout. Al fin y al cabo, tu estrategia de marketing debe llevar a tus seguidores a querer realizar una acción cuando vean tus publicaciones de compras, y es importante estar atento a las publicaciones que aportan más valor a tu marca. Dos métricas clave que las analíticas de compras pueden ayudarle a seguir son las visitas a la página del producto y los clics en el botón del producto. Si la página de su producto tiene muchas visitas pero pocos clics en los botones, puede ser un indicador de que el precio del producto es elevado o de que la descripción del producto no es lo suficientemente convincente.

CAPÍTULO 6: PUBLICIDAD EN INSTAGRAM

La parte final de este libro trata sobre la publicidad en Instagram y la revisión de si la publicidad en la plataforma tiene sentido para su marca y negocio o no. Hay un montón de beneficios de la publicidad en Instagram en términos de exposición a un público objetivo, la generación de clientes potenciales para su negocio, y la oportunidad de dirigir el tráfico a un sitio externo. Publicar anuncios es una decisión importante que debes tomar como propietario de una empresa o marca, por lo que siempre es mejor hacer los deberes y preguntarte si estás preparado para publicar anuncios y qué quieres conseguir con ello.

Normalmente tiene sentido publicar anuncios cuando su negocio está empezando a despegar, ya que los anuncios son simplemente un método de amplificar el esfuerzo que ha realizado para hacer crecer orgánicamente su negocio o marca hasta ese momento. No querrá gastar dinero en anuncios que no van a convertir clientes, ni en anuncios de baja calidad que no tengan una llamada a la acción deseable. También es importante comprender la mentalidad con la que debes empezar a anunciarte en la plataforma y que, a menos que se trate de un brillante golpe de suerte, no todos tus anuncios funcionarán bien o se convertirán. Además, es posible que en algún momento sus anuncios empiecen a perder rendimiento. Todas estas preocupaciones forman parte del proceso y no deben disuadirle de analizar qué ha ido mal e intentar conseguir de nuevo una fórmula ganadora.

Una vez que se haya decidido a dar el paso con la publicidad, esta sección le dará toda la información que necesita para configurar y ejecutar la primera de muchas campañas publicitarias.

En el primer capítulo de este libro has leído acerca de cómo vincular tu perfil de empresa de Instagram a una página de empresa de Facebook, y esto es extremadamente importante, ya que Instagram utiliza la plataforma publicitaria de Facebook para publicar anuncios. Si creaste una página de Facebook al principio, cuando comenzaste tu viaje de marketing en Instagram, las siguientes estrategias deberían ser fáciles de implementar, ya que toda la configuración, el presupuesto, la programación, la creación y la ejecución del anuncio se realizarán a través del propio Facebook.

Investigación

La investigación es siempre importante antes de aventurarse en algo nuevo, y usted ha leído a través de este libro acerca de cómo la investigación de sus competidores es importante. Dedicar tiempo a investigar lo que hacen tus competidores y los líderes del sector te ayudará a entender sus llamadas a la acción, sus niveles de compromiso y los tipos de anuncios que convierten.

Hay dos formas de investigar los anuncios de tus competidores. El primer método es acceder a su página de empresa de Facebook y hacer clic en "Transparencia de la página" para ver el historial de todos los anuncios que han publicado vinculados con Instagram y otras plataformas. Por lo general, si el anuncio sigue publicado, es muy probable que esté funcionando bien.

El segundo método de investigación es un poco experimental, especialmente si están utilizando una estrategia de remarketing. Empieza por ver su perfil en Instagram y haz clic en el enlace a su sitio web que aparece en su biografía. Cuando te redirijan a su sitio web, navega por algunos de sus productos y haz clic en algunos para leer sus descripciones. Sal y vuelve a entrar en Instagram, y cuando vuelvas a la plataforma puede que veas su anuncio de retargeting en tu feed de inicio.

Objetivos

Los objetivos de campaña son básicamente lo que necesitas que hagan los visitantes y seguidores cuando vean tus anuncios. Para la publicidad en Instagram, los objetivos de la campaña son un poco diferentes en comparación con los objetivos de la campaña de Facebook, y son los siguientes:

- **Notoriedad de marca** - Quiere llegar a más gente y dar a conocer su marca y su negocio.

- **Alcance** - Quiere que su anuncio llegue al mayor número de espectadores posible.

- **Tráfico** - Desea aumentar el porcentaje de clics en sitios web y tiendas externas.

- **Instalaciones de aplicaciones**: desea enviar a los usuarios a su tienda en línea para que realicen una compra.

- **Participación** - Quieres conseguir participación en tus publicaciones a través de me gusta, comentarios, compartir y guardar.

- **Conversiones**: desea que los visitantes tomen determinadas decisiones, como suscribirse a una lista de correo electrónico o realizar una compra.

Una nota importante que hay que mencionar es que si tu objetivo es vender productos o servicios en línea y quieres realizar una campaña de remarketing, debes instalar un píxel de Facebook, que es un pequeño fragmento de código que puedes colocar en tu sitio web para realizar un seguimiento de los visitantes.

Dirigiéndose a

La segmentación consiste en tratar de encontrar a las personas adecuadas a las que dirigir la publicidad y que tengan más probabilidades de actuar y realizar una compra. Instagram tiene las mismas opciones de segmentación que Facebook, que incluyen la ubicación, los datos demográficos y el comportamiento, entre otras opciones.

En el nivel básico, para empezar, debe seleccionar la ubicación, la edad, el sexo y el idioma. También tienes la opción de crear un público personalizado o un público similar basado en la configuración de ambas plataformas. A partir de aquí, tienes dos opciones para delimitar aún más tus criterios con Facebook Audience Insights o Google Analytics.

Creativo

Diseñar tus creatividades publicitarias para Instagram es a la vez un arte y una ciencia con el propósito de llegar a las personas adecuadas y motivarlas con el tono adecuado para que interactúen con tu anuncio. Instagram tiene cuatro tipos de anuncios entre los que puedes elegir:

- Carrusel - Estas son excelentes opciones para mostrar múltiples productos o múltiples usos de un solo producto.

- Imagen única - Las imágenes son sencillas si estás empezando con la publicidad en la plataforma y son bastante fáciles de configurar y funcionan muy bien.

- Vídeo único - Los vídeos son los mejores para enganchar a su audiencia con clips de 30-60 segundos y definitivamente tienen el mejor retorno de la inversión.

- Presentación de diapositivas: son ideales si dispones de recursos limitados y simplemente puedes montar un vídeo con imágenes fijas como si fuera una presentación.

Una vez que haya fijado sus objetivos, determinado su público objetivo y diseñado sus creatividades, es el momento de crear su primer anuncio con los siguientes pasos:

1. Si tienes tu perfil de empresa de Instagram vinculado a tu página de empresa de Facebook, haz clic en Anuncios de Instagram e introduce tus credenciales.

2. Dirígete a Facebook Ads Manager y haz clic en el botón " + Crear" situado en la parte superior izquierda de la pantalla.

3. Introduzca los objetivos de su campaña y cree un píxel si decide hacer retargeting.

4. Cree su conjunto de anuncios seleccionando las preferencias de audiencia y su presupuesto.

5. Haga clic en Continuar para elegir el tipo de anuncio que desea publicar y añada el pie de texto y el titular del anuncio.

6. Previsualice su anuncio para ver cómo quedará antes de publicarlo y realice los cambios necesarios.

7. Consulta otras opciones de distribución si quieres publicarlo también en Facebook.

8. Si todo parece correcto, haga clic en Confirmar.

Seguimiento

Ahora que has configurado y lanzado con éxito tu campaña publicitaria, como con cualquier otra cosa, es importante realizar un seguimiento y medir el rendimiento con el fin de editarlo y optimizarlo para el éxito. Deberías poder ver las métricas de rendimiento de tu anuncio de Instagram en el Gestor de anuncios después de realizar el pedido. También puedes utilizar el gestor de anuncios para personalizar y jugar con las funciones para que te muestre los resultados en función de tus objetivos. Si el anuncio funciona bien los primeros días, puedes aumentar la inversión cada tres o cuatro días y seguir controlando el rendimiento. Si el anuncio deja de funcionar o empieza a decaer, puede apagarlo para analizar dónde ha dejado de funcionar y volver a empezar uno nuevo.

CONCLUSIÓN

Ahora tienes toda la información importante a tu disposición en este libro para guiarte en la construcción de una sólida estrategia de marketing en Instagram. Constantemente surgen nuevas estrategias a medida que la plataforma evoluciona, pero este libro debería darte una buena base para empezar. Comprende que el marketing y el crecimiento de tus seguidores no darán resultados de la noche a la mañana, y que se trata de un plan de juego a largo plazo para el que debes estar preparado. En ningún momento debes tomar el camino fácil y recurrir a atajos mediante la compra de seguidores, ya que no se involucrarán con tu contenido y lo más probable es que sean bots que envían mensajes de spam y acosan a tus seguidores orgánicos.

Tómese su tiempo y experimente con el contenido, vea qué funciona y manténgase al día de las tendencias de la cultura pop para intentar entrelazarlas con su estrategia de contenidos si es posible. Céntrate en elaborar objetivos y metas sencillos con tu estrategia de marketing, y aprovecha siempre otras plataformas para dirigir y atraer tráfico adecuadamente. Dependiendo de tu presupuesto de marketing, puedes invertir en herramientas externas, software, aplicaciones y personas que te ayuden con tu marketing y publicidad en la plataforma para ahorrar tiempo, o si eres paciente y no tienes prisa, puedes hacer crecer orgánicamente tu número de seguidores con publicaciones y participación constantes.

Utiliza todos los tipos de publicaciones de Instagram a tu disposición lo mejor que puedas y apuesta siempre por la calidad frente a la cantidad. Recuerda que el contenido es el rey, y la calidad es clave a la hora de diseñar tu estrategia de marketing en Instagram para aumentar el número de seguidores orgánicos.

Cuando finalmente decidas publicar anuncios en Instagram, investiga siempre primero a tus competidores y elige los objetivos adecuados. Además, asegúrate de crear e instalar un píxel de Facebook si pretendes realizar una campaña de remarketing. Por último, empieza siempre con un gasto pequeño en anuncios y ve aumentándolo gradualmente si el anuncio funciona bien, haciendo los ajustes necesarios sobre la marcha.

Espero que hayas disfrutado aprendiendo sobre marketing en Instagram, ¡y te deseo la mejor de las suertes en tu empeño!